READING IN A SECOND LANGUAGE

Hypotheses, Organization, and Practice

Ronald Mackay, Bruce Barkman
R. R. Jordan
EDITORS

Newbury House Publishers, Inc. / Rowley / Massachusetts / 01969

Library of Congress Cataloging in Publication Data

Mackay, Ronald.
    Reading in a second language.

    Bibliography: p.
    Includes index.
    1. English language--Study and teaching--Foreign
students.   2. Reading.   I. Barkman, B., joint author.
II. Jordan, R. R., joint author.
PE1128.A2M256   428'.6'407   79-387
ISBN 0-88377-134-9

Cover designed by Diana Esterly.

NEWBURY HOUSE PUBLISHERS, INC.

Language Science
Language Teaching
Language Learning

ROWLEY, MASSACHUSETTS 01969

First printing: November 1979
Printed in the U.S.A.   5   4   3   2

Contents

Acknowledgments

We express our gratitude to the contributors whose work appears in this volume, both to those who allowed us to reprint material (Chapters 3, 5, 6, 7, 8, 9, 10, 11, and 12) and to those who provided hitherto unpublished studies for inclusion in this book, James Coady, Colin Harrison and Terry Dolan, Donald Sim and Marsha Bensoussan, and Salwa Ibrahim.

We are grateful to TESOL for allowing us to reproduce Chapters 3, 8, 11, and 12; the Regional Language Centre (RELC) in Singapore for Chapters 7 and 9; the Editor of *Language Learning* for Chapters 5 and 6; the Longman Group Limited for Chapter 10. Full acknowledgments appear on the first page of each of the appropriate chapters.

We would also like to thank Maryse Bosquet for preparing the index and Nathalie Fricot, who prepared the list of references.

Introduction

R. Mackay, B. Barkman,
and R. R. Jordan

The growing interest demonstrated by classroom teachers, curriculum planners, and applied linguists in second language reading can be traced back at least a decade or so to the time when the limitations of the audio-lingual method of second language teaching were becoming increasingly obvious and undeniable. It had been expected, or sometimes merely assumed, that skilled reading and writing would more or less automatically follow upon fluent oral production and understanding. When oral-aural proficiency was found not to be followed inevitably by comparatively high levels of reading ability, disappointed teachers began to ask pertinent questions. These questions resulted in an initially slow but now firm awareness that the factors involved in successfully teaching and learning second language reading have to be given consideration as being important in their own right independently of, as well as in relation to, factors affecting the development of oral-aural skills.

The importance of any individual's being able to read and understand his first language is unquestionable in a world in which education and virtually all the means for personal and social advancement as well as day-to-day survival depend, to a greater or lesser degree, upon literacy skills. In mother tongue reading a greater awareness has begun to develop of the large number of different skills used by an effective reader in order to cope with the varied purposes he has for reading and with the different kinds of written material he inevitably encounters.

For the English as a second language (ESL) teacher, efficient reading is now being seen as a legitimate goal of the ESL curriculum. Whereas at one time reading was understood to mean an ability to cope with the great literary works written in the English language, it is now being understood more in terms of matching the flexibility of the educated native speaker as he performs all the reading-related tasks presented by his environment. These include reading and understanding newspapers and popular magazines, personal letters, business correspondence, official documents such as driving license application forms, stories, academic textbooks, and scientific and technical reports. The linguistic and situational varieties of language that were absent from earlier materials have now started to appear in current second language reading texts.

A developing interest in communicative second language teaching has helped to provide the ESL teacher with a taxonomy for the different reader-writer relationships implicit in different genres of texts and the different situations in which and purposes for which they might have to be dealt with.

However, between the new sets of goals and objectives of the second language reading curriculum and the means and ways by which these might be reached there is a considerable gap. The precision with which communicative needs-analysis classification systems have permitted appropriate purposes for different groups of learners to be specified has not been automatically matched by an equally precise specification of the nature of the instructional materials and classroom exercises and activities which will ensure their fulfillment.

Fortunately, concurrent activity and advances in two areas relevant to the interests of classroom teachers and applied linguists have provided at least partial solutions.

Linguistics, influenced by views of language as only one part of the communication event, such as that described in Pike's "Language in Relation to a Unified Theory of Human Behaviour" (1967), began to turn away again from its concern with the sentence as the sole linguistic unit worthy of attention. Once again, influenced by anthropological and sociological views of language, suprasentence grammar was being talked of and at least partial descriptions of the syntax of textual cohesion were being made available, particularly that by Hasan (1968), later expanded into Halliday and Hasan's "Cohesion in English" (1976). Moreover, the increasing clarity of the distinction between grammatical cohesion and rhetorical coherence allowed applied linguists to continue developing ever more useful taxonomies of communicative acts and descriptions of their characteristic patterning in different genres of continuous prose.

These two branches of essentially the same development have resulted in new kinds of activities or exercise types being developed to facilitate second language reading instruction. Second language materials writers have always tended to make use of the units employed by the descriptive grammarian as the sole units of instruction offered to the learner. Descriptions of English ended at the sentence level and instruction focused correspondingly on exercising students in clause and other intrasentential patterns. Then exercises were developed to focus the learner's attention on intersentential and interparagraph and even larger relationships in a method similar to but more precise and detailed than that used in freshman composition and rhetoric courses in most American universities for decades. Of course, a great deal of work still has to be done in the description and the characterization of the grammatical and rhetorical features of continuous prose. Nevertheless, some curriculum developers, materials writers, and ESL reading teachers have started to incorporate those descriptions and even less rigorous attempts to account for the patterning of discourse into their instructional programs.

The second field of activity which provided a stimulus to the ESL reading scene was psycholinguistics. Whereas the dominant questions in ESL reading have always been, "How best can we teach students to read?" and "What are the most effective sets of instructional materials for the teaching of reading?" some psycholinguists involved in first language reading are asking different questions despite the fact that their ultimate goals are similar. These psycholinguists share the belief that for substantial improvements to be made in either classroom procedures or pedagogic materials, a clearer understanding is necessary of what it is that the successful reader does in order to understand written language. In other words, the psycholinguist's attention focuses not so much upon the teacher or the texts or the exercises as upon the processes engaged in and the strategies employed by the reader as he struggles more or less successfully to extract meaning from connected texts.

Learners' processes are notoriously difficult to observe. Applied linguists have tended to infer the processes and strategies employed by ESL learners from the errors they make in either oral or written production. A wealth of research in error analysis stimulated by Selinker, Corder, Richards, and others has provided interesting insights into and hypotheses as to how ESL learners cope with both formal and informal language instruction. Developments on this type of work have also opened up the possibility of observing not only errors but the learner's uses of the language both inside the classroom with teachers and other learners and outside the classroom in less structured situations. This work, however, has focused on spoken language and, in particular, interactions between two or more participants. Among other studies of second language reading, Hosenfeld (1976) examined American school-children learning to read French and Spanish in secondary school and developed a useful coding technique for recording their strategies. Cziko (1978) employed Goodman's oral miscue technique with English-speaking students of French to classify the kinds of errors they produce. From these errors he infers the extent to which different levels of proficiency were employing syntactic, discourse, and semantic cues in the text. Selinker has recently provided ESL with a new investigative direction in the study of reading processes. Stemming from his innovative work at the Hebrew University of Jerusalem in 1976, investigators have examined some of the difficulties encountered by students reading in English and the strategies used by them to overcome these difficulties. These studies, still in their infancy, were described by Cohen at the 12th Annual TESOL Convention in Mexico City in 1978.

Thus, only relatively recently have attempts to chart second language reading processes been engaged in. These draw heavily upon methods of research that have been developed for the observation of mother tongue reading.

What, then, are the current implications of the foregoing for ESL teachers? They are, we think, represented by the following assertions and questions:

1. A better and fuller understanding of what a second language reader does when he reads is needed.
2. The term "reading comprehension" needs to be defined in operational terms.
3. Given that second language reading seems to depend upon the interaction of linguistic proficiency and specific reading strategies or skills, an understanding of the relationship between these two factors is required.
4. What is the role of grammatical and rhetorical description of prose in the development of second language reading?
5. What can be learned for use in curriculum design and materials development from what is known of the strategies employed by successful and unsuccessful second language readers?
6. How best can ESL teachers develop an appreciation of the particular reading needs of their students?
7. To what extent can we distinguish between testing whether reading comprehension has occurred and teaching what is necessary for comprehension to be facilitated?

We think that it is in addressing and discussing these matters that this book contributes to the field of teaching English as a second or foreign language. We have selected and invited a wide-ranging collection of papers which we feel are relevant to the matters of current concern in second language reading and we have given them coherence in the editorial introductions to each of the three parts.

Section I, Hypotheses, introduces the second language teacher to the need for looking at reading, as a first or second language activity, in terms of what the learner appears to be doing and the kinds of information, both linguistic and nonlinguistic, that appear to be of importance to the success of the activity. We have purposely presented a hypothesis-generating approach in this section as opposed to a dogmatic one, in order to underline the tentative and uncertain stage in which the understanding of second language reading currently finds itself. Informed teacher observation of beginning readers is sorely needed to supplement model building and to generate hypotheses about second language reading. Experimental research is necessary to verify these hypotheses. Teachers will find many suggestions as to how they can contribute to our growing understanding of the reader and his difficulties in these four chapters.

Section II deals with the organization of programs to teach second language reading, Section III with specific classroom techniques and instructional activities which can be placed within the investigative framework of Section I.

The three sections provide a coherent picture of current thinking and developing practice in a branch of ESL which is just beginning to be given its deserved place in the scheme of ESL teaching as a whole.

There is one notable area which we have purposely decided not to handle directly in this collection. That is the area of testing learners' reading proficiency. Testing is a highly specialized activity which usually requires a knowledge of statistics and computational skills which most teachers have neither the time nor the overriding desire to master. Moreover, we feel that before a skill can be tested, its nature and manifestations must be adequately understood. Thus it is to this prior stage of understanding, the factors affecting the teaching and learning of reading in a second language, that this book addresses itself. For those who wish to go beyond these factors and become involved in the often delicate and difficult questions associated with testing, we would recommend any of the standard volumes on language testing such as those by Lado (1961), Harris (1969), Heaton (1975), or Valette (1967). Whereas these volumes tend to focus on discrete-point testing, Oller's more recent contribution, "Language Tests at School: A Pragmatic

Approach" (1979), discusses the advantages of pragmatic tests and tests of integrative skills over discrete-point tests. A foretaste of the underlying concepts and far-reaching implications of Oller's work for education in general as well as for ESL in particular was published under the title "Language in Education: Testing the Tests," Oller and Perkins (1978).

The purpose of this collection, therefore, is to provide a coherent (though necessarily incomplete) picture of the current state of thought and practice in ESL reading. The volume is intended to appeal to both the teacher who has daily contact with students in the classroom and the applied linguist whose duties may include developing curricula and planning instructional materials. A shared knowledge and understanding of the issues dealt with in this collection will encourage the success of the communal effort engaged in by teachers, researchers, and administrators alike, to promote functional reading skills in the increasing number of ESL learners.

SECTION I

HYPOTHESES

The chapters in this section contain discussions of some fundamental hypotheses concerning the nature of second language reading. The authors generally concur with Goodman's characterization of the reading process as a "psycholinguistic guessing game." In Goodman's view, the fluent reader takes advantage of the redundant features of language to reconstruct an author's message from a text. Such a reader does not process a text by identifying and interpreting each and every letter and word sequence in the text. Instead, he looks at a sample of the text and predicts the meaning of a larger part of it from what he has sampled and from his prior knowledge of the subject at hand. He then looks at another part of the text to test and confirm his prediction. The efficient reader is one who guesses correctly with minimal text sampling.

The authors in this section attempt to examine the nature of second language reading, to isolate the linguistic skills and subskills involved in reading comprehension, to develop classroom techniques based on Goodman's theoretical position, and to test the relative importance of different categories of words to second language reading comprehension.

In Chapter 1, Coady describes Goodman's model in detail and concludes that reading comprehension involves the interaction of the reader's conceptual abilities, his background knowledge of the subject being read, and what he does as he processes the text.

As beginning readers become more proficient, they rely less on abilities such as making appropriate correspondences between sounds and letters, and more on abstract strategies involving the use of syntactic cues and contextual meanings. Coady notes that fluent readers are thought to combine these strategies in different orders and amounts, depending on the nature of the text being sampled.

Some ESL readers are handicapped because their knowledge of English is insufficient to pick up the necessary linguistic cues. Other poor ESL readers seem to lack adequate processing strategies rather than knowledge of English.

In Chapter 2, Harrison and Dolan observe that information gained from tests of reading comprehension is not necessarily equivalent to reading comprehension itself, although it appears evident that it is only through such tests that insight into the nature of comprehension can be approached.

In an attempt to test the idea that reading comprehension requires a number of abilities, they devised a test to see if they could obtain evidence for eight supposedly distinct reading comprehension subskills. No clear pattern emerged from the factor analyses performed on this test. Although some evidence for separate subskills was present when other data were analyzed, Harrison and Dolan believe that these results are probably attributable to differences in subtest structure and testing procedures. They conclude that "classifications and taxonomies of comprehension skills must be treated with caution, since methods have yet to be devised to measure them reliably."

Various types of information gain tests are described. These tests generally require subjects to answer questions both before and after they read a passage, and the difference between scores under each condition is called the information gain. Such tests are said to minimize the effects of overall language competence on tests of reading comprehension, and to measure more exactly how much new information has been learned. Harrison and Dolan point out that these tests are not norm-referenced and that since each passage is used twice, the information-gain score reliability will be lower.

For L2 tests of reading comprehension, it may be perfectly appropriate to devise questions which test language competence as well as the comprehension of complex ideas. For the former, Harrison and Dolan consider cloze tests appropriate and for the latter, tests given in the subjects' mother tongue.

In the final section of the chapter, Harrison and Dolan recommend that improved reading comprehension be fostered by giving students immediate feedback through a reading laboratory approach and by setting small groups the task of completing cloze tests through discussion. They report that positive results emerged where these techniques have been tried.

In Chapter 3, Saville-Troike suggests that ESOL students are not likely to benefit much from an audio-lingual course which treats reading only as a reinforcement of oral-aural skills, especially if the students wish to use English primarily in the acquisition of information from written sources. She recommends instead that the reading component be structured with the objective of making ESOL students fluent readers in English. To accomplish this, she suggests concentrated training in the skills assumed important to good reading.

Goodman's model of the reading process provides the rationale for the types of training outlined in the chapter. For instance, sound-to-symbol correspondences are considered less useful to the advanced reader than to the neophyte. The good reader is supposed to hunt for clues to the message, which is presented, but not necessarily processed, in a linear manner. The clues are to be found in word recognition, derivational and inflectional morphemes, and knowledge of exposition techniques such as definition, explanation, comparison, and figurative meanings. Higher-level skills include recognition of grammatical units such as phrases, clauses, and words which habitually mark them. At this level, students should become aware of the roles of redundancy and expectancy in reading, as these are signaled by the grammatical and lexical patterning in texts. At the most advanced level, Saville-Troike believes that rhetorical organization and discourse structure should be taught, along with complex syntactic structures.

In Chapter 4, Sim and Bensoussan describe the administration of a 103-item reading comprehension test to 187 undergraduate students who had completed 50 hours of a 100-hour reading comprehension course at Haifa University. Their purpose was to determine whether the comprehension of function words was easier than that of content words, as some previous research using cloze techniqes had indicated.

Multiple-choice questions on L2 texts were set to test knowledge of function word uses and the connotative and denotative meanings of content words. In addition, some of the questions tested the subjects' ability to paraphrase parts of the texts and to determine the overall purpose of the texts. Difficulty indices were obtained for each question. The mean difficulty index for function word questions was higher than that for content word items, but the difference proved statistically insignificant.

The conclusion drawn is that the successful interpretation of content words is as important as the interpretation of function words in reading comprehension.

The theoretical questions which are raised in this section concern the nature and processes of reading comprehension. The difficulties in finding sound methods for investigating these questions become apparent upon careful consideration of the experimental studies described here. Harrison and Dolan are particularly aware of the necessity to formulate clear hypotheses and ways to test them, and of the importance of considering alternative interpretations of tests results. To date, no conclusive evidence which supports Goodman's model of the reading process or of reading comprehension has resulted from experimental endeavors. On the other hand, the progress in the development of techniques for measuring information gain is encouraging.

Ways to get at the process of reading comprehension await the further refinement of current hypotheses, especially with respect to the determination of how much of the text the reader perceives and how much he ignores, to mention two areas at a fairly low level of abstraction. Investigation of how the reader uses syntactic, semantic, and rhetorical cues will require advances in linguistic description and more sophisticated hypotheses about perception and learning than those in current use in the field.

CHAPTER 1

A Psycholinguistic Model of the ESL Reader

James Coady
Ohio University

This chapter describes the ESL reader from the viewpoint of a psycholinguistic model of reading. There is some mention of pedagogical implications and applications, but the major emphasis is on explaining the problems of learning to read in a foreign language in terms of a psycholinguistic model.

Goodman has described reading as a "psycholinguistic process by which the reader, a language user, reconstructs, as best as he can a message which has been encoded by a writer as a graphic display" (1971, p. 135). Goodman views this act of reconstruction as being a cyclical process of sampling, predicting, testing, and confirming. The notion of sampling from the written display is somewhat novel and is in direct opposition to models proposed by others such as Gough (1972) in which reading entails processing each and every letter. Goodman's argument is that the good reader takes advantage of the redundancy inherent in language which enables the reader to reconstruct the whole although he extracts only part of the graphic material. Thus, in this view, the reader is internally re-creating a replica of the textual message. This has been called an analysis by synthesis approach to language performance (Halle and Stevens, 1964; 1967).

Once such a reconstruction has taken place, it is necessary to test its accuracy against previous information. Previous information can refer to the information extracted from the text under consideration as well as to the store of information in long-term memory dealing with such a topic. Should the reader confirm that the reconstruction is indeed in agreement with previous knowledge, then the cycle of sampling begins again. If some inaccuracy or inconsistency is associated with the reconstruction, the reader can adopt some compensatory strategy such as rereading or suspension of belief.

One very immediate and clear implication of such a model is that any reader will have a large number of potential points at which uncertainty may arise. Hence Goodman (1967) refers to reading as a "psycholinguistic guessing game." He argues that all readers will read material in accordance with such a model and consequently will, at certain points, guess wrong. The effects of such a wrong guess can, of course, vary from inconsequential to quite serious. One of the key differences between proficient readers and poor readers is that proficient readers will recover quickly from such wrong guesses or miscues, and their overall performance will be little hampered by them. The poor reader, on the other hand, will not recover in such a successful manner and will instead fall into a vicious cycle of wrong previous information leading to wrong later predictions.

The most fluent readers will use a minimum sampling of text in deriving the meaning by using world, language, and reading knowledge as a substitute for all the redundant features of the text. A less skilled reader would probably have to sample much more from the text in order to derive the same amount of meaning.

Smith (1971) has argued that letter-by-letter or word-by-word reading will prove extremely detrimental because the meaning of one word will be forgotten before the next word is built and thus no meaningful relationships will be established between the words. No comprehension will be possible. This point is of extreme importance in the case of the ESL reader and will be discussed below.

The fluent reader approaches a text with expectancies based upon his knowledge of the subject. As he progresses into the material, he confirms or revises these expectations and builds still more on the basis of what has been read so far. This confirming of expectancy is done through the extraction of minimal samples from the page. Orthographic, syntactic, and semantic clues in the material are used in the reconstruction of the text. If there is an obvious flaw in the reader's interpretation, he may check back for the source of the miscue. Words may be processed on the basis of syntactic or semantic expectancy or broken down into roots or affixes or even broken down into the speech components (phonemes). The latter is probably rare for the fluent reader because there will be few words in his speaking or listening vocabulary which are not in his reading vocabulary.

Let us leave Goodman and Smith who are, after all, describing fluent and proficient readers and see how such an approach relates to the ESL student. First, let us view reading as essentially consisting of a more or less successful interaction among three factors: higher-level conceptual abilities, background knowledge, and process strategies. The result of the interaction is comprehension.

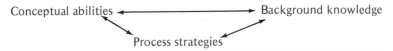

Conceptual abilities are important in reading acquisition. We can notice this especially in adult foreign students who may fail to achieve the competence necessary for university instruction because they lack intellectual capacity and not totally or necessarily because they cannot learn English. Unfortunately, beyond some study skills instruction, there is not much which can be done to remedy this situation in the typical ESL program.

Background knowledge becomes an important variable when we notice, as many have, that students with a Western background of some kind learn English faster, on the average, than those without such a background. This would follow quite logically from the psycholinguistic model just described.

In this discussion process strategies are considered as subcomponents of reading ability although they are also mental processes, part of the ordinary subroutines available to a speaker/user of a language for many purposes. For example, knowledge of the phonology of a language implies the ability to identify phonemes and use this knowledge for practical purposes such as listening. A knowledge of the phoneme-grapheme correspondences for a particular language is of more obvious need for reading. Some further examples of process strategies pertinent to reading are:

Grapheme-morphophoneme correspondences
Syllable-morpheme information
Syntactic information (deep and surface)
Lexical meaning and contextual meaning
Cognitive strategies
Affective mobilizers

The typical reader acquires the skills of reading by moving from the more concrete process strategies to the more abstract. In a psycholinguistic model the reader is reconstructing the meaning of a text based on the sampling he has taken. The more abstract language cue systems such as syntax and semantics signal meaning more overtly, and it is natural to expect the proficient reader to take more advantage of these systems. The display below (Shuy 1975) indicates how such a maturation might take place.

PROCESS STRATEGIES

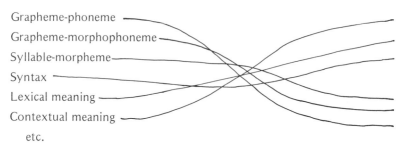

Grapheme-phoneme
Grapheme-morphophoneme
Syllable-morpheme
Syntax
Lexical meaning
Contextual meaning
   etc.

Relative change in use of process strategies over time is represented from left to right, e.g., beginning to advanced reader.

As the display indicates, process strategies are, in essence, paths to comprehension which readers must travel but not necessarily in the same manner or to the same degree. The claim made in this display is that ESL students typically begin by attending to more concrete process strategies such as phoneme-grapheme correspondences and word meaning. But gradually the student learns to take advantage of the more abstract process strategies such as context and syntax. This change takes place as the reader decides that a particular skill or combination of skills is not working as well in deriving meaning (comprehending) as another combination might. This change or shift, therefore, signifies awareness on the part of the reader that these skills are also strategies for successful comprehension—hence the choice of the term process strategies. Just as the relative use of a given process strategy such as phoneme corres-pondences might diminish as the reader becomes more proficient, the relative combinations can vary according to the type of material being read, the degree of comprehension desired, the time available, etc. The mature reader will shift and change the process strategies as the occasion warrants. The best combination for any given reading event should be decided on the basis of whatever delivers the most accurate reconstruc-tion. Accordingly, one cannot predict at any given time exactly which combination of process strategies a given reader is using. Moreover, there are certainly relative differences in proficiency in the various process strategies on the part of different readers, and this would lead to different combinations.

It is obvious that the ESL student is going to be deficient in process strategies which involve substantial knowledge of the target language. What about the other aspects of process strategies which relate to reading as a separate skill in and of itself? In other words, reading can be thought of as parasitic on language but not identical to it. How much of the nonlanguage content of knowing how to read transfers? Goodman (1971) claims that learning to read a second language should be easier for someone already literate in another language regardless of how similar or dissimilar it is. It has been the experience of a number of ESL teachers that such is, in fact, the case. The more mechanical aspects of reading transfer automatically to reading in a new language. For example, students who have learned to read in an alphabetic language do not have to "relearn" the principle of the alphabet. Note also the Lambert and Tucker (1972) research in which the children learning to read in French displayed a rather dramatic transfer of this ability to reading in English.

Yorio claims that difficulty in learning to read in a foreign language can basically be traced to lack of knowledge of the target language and to the fact that, "at all levels, and at all times, there is interference of the native language" (1971, p. 108). Hatch (1974), for example, found that phonological interference does occur even in silent reading.

Moreover, Yorio points out that for the second language learner:

The prediction of future cues is restricted by his imperfect knowledge of the language; moreover, because he has to recall unfamiliar cues, his memory span is very short; he therefore easily forgets the cues that he has already stored. These two factors make associations insecure, slow, and difficult. (1971, p. 110)

In short, success in reading a second language is directly related to the degree of proficiency in that language.

On the other hand, alarming numbers of students have a great deal of proficiency in English and yet read very slowly and with poor comprehension. Looking at this situation in terms of our model would lead us to infer that these students are using a poor combination of process strategies in their reading. In other words, we have a reading problem and not a language problem.

Perhaps we can understand how a student might have such a problem by examining a typical mode of instruction in ESL. A reading class will use a reader which has short stories followed by comprehension questions, vocabulary exercises, and occasionally language-oriented exercises such as identification of affixes. The implicit goal of such a lesson is total and perfect comprehension of the reading passage as well as highly accurate detail work on the exercises. It is interesting to note that in such a lesson the student may read the passage in five to ten minutes and then spend fifty to a hundred minutes doing the exercises and correcting them and discussing the passage in class. This ratio of 1:10 for the amount of time spent in actual reading in contrast to exercises and discussion is a very telling one. The pedagogical strategy which seems to emerge for the student is that one should read educational material very carefully and understand it as perfectly as possible and be prepared to answer all kinds of detailed questions. Since this is the strategy which we encourage in our students in their reading instruction, is it any surprise that ESL students tend to read slowly?

Even so, why should their comprehension be poor? An obvious question to ask is what they do with the extra time. Oller (1972), Tullius (1971), and MacNamara (1970) have found that the number of eye fixations and regressions do not differ between native language readers and ESL readers. The actual differences are found in the durations of the fixations. Thus it would appear that they do not extract larger numbers of samples from the text but rather spend more time on either the sampling of the text or the reconstructing. Since we do not see satisfactory comprehension, the additional time is evidently not being spent on putting the information gained into memory. Indeed, the comprehension loss seems to be attributable to a poor use of process strategies.

Kolers (1970) found that proficient bilingual speakers of French and English read and perceive in terms of meaning rather than graphic display. When texts contained both languages, they could read them as well as monolingual ones. But, if translation into one particular language was required, there was a delay. Kolers (1972) also found that while reading aloud the bilinguals would substitute an equivalent word in the other language when misreading and would not correct such substitutions. It appears that what is stored in memory is meaning and not words as defined by a particular language.

This finding is very much in agreement with a psycholinguistic model and has important implications for teaching reading, as can be seen by considering the dictionary usage of typical ESL students. At first, they rely heavily on a strategy of looking up and collecting words that they encounter. They much prefer to use a bilingual dictionary even if it is manifestly inferior to a monolingual one which is readily available. The explanation seems to be that the bilingual dictionary allows them to fall back on the native language for comprehension while the monolingual dictionary forces them into the "guessing" approach to reading. Although Rubin has pointed out that "the good language learner is a willing and accurate guesser" (1975, p. 45), ESL students will often avoid a monolingual dictionary because of the insecurity which it engenders. But, more importantly, their basic strategy seems to be the collection of words rather than the construction of propositional meanings. Moreover, one can question the habitual use of the dictionary because it tends to slow down the reading process. As Smith pointed out, too slow a speed in reading can prevent the necessary synthesizing of ideas. In short, by learning the word, they have lost the sentence.

There are some pedagogical implications which flow from this model of reading.

1. The teacher should always put primary emphasis in reading instruction on comprehension strategies. It is tempting to emphasize the more concrete process strategies because they are better known and more amenable to attention. But such emphasis can easily mislead the learner into concentrating on these lower-level process strategies instead of the higher ones. The basic problem with such a concentration is that the lower-level process strategies typically deal with the symbols which carry the meaning message. Spending too much time on them, as we have seen, can lead to an overall loss of meaning. In short, too much emphasis on concrete process strategies such as letter-sound correspondences can leave the student with a poor priority of strategies.

2. Since the various process strategies interact among themselves, the ESL student should take advantage of his strengths in order to overcome his weaknesses. For example, greater background knowledge of a particular subject matter could compensate somewhat for a lack of syntactic control over the language. The proficient reader learns to utilize whatever cue systems render useful information and to put them together in a creative manner, always achieving at least some comprehension. Thus a weakness in one area can be overcome by a strength in another. The poor reader, on the other hand, does not make the necessary compensations and allows his weaknesses to prevent any significant comprehension.

3. There is not any *one* way to teach reading. Readers are going to have differing strengths in the various process strategies and, moreover, utilize them in varying combinations. An eclectic approach with different types of materials has the best chance of supporting learning in such a situation.

4. Individualized materials are very useful in reading instruction because they allow the student to proceed at his or her own rate. There is frequent testing for comprehension, i.e., immediate feedback. And the teacher is available for helping individual students with their own particular problems.

5. Some initial emphasis on increasing the reading speed of the student is usually necessary to change the strategy of translation so commonly found in adults. At a more advanced level it is important to increase speed to avoid loss of comprehension of the passage as a whole. But the degree of speed to be used should vary according to the complexity of the material read, the purposes for reading the material, and the reader's background. Thus it is not a matter of simply increasing reading rate but rather of increased flexibility in rate of speed for reading. In short, comprehension is achieved by reading neither too fast nor too slow.

6. The subject of reading materials should be of high interest and relate well to the background of the reader, since strong semantic input can help compensate when syntactic control is weak. The interest and background knowledge will enable the student to comprehend at a reasonable rate and keep him involved in the material in spite of its syntactic difficulty. The benefit of such reading will be twofold: confidence in oneself and exposure to the very syntactic patterns which must be learned.

7. The teacher's main function in reading instruction is to get the student moving in the right direction and provide timely and appropriate feedback. After all, it is the student who must learn by doing. It is the student who must learn the possible combinations and interconnections among the various process strategies. This goal of learning to use them quickly and flexibly can be achieved only by practice, i.e., reading.

In conclusion, there are two ways in which learning to read a second language differs from learning to read a first language. First, there is the obvious need to learn the target language and avoid the pitfalls of the native language. Second, there is the fact that a great deal of the ability to read transfers automatically. That very automaticity has left the ESL instructor of reading with the impression that there is little or no need to teach the process of reading. We have only recently come to realize that many students have very poor reading habits to transfer from their first language, and thus, in many cases, we must teach reading skills which should have been learned in first language instruction. Moreover, there are aspects of the process strategies which are language- and culture-specific which must be taught. It is hoped that this examination of the ESL reader from the viewpoint of a psycholinguistic model of reading will demonstrate that reading is an important component in an ESL program and one which demands that the ESL teacher be a truly competent reading teacher.

CHAPTER 2

Reading Comprehension — A Psychological Viewpoint

Colin Harrison and Terry Dolan
School of Education,
University of Nottingham

The title of this chapter may be taken as indicative of the authors' interest in the fundamental question of what happens when a person reads. So far as possible, however, our intention is to set aside consideration of eye movement, visual information processing, motivation, memory, and attention, and to concentrate instead on what takes place beyond the word-recognition stage as the reader attempts to understand the meanings conveyed by the text.

There is a sense in which it is impossible to investigate reading comprehension, in that (as in subatomic physics) an uncertainty principle operates, and simply by attempting to observe the reader's response we are bound in some way to affect that response. This does not mean that it is impossible to obtain any insight into a reader's comprehension but rather than we must accept that the information we obtain will be limited and to some extent determined by the mode of investigation. A psychologist tends to be concerned with what can be measured, and it is not surprising therefore that investigations of reading comprehension have until fairly recently focused on test performance almost exclusively. Similarly, teachers have tended to assume that since it is important to be able to comprehend, children should do comprehension exercises in order to enhance their reading skills. More recently, however, the Bullock report (H.M.S.O. 1975) has questioned the value of reading tasks with unclear goals and a wholly arbitrary reading stimulus, and has firmly endorsed the concept of a general development of reading skills in all subject areas.

First presented at the Symposium on Reading in a Second Language, Nottingham University, March 1976.

Most teachers are happy to accept this recommendation, and many agree that the overall curriculum is the most fitting context for the growth of skilled reading. However, they feel uncertain as to exactly which "skills" are involved and how these might be promoted and measured. This uncertainty grows in teachers who consult the literature on research into reading skills, since, despite numerous and extensive investigations into the nature of reading competence, no clear-cut decisions have emerged. Some researchers claim to have isolated "skills" (even though their lists often differ from those of others who have looked at essentially the same data), some have denied the existence of separate "skills," and yet a third group seems to have ignored the findings of previous research and to have proceeded on pragmatic grounds to speculate "skills" at all sorts of levels.

The situation worsens as teachers turn to the procedure generally adopted by those who have carried out investigations. A list of hypothetical skills which are considered pertinent is drawn up and instruments are constructed to measure them. A large group of readers is then tested and performance on the various skills is interrelated. The resultant correlations are then factor-analyzed, and it is at this point that the teacher becomes quite lost. Factor analysis is mathematically complicated and the selection of the most appropriate analytic procedure calls for the kind of expertise rarely found outside departments of statistics. The outcome of the analysis is a list of factors or a single factor, whichever the case may be, a factor being an influence which appears to have determined performance on one or more of the items or tasks measured.

The literature reveals controversy about the factoring techniques used by researchers into comprehension. A good example is found in the disagreement between Davis (1944, 1946) and Thurstone (1946). Davis analyzed data and claimed to have isolated five factors. Thurstone took Davis's data, processed them using a different factor-analytic technique, and declared that only one robust factor was present. Several wide reviews of studies into comprehension have noted only limited agreement among researchers as to the number and identity of factors involved in the process of comprehension (Lennon 1962, Farr 1969). This is irritating for the teacher, especially as the most fundamental question about reading comprehension, namely, whether or not it is a unitary competence or a number of skills, remains unresolved. In any event, is it feasible to consider reading comprehension in the context of "reading" skills as opposed to one of "cognitive" skills which follow initial decoding? Some factor-analytical studies have been criticized as being mere manipulation of statistics generated by reading tests. Goodman (1969) considers reading as information processing which takes place when an individual decodes print and that it is quite artificial to fragment this complex processing into distinct components. Serious criticism of the factor-analytical approaches reported comes from Farr (1969), who points out that certain key variables have not featured in the data processed in those studies he reviewed for the International Reading Association. For example, these studies have generally failed to assess or control for the reader's interest level and familiarity with the content of the reading matter.

This was the background noted by the Schools Council project, the "Effective Use of Reading," when in 1973 it considered the nature of reading comprehension. The teachers' study groups, an integral part of the project, agreed fully with Maurice Waite, project officer and an experienced primary headteacher, that many teachers feel at a loss when it comes to promoting effective reading in children who have mastered decoding. Further, most of the commercially produced comprehension material and existing tests of comprehension tend to overemphasize elementary aspects, with a preponderance of items requiring the pupil to define the meaning of isolated words or to answer questions that can readily be resolved by reference to single phrases or sentences.

There are, however, certain exceptions in the case of comprehension tests. These include the Gates-MacGinitie tests in the United States (1965) and, more recently, the Edinburgh Reading Tests (1973). However, it is a feature of these tests that different passages are used to measure the different subskills specified, and several short passages are used to measure each one. It could therefore be argued that such tests are open to two criticisms:

1. The test situation is markedly different from the standard reading situation.
2. Differences between individual scores on the various subscales are likely to reflect differences between passages and item type (the formulation of items being generally standard for all items in any subscale but quite different from that of items in all other subscales), as well as any real differences in reader profiles.

If there are distinct subskills and if these are constantly in demand throughout the process of reading passages of connected discourse, it should be possible to formulate appropriate questions bearing on an extended piece of text such that each of the subskills is tapped by several questions. The project team prepared and redrafted tests based on four fairly lengthy (600-word) passages. For each passage some thirty questions were devised to cover the following eight putative subskills of reading:

Word meaning:	in isolation.
Word meaning (context):	the meaning of a selected word as it is used in a particular context.
Literal comprehension:	one which calls for only a verbatim response.
Inference (single string):	an inference is made from a single sentence or group of words.
Inference (multiple strings):	an inference is made from information drawn from a number of sentences/groups of words.
Metaphor:	responses are sought from a passage wherein interpretation cannot be made at a literal level.
Salients:	the ability to isolate the key points of the passage.
Evaluation:	the ability to make a judgment or come to a decision, after assessing the content of a passage and setting this against knowledge gained from previous experience.

These categories were arrived at as a consensus of those subskills listed in the New York City Board Bulletin (1964); they may be taken as representative of many similar taxonomies which have been suggested by experts in the reading field.

Several attempts were made to arrive at a satisfactory analysis with interpretable factors. The method used was an oblique procedure (Kaiser 1970), but principal components analysis with rotation to Kaiser's varimax criterion was also carried out as a supplementary check. In the various analyses, individual tests, pairs of tests, and all four tests together were analyzed, with items alone being examined, then subscale totals.

Our main conclusion was that it was not possible to see any clear pattern in the loadings and any attempt at interpretation would have been entirely speculative. Subsequently, similar analyses have been carried out on test results from larger samples of eleven-, twelve-, and fifteen-year-old children, but the results are no clearer. All these results lead us to question the suitability of this type of data for factor-analytic purposes. Scatterplots of children's scores on each item against others revealed that many correlations were, in fact, nonlinear. This occurred, for example, when children who achieved success on more demanding items scored poorly on less demanding ones. This is startling until one considers that one frequently reads a passage, skipping words which one does not understand, yet is still able to make inferences about the content and to note the salient features. However, linear relationships between variables are absolutely essential for valid factor analysis.

What then are the implications of this work? We were rather fearful of suggesting that the posited taxonomies of comprehension were without foundation, and therefore sought to replicate our analysis on other data. We reanalyzed Davis's 1944 data and also gave 250 children the Edinburgh reading test, which is based on five subtests, each related to a putative subskill of reading (it is perhaps interesting to note that those subskills had not been determined by measuring children's performance but by a committee of Scottish Education Department representatives and college lecturers).

We found in both cases a single factor emerged, with some hints of other factors in the Edinburgh tests. However, since each subtest had very different types of testing procedure and item structure, this related more to item-specific differences than to subtest content. Our conclusions therefore were that classifications and taxonomies of comprehension skills must be treated with caution, since methods have yet to be devised to measure them reliably.

The extent to which reading comprehension tests do in fact measure what they claim to measure has been examined in an important paper by Anderson (1972). His criticism of many comprehension tests was that they do not assess what a reader has comprehended from a passage in terms of new information, but rather measure a much more general overall language competence. This is a point which would be accepted by many teachers. Anderson differentiated among four types of comprehension questions, which he called verbatim, transformed verbatim, paraphrase, and transformed paraphrase. A verbatim question is one which could be answered satisfactorily by an exact quotation from the text. A transformed verbatim question is one which required a linguistic transformation in order to produce a satisfactory answer; e.g., appropriate changes may need to be made in verb tenses and person, but the answer does not require that crucial words be paraphrased. A paraphrase question is one which does require that certain words in the original text be replaced by others with substantially the same meaning. Finally a transformed paraphrase question requires an answer which incorporates both paraphrase and a linguistic transformation. Anderson's central thesis was that verbatim and transformed verbatim questions cannot really be said to test the reader's comprehension at all. This is because they can be answered without the meanings of crucial words ever being appreciated. In his own terms, the words used in verbatim responses may have been phonologically (acoustically) encoded, but there is no guarantee that they have been semantically encoded.

Anderson suggested that a printed visual stimulus is phonologically encoded, but if it is to be remembered for more than a few seconds, it must then be semantically encoded. His contention was that an effective reader must store meanings rather than strings of symbols or speech sounds. The task of the comprehension test constructor, therefore, is to devise questions which can be answered if a person has semantically encoded the meanings of the text, but cannot be answered if the encoding was simply visual or phonological. If this is not done, claims Anderson, there is no guarantee that the test is examining reading comprehension at all.

Some of the weaknesses of standardized tests have also been explored by Tuinman (1973), who has asserted that a test cannot properly be described as one of reading comprehension if high scores can be obtained by subjects who have never seen the passage on which the questions are based. He reports scores as high as 65% correct on multiple-choice comprehension tests under this "no passage" condition, when the score on a random response should be only 25% correct. The discrepancy, he feels, is related to the fact that what is being tested is a general language competence, rather than what has been gleaned from the passage. Tuinman accepts that information about the passage is included in many of the questions, but presumably this too represents a severe structural weakness if it tends to make reading of the test passage unnecessary.

One way of bringing some clarification to the issue of what aspects of the reader's response are examined in a test is to differentiate between *comprehension* and *information gain* (IG). There are a number of ways of attempting to assess IG, but in general the concept involves a comparison between the reader's state of knowledge before and after reading the test passage. Thus we could, following Tuinman, administer a standardized test under the "no passage" condition, followed by the same test given when the subjects are able to read the passage, and subtracting the first score from the second would give a measure of IG. Another measure of IG is obtained by playing "Shannon's Game" (see Shannon 1951) twice. The subject is asked to guess successively each word in the test passage, and is given as a clue all the preceding words up to the target word for each guess. For a 370-word passage he thus makes 370 guesses. The whole exercise is repeated, and the difference between the percentage of correctly guessed words is taken as the index of IG. A third method, used by Coleman and Miller (1967), is to obtain percent correct cloze scores before and after the subjects have had an opportunity to read the passage in its original form, and the difference between the two is taken as the IG score. (Briefly, cloze procedure involves systematically deleting every nth word in a passage, usually the fifth, seventh, or tenth, and asking the subject to suggest a suitable word for each one omitted.)

Measures of IG are useful when the tester wishes to take each subject as his own control, and to compare performance under different conditions, for example, on passages with different content, interest levels, or prose difficulty levels. It seems that to a certain extent the effects of overall language competence are canceled out, and that IG scores offer a truer index of the extent to which the reader has assimilated new information. However, even allowing for the criticism that in psychological terms this account of IG is oversimplified, there are two other problems associated with attempting to use IG scores under test conditions which must be brought out. First, IG scores are not norm-referenced and therefore cannot be used in a general way to compare one reader's performance with that of another. Second, there is a statistical point connected with gain scores; since they involve using a test twice, they allow a double opportunity for error to creep in. A multiple-choice comprehension test, for example, probably has a reliability of about .85, and since we are using the test twice we must accept that the gain score will have a reliability which is rather lower. These warnings are not meant to imply that measures of IG are of little value, but rather that those using them must be aware of their limitations.

When we consider some of the implications of what has been said so far for the development and testing of reading comprehension in L2, it seems clear that something of a shift from the rather inflexible positions of Anderson and Tuinman is called for. The reason for this is that the purposes of comprehension testing in L2 seem to be rather broader than those in L1. It could be argued that it is perfectly proper to include questions of literal comprehension, or Anderson's verbatim and trans-formed verbatim questions, when the aim of the test is expressly to examine overall language competence in L2, rather than the ability of the reader to comprehend complex ideas. It may well be, for example, that the content of the passage, were it in L1, would be immediately comprehensible to the reader. His problems in comprehension may be wholly related to aspects of grammar and syntax which are trivial for the L1 user. Thus a comprehension question which would be testing the minimal level of reading ability in L1 might conceivably be worth posing for certain L2 language users.

In this context one should note that cloze procedure would seem to be a useful instrument for assessing (or fostering) L2 competence. As Osgood has noted (1959), cloze procedure is a measure of the communality of the language systems of the writer and testee, and while this fact slightly reduces the usefulness of cloze as a measure of reading comprehension in L1, it by no means reduces its potential value in an L2 context, since it is often this communality which the L2 examiner is seeking to evaluate.

In other kinds of testing situations, when the examiner wishes the L2 reader to focus on the content of the passage, and he is not interested in testing language production as such, we can see, following Anderson, that there is no real necessity for the test to be conducted in L2 at all. Since in this case the examiner is interested in the passage meanings, there would seem to be no reason why all the questions and answers should not be in L1, but based on a passage in L2. This is in fact how one conducts an undergraduate seminar on Wittgenstein or Kant, and it seems reasonable to describe the activity as a reading comprehension exercise in the fullest sense.

Much of what has been said so far has related to the examination of comprehension under test conditions. This has been a natural emphasis, since the great majority of studies of reading comprehension have used test scores as a crucial variable. In our final section we consider some ideas which are more closely related to the problems of establishing and fostering reading comprehension.

Just as we have suggested criticisms of certain comprehension tests, so shall we admit to having grave doubts about one belief widely held among language teachers, namely, that doing reading comprehension exercises enhances reading comprehension. Generations of schoolchildren have spent the greater part of their total contact with second language texts working on reading comprehension exercises, and yet these are open to most of the criticisms offered above of standardized comprehension tests, and perhaps some others as well. We know that in mother tongue language work at school, students who are doing a reading comprehension exercise actually spend the greater part of their time writing, not reading (Lunzer and Gardner, in preparation). Furthermore, they tend not to read a passage for overall meaning, but rather to read in small bursts near the point in the text at which a cue word in the question suggests the answer may be found. In many instances this is possible because a question can be answered with a verbatim or transformed verbatim response, and because the questions follow a highly predictable pathway through the passage itself. It has already been accepted that in an L2 context verbatim or transformed verbatim comprehension questions may serve a useful purpose, but if there is no reading for overall meaning, the argument that the exercise is developing overall reading comprehension must be a weak one.

From a psychological point of view, the delay in giving the student feedback about the level of his performance on a reading comprehension exercise is also a great weakness. A good mark may encourage the student, but meticulous correction of errors and misunderstandings may be entirely wasted if the student has forgotten most of what was read and why he chose the answers he did. One real problem for a poor reader in any language is that he may well have an imprecise notion of what it is to comprehend adequately, and may not be clear himself whether or not he has understood what he is reading. If this is the case, attempting to answer comprehension questions on his own is not necessarily going to strengthen this awareness. A partial solution to the problem is for the teacher to introduce a "reading laboratory" approach, with self-corrected exercises which allow the answers to be checked as soon as the student has responded to the multiple-choice questions. As a recent study by Fawcett has shown (1977), such a course at the very least enables students to perform better on standardized comprehension tests than their counterparts who have simply received their normal English lessons. Nevertheless, many teachers have accepted the Bullock Report's criticisms of reading laboratories which draw attention to the arbitrary nature of the reading stimulus, and to the minimal claims to literary merit of the texts used.

An alternative approach to developing reading comprehension which the present authors have investigated is through structured small group discussion of texts, following silent reading. Certain techniques, first described in the work of Stauffer (1960), and more recently developed and extended in the United Kingdom (Walker 1974, Harrison 1976), have been found to be very valuable in an L1 context, and might well prove equally useful in L2 work. The aim of the activities is to encourage close reading of the text in a noncompetitive atmosphere. A group size of between six and eight is usually large enough to ensure a breadth of response while allowing each member reasonable opportunity to participate. A number of approaches are possible, but only the two most widely known, group cloze and group prediction, will be described here.

For the group cloze activity, words are deleted from a passage and the task of the readers is to study the text and arrive at a consensus view of the most suitable word to fill each blank. No constraints are laid down in relation to passage content or length. Deletions may be every fifth, seventh, or tenth word, depending on the difficulty of the passage and the nature of the audience. With difficult passages deletions should not be commenced until about the hundredth word. Subgroups of two, three, or four children prepare their answers, with stress being laid on the need for convincing argument within the group before decisions are reached. The chairman (usually this will be the teacher at first, but ideally the role should be taken by others) calls the subgroups together to thrash out a final version. The chairman possesses the original version, but he must try to avoid notions of "right" and "wrong." Group prediction exercises involve releasing installments of a short passage, one at a time, to a group of readers. The task is to respond to questions put by a group chairman about what has been written in the passage, and to make inferences from what is read and thus anticipate what might happen in later installments. All reading is silent and no writing is involved. Following reading and discussion of each installment, the chairman collects the installments so that no reference back is possible. Readers are encouraged to justify their responses, and other members of the group are encouraged to challenge the responses.

The authors have collaborated with a large number of teachers who have tried out these activities with children from all ages between seven and eighteen, and gradually certain positive aspects have emerged. First, children enjoy doing the activities; they enjoy sharing their responses with each other and engaging in what appears to be some literary detective work. Second, and this is no doubt a contributory factor to the first point, the poorer readers are able to contribute, and yet also gain in sharing the insights of the more fluent readers. Similarly, those children whose writing skills are weak but who can read reasonably fluently are able to make a full contribution, whereas they would be hampered in tackling a written comprehension test.

Of course, we would not claim that these group reading activities should set the framework for all reading. Neither would we suggest that each of the possible benefits noted above is observed regardless of the content of a passage; if a piece is bland and boring, or too complex or technical for a group of readers, they will not learn from it. The teacher must always make a number of judgments about whether a passage or book is suitable for the individuals in a group. What we do say is that no reader will learn from a text unless he actually engages with it, and that these activities seem to encourage this engagement or reflection in a way that individual silent reading may not.

The suggestions that have been made in this final section are already being tried out by a number of L2 specialists in the United Kingdom, and it will surprise no one who has worked in the public examination field to learn that examination boards are taking an active interest in the development of cloze tests as an instrument for gauging competence in a second language. If this trend continues we shall perhaps see cloze tests at O or A level, and these would no doubt be rapidly followed by textbooks offering practice in cloze technique. This in turn could lead to a use of the procedure which would be mechanical, private, isolated, and unreinforced, and which would take no account of the reasons advanced in this chapter for its use in a teaching context.

The task in developing reading comprehension is to encourage a vital response rather than a mechanical or unchallenged one. Our belief is that in a fluent reader the critical and reflective response is internalized; what group reading activities offer is an externalization of the process of critical reading, which can be shared and enjoyed by those who take part, and which is potentially a valuable learning experience, since it offers the poorer reader models and strategies which he can use in his own private reading.

CHAPTER 3

Reading and the Audio-Lingual Method

Muriel Saville-Troike
Department of Linguistics,
Georgetown University

Linguists these days sometimes enjoy taking pokes at the audio-lingual method, and I admit to being no exception. I considered calling this chapter "The R-ful/oral Method." The fact that there isn't any R in TESOL is *not* merely incidental to this presentation. In spite of its crucial role in advanced English language learning contexts, such as those the students in the DLI (Defense Language Institute) English Language Program are being prepared for, fluent reading has seldom been a product of the audio-lingual method.

I would like to explore some reasons for this weakness, defining "the state of the art" in teaching reading today, and suggesting changes in our TEFL methodology in the light of current pedagogy, which may improve the reading competence of our more advanced students.

The primary reason for our neglect of this area seems to be a historical one. Older teaching methods emphasized the written forms of language, largely ignoring speech, and the audio-lingual approach was a reaction to this book-centered orientation. In addition, the schools of behaviorist psychology and structuralist linguistics were in vogue at the time, and their respective views of language learning as a process of habit formation and of language itself as speech, provided a rationale for the new methodology.

First published in *TESOL Quarterly*, Vol. 7, No. 4, 1973. Copyright 1973 by Teachers of English to Speakers of Other Languages. Reprinted by permission of the publisher and Muriel Saville-Troike.

In the resulting shift of emphasis in foreign language teaching to the acquisition of oral skills (listening and speaking), reading and writing have been sadly neglected or even ignored. This has occurred in spite of the fact that transformational grammar for more than a decade has insisted that language is a mental phenomenon, and that speech and writing are two separate manifestations of language. Similar developments in cognitive psychology have emphasized the same view. The fact that reading instruction in TESOL has been so neglected can only be attributed to the long isolation of the field from continuing developments in linguistics, so that many people in TESOL who are still basing their practices on the theories of the fifties are unaware that these are no longer all equally valid in the seventies.

History tells us that people can learn foreign languages in many different ways, but the choice of methods usually determines which teaching objectives are most satisfactorily realized.

The audio-lingual method has placed a high priority, and rightly, on oral communication, and *good* audio-lingual programs have succeeded in producing fluent speakers of English and other foreign languages. But these programs must additionally recognize reading as a skill in and of itself instead of as merely reinforcement for orally introduced structures and vocabulary if they are to produce fluent readers as well.

It is a cliché of reading instruction that one first learns to read and then reads to learn. All advanced students preparing to *use* English as a *tool in learning* must:

1. Understand the vocabulary and structures unique to the milieu of college texts, technical manuals, and other written material required in their professional training and its realization.
2. Read at a rate which will not be a handicap to learning.
3. Process deeper levels of interpretive meaning within English-speaking cultural contexts.

These skills, while quite teachable, do not coincide with the audio-lingual goals of instruction, and to expect students to "catch" them in their contact with English much as they would a communicable disease is inefficient, unfair, and unrealistic. We can do better.

Reading is sometimes referred to as a "passive" skill, but there is in fact relatively little about the reading process which can be classified as habitual response. Left to right directionality would come in this category, as would the recognition of letter shapes, punctuation marks, and common patterns of arrangement.

Sound/symbol correspondences may also be classified as habits, but while "sounding out" words may be considered a good habit in beginning stages of reading instruction, learners must evidently shift from phonetic to lexical interpretation of spelling patterns before they can be said to be fluent readers (Chomsky 1970). Some educators are suggesting that reading out loud may be detrimental to a beginning reader by impeding the shift (Cazden 1972), and all reading experts agree that subvocalization during silent reading is a *bad* habit calling for remediation.

In contrast, I would like to quote from a well-known text on teaching English as a second language:

In reading, and this happens in reading our native tongue, too, we subvocalize; that is, we make sounds in our throat. We read faster, therefore, if we know how to make the sounds without stumbling over them and if we have learned to read in thought groups.

We in TESOL have insisted that reading is based on oral language, and I will still maintain that reading content at beginning levels should be first introduced in meaningful oral contexts, but we do our more advanced students a disservice by not recognizing and providing for the extensive differences between oral and written language and its processing, as well as for the similarities.

Reading, like listening, is a receptive skill. Like listening, reading involves the use of incomplete data input in predicting and anticipating what probably follows—what the receiver has not yet heard or seen. Input is phonetic for the listener and graphic for the reader, but for the good reader there seems to be no intermediate phonological level of processing. Psycholinguists do not know precisely how we read, but they do tell us there isn't nearly enough time in the process for the fluent reader to make sound/symbol connections, and that "the immediate memory span is virtually identical for words of one to four syllables." (Gough 1972) We must conclude that whatever the form of written language stored for recognition, it cannot be in phonological or phonemic segments. Additional evidence for the independent processing of speech and writing can be found with the many graduate students who have learned to read a foreign language, such as French, without being able to understand a spoken sentence, or with the deaf who learn to read, but never hear language.

It is true that most readers can encode the graphic symbols into phonemic representations and read out loud what is written on a page, but this is not the same process as either speaking or reading and may be learned by someone who does not speak the language at all, or even understand it. Goodman's example for this case is the bar-mitzvah boy who has learned to recode Hebrew script as chanted oral Hebrew but has no understanding of what he is chanting (Goodman 1972). Most of us can read a story out loud to our children while planning our schedule for the remainder of the evening or thinking about a problem that arose at the office during the day. Although reading is dependent on graphic input, I wish to limit the term "reading" here to reconstructing the meaning of the writer, to processing the semantic content.

As in listening, reading involves the use of syntactic information in determining meaning, and both listeners and readers should process words in groups rather than as single lexical items. While oral language is necessarily decoded in the same order as the sequence of speech, however, a good reader is by no means limited to a string of words as they pass in front of his nose. His eyes will jump back and forth, taking in just enough cues to anticipate what's coming next, skipping back for more if a tentative decision on meaning has to be rejected or refined. The span of his glance increases with the predictability of the grammatical form, becoming quite large in such constrained contexts as the end of a passive sentence where "by the (agent)" almost *has* to occur. His eyes will check back frequently in a complex sentence in which much has been inserted between the beginning of the subject and the verb, what linguists call "left embedding." (Kavanagh 1968)

It is, in fact, this very characteristic of writing that leads to its differentiation from spoken language. Writing is not simply "talk written down," but rather once a society becomes literate, the written variety of the language comes to lead a life of its own. The fact that we do not have to rely on short-term aural memory for processing sentences frees writers from the limits of aural memory and permits them to construct sentences whose length, density, and complexity would be unlikely or impossible in a purely oral mode.

Such complex sentences are quite common in college texts and technical manuals, but ordinary oral drills can never prepare readers for them, since they are practically nonexistent in colloquial speech. Structures unique to written English should be introduced and analyzed in written contexts, as should technical or literary terms students will only need to recognize and never have to produce. The structure of written English should be approached as systematically with our more advanced students as we hope the structure of spoken English was when they were beginners.

We have been focusing first on the structure or grammar of written language, the order of words and their interrelationship, but of course they do carry meaning which must be decoded during the reading process. We have all seen nonsense sentences such as "The wiltish toffs slocked rumbly" used to illustrate structural meaning, but no one suggests that this is all there is to language. The semantic content of individual words and expressions remains an essential building block in our structures, and studies show us there is a higher correlation between reading achievement and the recognition of individual lexical items than between reading achievement and knowledge of grammar, speaking fluency, or any other linguistic skill. I will have more to say about this with regard to methodology, but I would first like to call attention to yet another level of meaning in reading—essential for teaching English as a foreign language, but seldom (if ever) given adequate consideration. It may be called "sociocultural meaning."

Speech is usually considered as preeminently a social activity, while reading, on the other hand, is often viewed as a nonsocial activity which someone can do by himself in a corner. But this distinction is misleading for our purposes, since written, as well as spoken, language has sociocultural content often unrecognized by native speakers of the language because it operates at an unconscious level. This content is essential for foreign students to understand if they are to interpret the meaning of an English sentence (or longer construction) as intended by the English-speaking writer.

The significance of sociocultural information is most important in imaginative writing, probably reaching its zenith in satire, while it is probably least significant in technical and scientific writing, though even here allusive intrusions may occasionally interfere with comprehension, particularly in less formal prose. *To shrug something off* may puzzle a Chinese who has never seen this gesture or *to receive a nod* may confuse a Turk for whom this is usually a sign of negation.

One of the most important sociocultural features of meaning is the "value" or connotation we attach to words, which are usually culture-specific and not easily translatable from language to language. An example is the humorous paradigm

He is old.
You are middle-aged.
I am mature.

Words that appear to be synonyms when looked up in a bilingual dictionary often have vastly different meanings in usage. Many of these so-called "loaded" words have at one time been quite emotionally neutral, and then taken on negative cultural connotations and been replaced by euphemisms, as *hoarding* has been replaced by *stockpiling* in recent years. Understanding the culturally different values assigned to referentially synonymous pairs *smile* and *leer, intercede* and *interfere, conciliation* and *appeasement, attorney* and *shyster* is essential if an advanced student of English as a foreign language is to understand the tone and intent of much of what he reads. The Spanish speaker for whom the word *propaganda* is completely neutral will be badly misled if he does not recognize its negative connotation in English.

It also seems important for language students to be able to separate what is *asserted* by the writer from what is *presupposed.* In the sentence "King Charles of France drove a white Mercedes" the writer asserts:

1. King Charles drove.
2. He drove a Mercedes.
3. The Mercedes was white.

The writer additionally presupposes that France, at the time of writing, had a king named Charles, that he could drive, and that at the time the personage lived, Mercedeses existed. These presuppositions are taken to be shared between writer and reader and not new information. It seems profitable for advanced students to pursue such analyses, although all languages seem to have similar conditions on assertions and presuppositions, and cultural interference is not much of a problem at this point.

Recent references to "King Richard," however, contain many implications which depend on presupposed information common only to our culture, as uniquely American as our collective attitude toward monarchies and our recent legislative hassles.

It is probably at this level of sociocultural meaning that most misunderstandings occur. Much confusion may result from allusions to "the patience of Job" or a character from Greek mythology, as in the recent headline "Wounded Knee Is McGovern's Achilles' Heel," if the student is from an Eastern culture; and such common expressions as "to kick the bucket" or "to keep tabs on" are meaningless if one is limited to a literal interpretation. Very commonly, students are misled in their interpretation by previous cultural experience, a type of interference which frequently goes unnoted and uncorrected by either student or teacher.

Improving the reading skill of any student begins with identifying his weaknesses, and then implementing appropriate methods for strengthening these skills. Students in an advanced English program will vary greatly in their needs, depending on prior reading methods used with them and on the nature of their native-language reading skills.

Except for calling attention to its primary function in the teaching of reading, I will not take time to discuss diagnostic testing. Suffice it to say that knowing what reading skills to teach, and where to begin, depend largely on the use of adequate diagnostic measures.

The first level to test for is word recognition. Students should recognize many words on sight, be able to "sound out" most new words presented in isolation, be able to identify morphemic and contextual clues to meaning, and be aware of the various meanings a word may have, including figurative meanings.

Although reading aloud is usually recommended for establishing the sound/symbol relation which is beneficial in decoding new words, research has indicated that enough potentially bad side effects may occur for me to discourage this practice. Listening while looking may be a better way of achieving the same objective. I would suggest providing students deficient in this skill with tape recordings of their reading assignments and supplemental material so that the two receptive language skills (listening and reading) can be correlated. The intonation of the taped native English speaker will provide additional clues for the syntactic and semantic interpretation of more complex sentences not yet within the students' competence. Listening to inaccurate peer models reading aloud in the classroom is at least as doubtful in value as reading aloud itself, and it must be remembered that the process of attaching sound to symbol is only a temporary state in learning to read. It should be used by advanced readers only when they encounter a new and difficult word which they cannot decode from the context. Having students read aloud, if done at all, should be seen as a testing device rather than a teaching procedure.

Morphemic clues, listed above as part of word-recognition skills, are those within the form of words which signal part of the meaning. These include plural and possessive suffixes, verb inflections, comparative forms, and derivational affixes. Students first need to identify each as they develop word recognition skills, understand the function of each in context, and then practice for quick recognition of such structural clues. Using flash cards, transparencies, or some other technique which limits the visual image to only a second or two for each sentence, students should learn to distinguish signs of tense, possession, or negation, locate words that tell *how many* or *what kind*, or identify the sentence as a statement, question, or command.

Contextual clues allow good readers to deduce the meaning of unfamiliar words. Too much emphasis can be placed on this skill at beginning and intermediate levels to the detriment of fluency. Unfamiliar words often cause the less advanced reader to come to a screeching halt. Even if told just to guess at new words, most students will look them up if the opportunity arises and write a translation "equivalent" above the line in their text. The unnatural eye movements and bilingual processing then required in subsequent reading of the page should be avoided. All students still having difficulties at the level of word recognition should have the new words in a passage introduced *in advance of reading it.* They can look them up in a dictionary, use them in original sentences, and, if desired, enter each on a 3x5 index card to have handy for reference when they need it in reading and for vocabulary review. When the words are encountered in the text at this level, only the structural and semantic context should be new.

In the direction of deducing the meaning of words from context, students should be taught to recognize and interpret such explicit clues as actual definition, explanation, comparison, or contrast in the text. Guessing word meanings from structural and semantic probability should not be required in a foreign language until all words within the understanding of students are easily recognized in print.

A final skill at this level is recognizing figurative meanings as such. I do not suggest trying to teach what all the expressions mean—there are far too many—but just their identification and the understanding that they must be interpreted differently from other words.

The second level to test for is phrase-reading skill, the ability to process meaningful groups of words at a glance instead of word-by-word decipherment. To read at this level of proficiency, students must be able to recognize meaningful grammatical units, predict what will follow from incomplete linguistic input, and be selective in their perception of what elements are most important to meaning.

Students deficient at the phrase-reading level of reading competence may either perceive only words as meaning-bearing units or they may visually group words in meaningless combinations. It is important for students to recognize the function words which mark sentence elements: noun markers, such as *a, the, any,* and *few*; verb markers, such as *is, have, had*; phrase markers, such as *up, down, below*; clause markers, such as *if, because, when*; and question markers, such as *who, what,* and *why.* (Lefevre 1964) The grammatical analysis of basic sentences will help, at least to the extent of discovering how a particular unit is recognized as the subject, how it relates to the rest of the sentence, and where it occurs in normal sentence order. Other units are perhaps best brought in focus as answers to questions: What did they do? How many did it? Where? When? Such questions should be asked of sentences reflecting normal English word order until students can respond without hesitation. Common inversions should then be added in the question drills, such as sentences with initial adverbials and passive constructions. Needless to say, perhaps, the recognition of these components of relatively simple sentences is an essential prerequisite to processing the complex structures often encountered in written English.

Recognizing meaningful groups of words is a big step in the direction of recognizing redundancies in the language and using them to predict what follows. This is an essential step to fluent reading, but one which some students never take if merely left to their own devices. The recognition of both semantic and syntactic redundancy can be taught.

Intermediate students should be able to use their knowledge of the structure of English to know which words are most important in a sentence. They should recognize punctuation as a clue to meaning and have some idea of what kind of information they can anticipate after a comma, dash, colon, or semicolon. They should recognize such logical indicators as *but, if . . . then,* and *therefore,* and understand how they relate parts of a sentence. Students can best be forced to practice the expectancy task in reading through writing: the instructor can duplicate passages from fairly easy material, leaving a blank space for at least one word in each sentence which has a low information load. Students should fill in the blanks with words they think the original writer would have used. A slightly more difficult task involves completing sentences with appropriate phrases or clauses.

Advanced students additionally profit from techniques traditionally used in beginning courses in composition for native English speakers: as they are reading, have students note only the main ideas; have them note how often they are repeated, recognizing paraphrases; point out the patterns of organizations in paragraphs, how the ideas go together. (Handbooks for composition are often good sources for such reading material.) Students should recognize such relationships among sentences as time order, comparison and contrast, enumeration, or cause and effect. They need these skills to decode such sentences as the following: "If the gasoline supply is shut off, there is no gasoline in the charge to ignite and therefore no power event occurs and the engine stops."

This is a point where a contrastive analysis of discourse structure in English and the learner's language would be useful. Many of the rhetorical principles which guide (often quite unconsciously) the structure of writing in English are not used or are used quite differently in other languages. Since an awareness, again unconscious, of these principles serves to guide our reading like a compass which gives us our bearings, it elevates the redundancy of what is read by increasing the expectancy of what is to come. By making students sensitive to the structure of discourse, especially where it differs from that in their own language, we can help them to gain an overview in this reading and avoid getting bogged down in sentence-by-sentence decoding.

Selectiveness in perception is also an important factor in fluent reading. As in listening, students must learn to recognize the important meaning-carrying elements at a glance and not give each word equal attention.

It is difficult to say whether a slow pace of reading is just symptomatic of word-by-word processing or whether it also causes it. Besides the fact that a faster pace generally improves comprehension and of course facilitates learning *through* English, it also guarantees that a phrase level of reading must be taking place. Increased speed can be encouraged through flash card techniques which require seeing an entire phrase at a glance, and through regular timed reading exercises followed by comprehension questions. Such drills can be highly frustrating to students not yet able to process phrases as syntactic units, but beneficial to those who have reached this level of competence.

Even most who qualify as advanced students of English as a foreign language have difficulty processing some of the more complex sentence structures which seldom, if ever, occur in speech. (Take, for example, the preceding sentence!) Common problems include ellipsis, complex noun phrases, relative clause and participial modifiers, and cleft and pseudo-cleft inversions.

The first step as instructor is to make sure the previously mentioned skills of word recognition and phrase reading are under control, for the processing of complex syntactic structures requires these as a base. Several different approaches may be taken from that point.

One, from a syntactic perspective, is to work up from simple sentences to the complex structures (Eskey 1970). A complex sentence is read from the text; then one or more simpler sentences with similar meaning are supplied by the instructor. Students are asked to inductively relate the simpler to the more complex with regard to differences in form and meaning. This essentially amounts to paraphrasing a complex sentence in simpler form.

Take this complex sentence as an example: *That John was believed by Mary to have been bitten by the dog is not true.* It might be paraphrased: *It is not true that Mary believed the dog bit John.* The differences in meaning which would be noted should include the shift in focus as the word order is changed.

A semantic perspective on instruction would have students tackle complex sentences as combinations of propositions. They would read the sentence, and then say or list the different propositions included in it. This procedure is similar to the identification of *assertions* and *presuppositions* discussed earlier.

The following sentence occurs in an intermediate-level reading lesson: "Of course, the weather is quite important to people who work outdoors, such as farmers or house painters." From this semantic point of view, this sentence could be broken down into its basic propositions.

1. The weather is important to some people.
2. It is important to people who work outdoors.
3. Farmers work outdoors.
4. House painters work outdoors.

The initial phrase "of course" means that the writer feels the information which is to follow should not be new to the reader.

Another syntactic approach is to begin with simple sentences and teach students how to combine them in more complex structures. This technique, which was common in the 19th century, is called "sentence synthesis." Students, on encountering complex sentences in texts, should then be better able to break them down into multiple simpler sentences. They would need to recognize different types of transformations in English and be able to reconstruct more basic forms.

An advanced assignment using this technique might call for students to combine the following sentences into a single complex sentence:

1. Proponents are expressing fears in Texas.
2. They are proponents of education.
3. The education is equal.
4. They fear something.
5. The Rodriguez decision may cause something.
6. The legislature would not act on proposals.
7. The proposals would equalize tax burdens throughout the state.
8. The proposals would equalize education throughout the state.
9. The state is big.

The resulting synthesis would be: Proponents of equal education in Texas are expressing fears that the Rodriguez decision may cause the legislature not to act on proposals which would equalize tax burdens and education throughout the big state.

The processing of complex sentences can be guided with questions (Who? What? Where? When? How?), and students should be taught to use this procedure independently.

An inductive contrast between the complex English structure and the student's native language may be additionally helpful at this point in insuring comprehension.

Finally, a pervasive goal of instruction through all levels of reading proficiency is improved comprehension. I would like to offer some specific suggestions in this general area.

1. Provide advance guidelines for reading, including questions to be answered and points to look for.
2. Continually have students use information from their reading in class discussions and written assignments.
3. Test only on important points in the reading, and not on minor details.
4. Encourage students to read extensively at a level which is easy and enjoyable for them.
5. Sele. reading material which is relevant to students' experiences, interests, and needs.

I have tried to indicate that the audio-lingual method, by focusing so exclusively on the productive aspect of language in the oral mode, has in its own way distorted the emphasis of language teaching as much as did the much-maligned grammar and translation method. Except for the restricted purpose of person-to-person communication, training in oral production to the exclusion of other modes is of limited value. For the person outside an English-speaking environment who wishes to use the language as a tool for acquiring information, fluent reading ability is probably the most important single skill he can acquire. It has been more than a decade since the linguistic and psychological theories on which the audio-lingual method was based were first called into question, and the method itself is now undergoing intensive reassessment. It is my belief that out of this reassessment, which is long overdue, the role of reading will assume a more significant place than it has had in the recent past.

CHAPTER 4

Control of Contextualized Function and Content Words as It Affects EFL Reading Comprehension Test Scores

Donald Sim and Marsha Bensoussan
University of Haifa

Introduction

For the purposes of this study, reading comprehension is considered as the ability of the student to understand both content words (nouns, verbs, adjectives, and adverbs) and function words (prepositions, pronouns, conjunctions, and auxiliary verbs). Content words contain the message or idea, whereas function words connect the ideas cohesively in a larger context. A facility in interpreting the interaction of the two kinds of words is necessary for effective comprehension of the context in which they operate.

Based on this consideration of the nature of reading comprehension of expository prose at an academic level, teachers in institutions of higher education spend a proportion of class time teaching the meaning, contextual use, and relation of selected function words to the cohesive properties of a text (Halliday and Hasan 1976). Oral questioning, written exercises, and a body of teacher opinion support the notion that function words, in particular, are not handled with facility by students when reading expository prose texts.

Yet previous studies based on the cloze procedure (Aborn 1959, Louthan 1965) have shown that function words are easier to replace than content words.

By implication, then, it might seem that they are also easier to read. As this appeared to gainsay current teaching practice, an experi-

The statistical supervision of this experiment was directed by Dr. Baruch Nevo, Head of the University, to whom we are grateful. His critical comments were penetrating and useful. We also wish to thank the teachers and students who participated in the administration of the examination.

mental test was undertaken to elicit indications as to whether control of contextualized function words had a greater, a lesser, or the same effect on comprehension success as had control of content words.

The purpose of the study, accordingly, was to determine whether, using a noncloze procedure, students score higher on questions testing function words than on questions on content words. A noncloze procedure was used to examine the matter, since we were concerned with recognition and decoding in reading rather than with substitution in writing. Multiple-choice questions were therefore used as an objective noncloze method.

The experiment assumed that students who have not fully mastered the reading skill that is needed to decode or interpret function words have more difficulty in reading texts than students who have mastered this skill, and that this is no less important a lexical skill than content-word decoding or interpretation.

Previous preliminary research (Sim 1973) indicated that function words cause difficulty in reading comprehension at an academic level. In experiments at the Universities of Manchester and Haifa (1972-1973), texts containing selected function words and the same texts from which the function words had been "written out" were administered. The content and questions were the same for both versions, which were randomly distributed. Indications were that texts containing the selected function words presented greater difficulty, as reflected in student scores. Further indications of this were sought in the present experiment.

Accordingly unseen tests of advanced reading comprehension were constructed with types of questions designed to test control of function and content words. Additional paraphrase and purpose questions assumed control of both types of words. Examples of the types of questions are given under Method below. Results on these tests would, it was considered, indicate the relative difficulty experienced by students in answering function- or content-word questions and, by extension, in reading function and content words in context.

It was thought that if incomplete mastery of the contextual operation of function words affected test scores at least as much as incomplete mastery of content words, there would be justification for spending prime teaching time and resources in teaching the use of function words in contextual cohesion.

Method

A test battery of 2½ hours, including 11 texts and 103 questions (a specimen text containing questions is included as Appendix A), was administered to 187 undergraduate students at Haifa University who had completed half of a 100-hour English reading comprehension course at the time of taking the test.

Students were permitted to use English-English dictionaries to reduce the element of lexical uncertainty and thus further validate test results. It was assumed that students who answered items incorrectly, even with the help of a dictionary, really did not know the meaning, or even how to find the meaning, of specific vocabulary items in context.

The 103 questions on the test battery, derived from 11 texts covering a range of content areas, fell into five categories, arbitrarily entitled as follows:

1. *Questions on function words*, used in a logical sequence.
2. *Questions on content words*, used denotatively for meaning.
3. *Questions on content words*, used connotatively for tone and implication.
4. *Part-text questions* on the ability to recognize a paraphrase of short stretches of text.
5. *Whole-text questions* concerning the author's purpose and manner of achieving that purpose.

The last two types were included as general questions, typically asked in unseen tests.

These question types have evolved over a period of time as questions habitually asked in reading comprehension tests in the circumstances in which such tests are normally administered. There was therefore no particular bias introduced to satisfy the hypothesis.

The following are examples of each of the five types of questions:

1. Function-word Question
   As a matter of fact, however. These words introduce a paragraph that
   1. contradicts the ideas stated previously
   2. continues the ideas stated previously
   3. results from the ideas stated previously
   4. agrees with the ideas stated previously

2. Content-Word Question: *Word Meaning* (The student is asked to choose the appropriate meaning in the context from among four different definitions given in the dictionary)
   climate. This word means
   1. weather conditions
   2. conditions of temperature

     3.   atmosphere of opinion
     4.   meteorological atmosphere

3. Content-Word Question: *Tone and Implication*
   ultimate abdication. These words show the author's
     1.   approval
     2.   disapproval
     3.   objectivity
     4.   exaggeration

4. Part-Text *Paraphrase* Question
   An argument in favor of the primacy of spoken language is that
     1.   people are more careful of their style
     2.   the content is more interesting and valuable
     3.   most conversation is trivial and ungrammatical
     4.   we speak more than we write

5. Whole-Text *Purpose* Question
   The aim of this passage is to
     1.   present some arguments against a widespread impression
     2.   present the history of language
     3.   show how language develops
     4.   show that writing and speech are basically similar

All questions underwent computerized Item Analysis (Nevo, ITANA, 1975), yielding a Difficulty Index for each item. (See Appendix B for detailed Item Analysis.)

Results

A Review of the Figures in Appendix B (n = 187)

Question type		No. of items	Average of difficulty indices
1.	Function word	13	59.2
2.	Content word—*meaning*	22	53.8
3.	Content word—*tone and implication*	12	50.2
4.	Part-text—*paraphrase*	43	53.2
5.	Whole-text—*purpose*	13	55.1
		103	

The difficulty index is obtained by calculating the percentage of students answering the question correctly out of the total number of students attempting to answer it.

On examination of the indices, the average difficulty for Function Words is 59.2 and for Content Words, 53.8 and 50.2. Although the figures appear to show that the former are easier than the latter, this in fact is not statistically significant. An F test (Hays 1963, pp. 371-378; F = .54) for the significance of differences among the five averages of difficulty yielded no significant difference. That is to say, within the limits of the experiment, function-word questions appear to be as difficult as content-word questions.

Discussion

If we suppose that the process of reading expository prose involves the ability to follow a logical argument, function-word as well as content-word questions should be included in tests of reading proficiency. This argues that in measuring a student's level of reading proficiency, a test should attempt to elicit the student's understanding of the cohesive relationship between the components of a text, as well as an understanding of each component separately. It would seem that for this purpose decoding or interpreting function words is no less important a lexical skill than content-word decoding or· interpretation, while facility in interpreting the interaction of the two kinds of words is necessary for effective comprehension of the text in which they operate.

While there is no evidence to suggest that teaching the contextual operation of function words is more important than teaching content words, the results, within the limits of the experiment, support the contention that function words, being an apparent cause of reading difficulty, need to be taught and tested to the same extent as content words.

Further investigation is required to determine to what extent such teaching should be undertaken and at what stage in the curriculum it should be stressed.

Appendix A

Force and violence are often wasteful because they do not necessarily teach or influence the subjects to act exactly as those who inflict the coercion wish. Force cannot teach children mathematics, nor can it even be used to teach soldiers how to use force. With only sighs and quivers from the population, effects are achieved that would have bloodied every street in medieval England. The history of lands and times when physical coercion diminished, relative to education and economics, is the story of politics that has learned more ingenious and sophisticated ways to accomplish its purposes. (from *Political Behavior*, by Alfred de Grazia).

Questions	Question type	Difficulty index
67. The main idea of the passage is that force and violence	5	64
1. can make people change their behavior		
2. are the major weapons of politics		
— 3. are not so effective as education and economics		
4. cause sighs and quivers from the population		
68. *Force and violence are often wasteful* because they	4	81
1. cannot be used by soldiers		
— 2. are not necessary to achieve a desired effect		
3. have bloodied every street in medieval England		
4. have no meaning in the modern world		
69. Medieval England is given as an example of a place where	4	62
1. democracy was strong		
2. the people studied education and economics		
3. force was rarely used		
— 4. force was often used		
70. According to the last sentence, modern politics	4	75
1. no longer tries to influence people		
2. accomplishes its purposes using coercion		
— 3. influences using methods more sophisticated than force		
4. is a history of lands and times of physical coercion		
71. *more ingenious and sophisticated ways.* Among these, the author includes	4	40
1. the story of politics		
2. the history of lands and times		
— 3. education and economics		
4. physical coercion		
72. *its purposes.* The author refers to the purposes of	1	69
1. history		
2. lands and times		
3. education and economics		
— 4. politics		
73. *coercion* is another word for	2	69
— 1. violence		
2. subjects		
3. quivers		
4. effects		

— indicates correct answers

Appendix B   Item Analysis of Test

Function Word Questions

Text	Question	Difficulty index
3	17	53
4	28	66
6	48	51
7	58	56
7	60	45
9	72	69
9	74	99
10	78	75
11	93	77
11	98	59
11	100	66
11	102	26
11	103	39
Average		59.2
Standard deviation		16.8

Total: 6 texts, 13 questions

Content Word Questions: *Word Meaning*

Text	Question	Difficulty index	Text	Question	Difficulty index
1	4	59	11	90	64
1	6	18	11	91	47
2	12	17	11	92	75
3	19	64	11	94	27
4	23	81	11	95	66
4	24	72	11	96	55
6	42	49	11	97	42
6	49	37	11	88	55
6	52	46	11	101	30
6	53	77	Average		53.8
9	73	69	Standard deviation		16.9
9	75	19	Total: 8 texts, 22 questions		
10	79	54			

Content Word Questions:
Tone and Implication

Text	Question	Difficulty index
1	2	76
1	5	38
3	15	54
5	40	43
6	43	66
6	47	46
7	59	58
10	80	50
10	81	45
10	83	48
10	84	33
10	87	45
Average		50.2
Standard deviation		11.9

Total: 7 texts, 12 questions

Part-Text *Paraphrase* **Questions**

Text	Question	Difficulty index
1	1	45
1	3	75
2	9	56
2	10	88
2	11	36
3	13	69
3	14	26
3	16	36
3	18	59
3	20	62

Part-Text *Paraphrase* **Questions**
(continued)

Text	Question	Difficulty index
4	21	40
4	22	54
4	25	66
4	26	73
4	27	72
4	29	50
4	30	68
5	32	32
5	33	26
5	34	25
5	35	34
5	36	31
5	37	44
5	38	42
5	39	33
6	41	68
6	44	63
6	45	90
6	46	28
6	50	62
7	56	33
7	57	61
8	62	66
8	63	34
8	64	53
9	68	81
9	69	62
9	70	75
9	71	40
10	77	66
10	82	60
10	85	48
10	86	45
Average		53.2
Standard deviation		17.9

Total: 10 texts, 43 questions

Whole-Text *Purpose* Questions

Text	Question	Difficulty index
2	7	62
2	8	44
4	31	27
6	51	54
7	54	49
7	55	73
8	61	80
8	65	61
8	66	30
9	67	64
9	76	57
10	88	57
10	89	58
Average		55.1
Standard deviation		15.0

Total: 7 texts, 13 questions

SECTION II

ORGANIZATION

The chapters in this section concern the organization of second language reading classes and materials. Guidelines are presented for the selection of reading passages that are in keeping with the interests and needs of the students. The kinds of linguistic knowledge and extralinguistic information that appear to be necessary for efficient reading in a second language are also discussed.

In Chapter 5, Clarke and Silberstein consider the objectives and general content of ESL reading courses in the light of current theoretical perspectives on the reading process. The fluent reader is assumed to read with a purpose. His approach to a given passage will vary, depending on the purpose.

The authors describe techniques for fostering the general strategies of scanning to get specific facts, skimming for the general idea, reading for thorough comprehension, and critical reading. They also indicate the types of materials that provide appropriate training and practice in each of these strategies and in the language skills that they assume students must have in order to use the strategies in the interpretation of texts. Sample lesson plans for a week's reading classes are given, in an attempt to relate materials and teacher and student activities to the theoretical framework.

In Chapter 6, Eskey describes a highly useful model of the reading component in courses for advanced learners of English based on recent thinking on the nature of the reading process. The model is designed to ensure instruction and practice in the language skills that appear to be necessary for efficient reading.

Eskey's model includes intensive classroom instruction in text structure, grammar, vocabulary, and the target culture and extensive reading practice outside the classroom. The role of the teacher is to activate the learner's capacity to develop his own learning strategies for efficient reading, rather than merely to provide a set of techniques for coping with the texts. The reading materials assigned to the students should be selected because they conform to the known areas of interest and to the professional concerns of the learners.

In Chapter 7, Mackay points out that certain categories of linguistic markers tend to be neglected in the second language classroom, although an understanding of them is essential to the successful interpretation of spoken or written texts. These include intersentence ties which contribute to the lexical, grammatical, and semantic cohesion of a text. Mackay illustrates these neglected linguistic categories by referring to authentic texts taken from the field of environmental studies. (He also offers detailed examples of techniques by means of which these language features can be exercised appropriately.) He is in this chapter particularly interested in learners for whom a reading knowledge of English is a necessary auxiliary skill contributing to professional and academic studies. Mackay suggests that the full development of the comprehension skills may be impeded if instruction in how various linguistic devices contribute to textual meaning is neglected.

In Chapter 8, Been proposes an approach to "reading for meaning" which was developed for use in an adult teaching situation, where reading instruction is currently a vehicle for vocabulary enrichment and expansion of the learners' knowledge of English syntax. Been considers that classroom techniques used with reading passages, such as reading aloud, explanation of vocabulary items, and literal comprehension questions, are not likely to produce fluent readers, however useful these classroom activities may be in extending general English skills, or "reading for language."

To promote "reading for meaning" as well, Been suggests first that questions providing "context support" be asked, before a passage is read. The questions would help the students search for specific information. The second part of the approach is to provide graphic cues which would encourage the development of good reading strategies by drawing the learners' attention to the important words (in large type) and by directing their attention away from redundancies (in small type). The ordinary linear processing strategy would be promoted by using regular type.

Been presents some intriguing sample materials. As she is careful to point out, however, this approach to "reading for meaning" has yet to be proved effective experimentally.

These descriptions of how to organize second language reading courses and materials point up a change in attitude toward what the purpose of reading instruction in a second language should be. In the past, reading selections and classes were viewed primarily as a way to provide further practice in the language, or as additional samples of the second language to be used in intensive oral practice or for vocabulary expansion. The chapters in this section assume that instruction in reading a second language should have as its primary purpose the improvement of the students' ability to acquire information from written sources accurately, rapidly, and efficiently. The materials selected for this purpose should reflect the characteristics of the written language, taking into account how written texts differ from the spoken language. Techniques of instruction should emphasize the essentially individual, private nature of reading, and considerable amounts of time should be allotted to silent reading as well as to specific instruction in the linguistic and rhetorical features of the written language.

CHAPTER 5

Toward a Realization of Psycholinguistic Principles in the ESL Reading Class

Mark A. Clarke
and Sandra Silberstein
English Language Institute —
University of Michigan

Theoretical Premises

There is no "psycholinguistic method" for teaching reading; the value of psycholinguistics lies in the insights it provides into the reading process (see, for example, Smith and Goodman 1973). In the past the reader was viewed as working through a text in a rigid, word-by-word fashion, decoding information in a precise manner from print to speech to aural comprehension. Frank Smith (1973) emphasizes two important contributions of psycholinguistics which make such an interpretation impossible.

First, it has been established that there is a severe limit to the amount of information that we are able to receive, process, and remember (Miller 1967). The reader, therefore, does not use all the information on the page but rather must select the most productive language cues in determining the message of the writer. From this it follows that reading is necessarily a rapid process which could not proceed word by word.

Second, research has shown that reading is only incidentally visual (Kolers 1969). More information is contributed by the reader than by the print on the page. That is, readers understand what they read because they are able to take the stimulus beyond its graphic representation and assign it membership to an appropriate group of concepts already stored in their memories.

First published in *Language Learning*, Vol. 27, No. 1, 1977. Reprinted by permission of the editor of that journal and the authors.

Goodman (1970) summarizes the psycholinguistic perspective of reading:

Reading is a selective process. It involves partial use of available minimal language cues selected from perceptual input on the basis of the reader's expectation. As this partial information is processed, tentative decisions are made to be confirmed, rejected or refined as reading progresses. (p. 260)

From this paragraph, which describes the proficient native-language reader, inferences can be drawn which are important in the preparation and use of second language (L2) reading materials.

First, the definition assumes that reading is an active process. The reader forms a preliminary expectation about the material, then selects the fewest, most productive cues necessary to confirm or reject that expectation. This is a sampling process in which the reader takes advantage of his knowledge of vocabulary, syntax, discourse, and the "real world." Skill in reading, therefore, depends on precise coordination of a number of special skills. Providing students with practice in these skills and helping them to develop consistent "attack strategies" should be the focus of any reading program.

The second inference, closely tied to the first, is that reading must be viewed as a twofold phenomenon involving process—comprehending—and product—comprehension. (For a discussion of this distinction see Goodman and Burke 1973.) The process of working through a reading task, with the mistakes and false starts that this involves, is often as important as producing correct responses to post facto comprehension questions. Our responsibility as reading teachers, therefore, goes beyond presenting our students with passages followed by comprehension questions. We must construct reading tasks which reward students as much for trying as for getting the correct answer.

Third, reading involves, as Goodman (1970) stated, an interaction between thought and language. The reader brings to the task a formidable amount of information and ideas, attitudes and beliefs. This knowledge, coupled with the ability to make linguistic predictions, determines the expectations the reader will develop as he reads. Skill in reading depends on the efficient interaction between linguistic knowledge and knowledge of the world. Two things follow from this. Students must have "conceptual readiness" for each task: reading activities must either hook into the students' knowledge of the world, or the teacher must fill in the gaps *before* the task is begun. Furthermore, this perspective underscores the importance of individualized reading tasks since it is recognized that each student brings special strengths and weaknesses to every activity.

Fourth, psycholinguistic theory emphasizes the importance of using semantically complete readings. Research shows (see, for example, Menosky 1971, Goodman and Burke 1973) that reading errors change significantly as the reader progresses into a passage, supporting the position that the reader builds on a previous store of knowledge by adding information from the reading. This finding suggests that successful reading lessons depend not only on the students' efficient use of strategies and knowledge but also on the nature of the reading passage. The easiest passage is not necessarily the shortest, but rather the one which is conceptually complete.

Following directly from this perspective, our goals as reading teachers are: (1) to train our students to determine beforehand their goals and expectations for a given reading activity; (2) to teach our students to use reading strategies appropriate to the task at hand; (3) to encourage our students to take risks, to guess, to ignore their impulses to always be correct; and (4) to give our students practice and encouragement in using the minimum number of syntactic/semantic clues to obtain the maximum amount of information when reading.

In the confusion of preparing and presenting lessons to large, heterogeneous classes, it seems almost impossible to adhere to a productive theoretical framework. How do we build bridges between theory and practice? How do we introduce our students to effective reading strategies? How do we teach the group while assisting individuals? Most importantly, how do we build bridges between the classroom and the real world; how do we develop an independence in our students that allows them to leave our classrooms with a modus operandi which serves them well in new and more challenging environments? These issues are examined in the next section.

Achieving Goals

Learning Environment

Our ultimate goal is to foster independence in our students. An independent student not only uses various skills and strategies on cue but is able to determine for himself his predictions for a reading, his goals, and appropriate reading strategies. The following learning environment encourages such independence.

We advocate a learning environment that involves all individuals—teachers as well as students—in a cooperative process of setting and achieving goals. Classroom activities should parallel the "real world" as closely as possible. Since language is a tool of communication, methods and materials should concentrate on the message, not the medium. In addition, the purposes of reading should be the same in class as they are in real life: (1) to obtain a specific fact, or piece of information (scanning); (2) to obtain the general idea of the author (skimming); (3) to obtain a comprehensive understanding of a reading, as in reading a textbook (thorough comprehension); or (4) to evaluate information in order to determine where it fits into one's own system of beliefs (critical reading). Our students should become as conscious as we are of the purpose for reading, so that they will be able to determine the proper approaches to a reading task.

Role of Teacher

Following the admonitions of Earl Stevick (for example, 1973, 1974a, b, 1975), we utilize a paradigm of L2 classroom activity which minimizes teacher intervention, forcing the students to use and develop their new language skills. Within this paradigm we see three roles for the teacher: the teacher as teacher, the teacher as participant, and the teacher as facilitator.

The teacher as teacher is necessary only when the class is attempting to resolve a language problem, for it is only in this situation that the teacher is automatically presumed to possess more knowledge than the students. This role can be minimized if the students' attack strategies and reading skills have been effectively developed. If the task is realistic, and if the students have learned to adjust their reading strategies according to the task, there should be little need for teacher intervention.

The teacher is a participant in activities in which the knowledge and opinions of all persons in the class are of equal weight. Such activities would include discussions arising from reading activities, forming judgments about ideas encountered in readings, and activities which emphasize learning about a subject through the medium of the L2.

The teacher is a facilitator when creating an environment in which learning can take place, where linguistic expertise is required only in the event of communication breakdown. Often assignments can be discussed and corrected without teacher participation. Individualized assignments or small group sessions also require little direct teacher intervention.

This paradigm of the L2 classroom has two important advantages. First, it puts teachers in their place, emphasizing the individuality of students and reducing the compulsion we sometimes feel to control classroom activity. This relieves us of feelings of guilt and frustration occasioned by unsuccessful attempts at coercing the students to keep together. Second, it puts the responsibility for learning squarely on the shoulders of the students, which is where it belongs.

Materials

The problem of materials is one faced by all teachers. While it may be true that a good teacher can make almost any set of reading materials work in class, it is obvious that properly conceived reading exercises free the teacher to work more efficiently with students to solve individual reading problems. As reading teachers we generally find ourselves in one of two situations: either we are trying to adapt a textbook to suit our needs, or we are trying to find readings and write our own exercises to fill gaps in our curriculum. The following sections discuss the evaluation, preparation, and use of materials in the L2 reading class.

Evaluating Reading Selections. Whether we are looking for readings from the "real world" or deciding which selection to use from an assigned text, there are two factors that need to be considered before a reading is taken into the classroom.

Is the reading selection appropriate to both the proficiency level and the interest of the students? Both aspects of a reading, linguistic difficulty and semantic relevance, should be weighed before it is selected for use. There is evidence to suggest that relevance is a more important criterion than difficulty in selecting readings (Niles 1970). A student with the requisite amount of knowledge and interest in a subject is more likely to force himself through a difficult passage than through a relatively easy selection in which he has no interest.

Can the selection be made to provide practice in the skills which you need to reinforce? Given the demands of day-to-day teaching it is easy to fall into the trap of using a particular type of exercise because it is easy and enjoyable. It is at this point, however, that we need to shift to a different type of task since ease of execution is one indication that students have mastered a particular skill. It is also important from the viewpoint of classroom dynamics to vary the focus of skill work in a realistic way, thereby emphasizing the fact that outside the classroom reading goals and tasks vary greatly from one type of material to the next. It is also true that a single reading might provide practice in a number of skills. A menu, for example, is usually scanned, but skimming for a general idea of the type of restaurant, and the range of prices, is also realistic. Poetry is often used in reading classes only to increase students' literary appreciation, but it is an excellent vehicle for working on vocabulary-from-context skills, getting the main idea, or drawing inferences. An essay might be skimmed initially to determine the author's attitude toward an issue, followed by careful, then critical reading to determine such things as who the intended audience is, if the author's presuppositions are valid, and ultimately whether or not the reader agrees with the author.

By varying the tasks students are expected to perform, we not only make classes interesting but also show students that skills can be used with a wide range of materials and that the same reading might profitably be attacked several ways.

Preparing and Using Materials.   Once we have decided to use a reading passage, we need to make a number of decisions concerning the tasks we ask our students to perform with the selection. First, the selection determines what we try to do with it. If we want students to practice determining the main idea of a passage, we must find readings which are well-organized with topic sentences and supporting details. If a selection contains many facts and figures, it would probably work well in a scanning exercise. We should not force students to perform an unrealistic task with a reading merely because we have determined that it is time to work on a particular skill. If we want to work on skimming, for example, it is our responsibility to search until we find an appropriate reading.

Next, we must be careful to teach, then test. A common problem with reading texts is the tendency to ask students to produce a vocabulary item or to exhibit proficiency with a skill before they have been given adequate exposure and practice. Whether we are writing our own materials or adapting textbooks, we must make a consistent effort to introduce, model, reinforce, and review new learning tasks before we expect students to perform on their own. A good rule of thumb is to initially evaluate all exercises to determine exactly what is being required of the students, then to mentally review previous learning activities to make sure students can reasonably be expected to perform that task. Many cloze-type tests which pass for vocabulary review exercises actually require a firm grasp of syntax skills which may not have been explicitly taught. Students' failure to do well on such exercises may indicate weaknesses in knowledge of the structure of the L2, not in knowledge of vocabulary. In addition, cloze exercises require productive knowledge of vocabulary while students may not yet have been provided with the opportunity to develop productive control of these items.

Third, exercises should be written and used to provide maximum individualization. Reading involves an interaction between thought and language, a point of view which places great importance on the information and experiences that each reader brings to a task. Furthermore, we can assume that no two human beings learn languages at the same rate or in quite the same way. These two facts offer a strong case for individualizing instruction; while it is clearly impossible to prepare a separate lesson for each student, there are a number of things we can do to increase the individualization of our teaching. By producing a large number of exercises arranged hierarchically according to difficulty or by adding to the number of exercises or exercise items already in a text, we make it possible for each student to do as much as he is able to do. This gives all students ample practice. In addition, class time can be arranged so as to give teachers the opportunity to work with individuals and small groups. Of course, it may sometimes be necessary to find or produce exercises for individuals, to assign extra work to faster students or remedial work to slower students.

Finally, it is important that we develop flexibility in sequencing the use of exercises which accompany a reading. Typically, textbook exercises follow the reading selection. However, students can benefit by working with selected vocabulary and comprehension activities as well as discussion/composition topics before they begin to read. Students are more likely to experience success with a reading if they are familiar with selected vocabulary items before they begin reading. Likewise, attempting to answer comprehension questions before reading challenges students to read a passage to confirm or refute their guesses. If discussion/composition questions are discussed before the selection is read, students are given the opportunity to think the issues through in advance and thus are able to read far more critically.

Working through exercises before students attack a reading can be the single most effective tool in getting them to take the risk and read to the end. As long as we maintain a sound theoretical perspective of the work we ask our students to do, we should not feel obligated to follow the "accepted" textbook sequences of: reading, comprehension questions, vocabulary, discussion, and composition.

Developing Reading and Language Skills. At the intermediate and advanced levels we can assume that students possess a basic competence in English and that our primary task is to teach reading. Reading is, however, a language process, and reading teachers are inextricably bound up in the teaching of the second language itself. Although in practice it is impossible to separate reading instruction from general language instruction, for the purposes of discussion it is convenient to consider materials development as being composed of two tasks: the development of reading skill exercises (scanning, skimming, reading for thorough comprehension, and critical reading) and the development of language skill exercises (vocabulary, structure, discourse), both of which enable students to read more efficiently by using a minimum number of linguistic clues to obtain maximum information. First let us turn our attention to reading skills.

Reading Skills.   *Skimming* is quick reading for the general drift of a passage. It is an activity which is appropriate when there is not time to read something carefully or when trying to decide if careful reading is merited. It is reading with a general question in mind: "Does this book treat generative semantics or merely transformational grammar?" or "Is this author for or against capital punishment?" Since we assume that students skim in their own languages, we see our task as helping them to transfer this skill to English. Although tips such as "Take advantage of chapter titles and subheadings," "Read first and last sentences in the paragraphs," and "Let your eyes travel quickly, catching adjectives and adverbs" are useful, the only way to improve this skill is to be forced to read more and more rapidly and to formulate appropriate questions before beginning. At first we must provide the skimming questions and coach students through passages; later students are expected to form appropriate questions and predictions and to push themselves to read quickly. (Many times textbook comprehension questions are general enough to be good prereading skimming questions.)

Scanning is similar to skimming in that the reader is pushing himself through a selection at an initially uncomfortable rate, but the search is more focused since the information needed is very specific—usually a date, a number, or a place. Before scanning the reader forms preliminary questions such as: "When will the candidates debate the tax reform bill?" or "What was the final score of the rugby match?" In addition to teaching students to take advantage of textual clues, as they do in skimming, we should also make them aware of the graphic form the answer is likely to take: written number, numeral, capitalized word, or short phrase containing key words. As in skimming, students gradually become less dependent on our cues until they become self-sufficient. It is important to use selections which can be realistically scanned (that is, those containing specific information) and selections which are commonly scanned in "real life": for example, the sports page, menus, classified ads, and telephone books. (Many textbook questions meant for general comprehension are good scanning questions because they focus on minute points.)

Reading for thorough comprehension is reading in order to master the total message of the writer, both main points and supporting details. It is that stage of understanding at which the reader is able to paraphrase the author's ideas but has not yet made a critical evaluation of those ideas. This type of reading is the primary concern of most reading classes. In fact, the most common weakness of reading courses is that this style of reading—the careful word-by-word approach—is practiced exclusively, without recognition of the fact that it is not necessary for some tasks and insufficient for others. Of course, holding students accountable for what they have read is valid. However, when developing thorough comprehension questions, a number of pitfalls should be avoided. We must make sure the questions reflect the focus and direction of a passage and that the information demanded by a question is accessible to the students during a careful reading. A good rule of thumb to follow when developing exercises is to read the passage and construct initial questions on the major points without looking back to the selection; we can hardly expect students to retain more after one reading than we have. Certain materials (such as research articles or textbooks) require careful reading and study, and we should expose students to a number of such readings. We do so, however, only after we are confident that they understand the situations in which such study is warranted.

Finally, *critical reading* requires us to push our students beyond the "thorough comprehension" stage of reading, to encourage them to react to readings with the same critical judgment they probably exercise when reading in their native languages. This critical reading ability is often suspended when students undertake reading tasks in a second language, perhaps because they feel a great sense of accomplishment merely at having deciphered the author's message. In order to build critical reading skills, we need to find readings which argue a point of view or which presume certain attitudes on the part of the readers. Examples of critical reading questions are: "For what purpose and for what audience is this intended?" "What knowledge and attitudes does the author presume of the audience?" "Are you convinced by the evidence presented by the author to support the claims made?" "Does your own experience support the conclusions reached by the author?" and "Do you share the author's point of view?" Such questions open up for students a completely new perspective of the selection, and lead to discussion in which they must use vocabulary and information from the passage to support their opinions. Many ESL reading texts for example, are guilty of hindering students' critical reading skills by taking the author's credentials for granted, by not asking students to critically evaluate the issues. (Critical reading demands a certain amount of class discussion time if students are to answer questions such as those posed above.)

Language Skills. Our students' efficiency in using reading skills is directly dependent upon their overall language proficiency—their general language skills. In addition to presenting exercises such as those mentioned above, we must also systematically treat specific language problems in the mode of reading. There are three areas of language skills work on which we focus: vocabulary, syntax, and discourse. At this point we turn specifically to *English* as the target language for consideration.

Vocabulary work is the easiest to devise and the easiest to abuse. Virtually all texts in English as a second language (ESL) work with vocabulary items, but it takes a teacher with a strong theoretical commitment to use such exercises effectively. A basic premise which should not be violated is: *work with real language contexts.* Words are vehicles of meaning and as such rarely occur in isolation. Three types of vocabulary attack strategies emphasized are: obtaining meaning from context, from morphological analysis, and from monolingual English dictionaries.

Guessing vocabulary from context is perhaps the most important of the vocabulary attack skills. Students must be made aware of the number of language clues available to them when they are stopped by an unfamiliar word. They should realize that they can usually continue reading and obtain a general understanding of the item. In context work, there are syntactic and semantic parameters of which we should make our students aware. We can emphasize the redundancy of language by demonstrating the types of contexts which can provide the meaning of an unfamiliar word:

synonym in apposition: Our uncle was a *nomad*, an incurable wanderer who never could stay in one place.
antonym: While the aunt loved Marty deeply, she absolutely *despised* his twin brother Smarty.
cause and effect: By surrounding the protesters with armed policemen, and by arresting the leaders of the movement, the rebellion was effectively *quashed.*
association between an object and its purpose or use: The scientist removed the *treatise* from the shelf and began to read.
description: Tom received a new *roadster* for his birthday. It is a sports model, red with white interior and bucket seats, capable of reaching speeds of more than 150 mph.
example: Mary can be quite *gauche*; yesterday she blew her nose on the new linen tablecloth.

Without burdening the student with linguistic jargon we can teach students to recognize the punctuation, syntax, and discourse clues which operate in each of the above examples. Most importantly, they must be taught to recognize situations in which the meaning of a word or phrase is not essential for adequate comprehension of the passage.

If context does not provide the meaning of an unfamiliar word, morphological analysis will often provide a clue. Many ESL texts provide lists of stems and affixes with accompanying exercises. These can be used to systematically introduce the most common stems and affixes. In subsequent reading tasks, students' familiarity with morphological items can be increased by continued practice in deciphering unfamiliar words.

Finally, if all else fails and if students feel they cannot continue without knowing the meaning of a word, the dictionary can be used. Students require a systematic introduction to dictionary work if they are to become efficient dictionary users. Practice in scanning for words, and in the use of syntactic and semantic clues to select the proper definition for a given context should be provided.

In using ESL reading textbooks, we become more effective if we are aware of a number of common weaknesses of the vocabulary exercises. Often the rationale for choosing the words to be glossed seems arbitrary; one doesn't know if the words are glossed because they are difficult or because they are useful. It is often unclear if students are· expected to make these items part of their active vocabularies. What vocabulary "teaching" there is consists of lists of words in isolation or with definitions. Neither format successfully teaches vocabulary. Many vocabulary exercises test without any teaching and are often unrealistic in two ways. Either the task itself is unrealistic ("Form a sentence with the word *dilemma*") or the presumed ability to do the task is unrealistic (asking students to produce vocabulary of which they have only a receptive command).

In such cases it is up to the teacher to determine how much vocabulary building should take place and then to provide contexts in which words can be introduced and subsequently reinforced. Introducing unfamiliar vocabulary in several sentences, each providing a clear context, has proved to be successful. (Of course, prereading vocabulary work should be restricted to only those items whose meaning is not accessible from the passage.) Assuring that vocabulary items appear again and again in comprehension and discussion activities serves as reinforcement. If a word appears in a technical context in a reading but would be of use to students in more generalized contexts, the teacher should provide such contexts for the learner. This can be done orally or in writing. Items which do not impede communication of the author's ideas and which will not prove useful later should be ignored. Items which impede understanding but which are rarely used in English should be quickly glossed by the teacher and then ignored.

Syntax work in reading classes is conducted on a diagnostic basis: only when a syntactic structure causes a communication breakdown do we work with it. When encountered in a reading, structure problems should be pulled out and explained. If a particular structure persists in causing comprehension difficulties or if the whole class is troubled by it, relevant exercises from grammar texts or teacher-constructed drills should be presented for intensive work. It is important, however, to emphasize grammar work as a tool for improving reading skills and to constantly reinforce the tactic of analyzing difficult prose for recognizable grammatical elements. Likewise, grammar exercises in reading texts should be analyzed to determine if the syntactic elements studied actually cause reading problems. If they do, the teacher should make explicit their value to the students and should build the necessary bridges between the exercises and the reading. If the exercises treat grammar points which do not give our students trouble when they read, we should not hesitate to skip the exercises entirely.

Discourse analysis consists of making students conscious of the effect of organization on the message of a writer. Rough outlining can be of value in showing students how one idea leads to the next. Many times this kind of work can be tied into the students' writing classes, where they may be working with such organizational schemes as comparison and contrast, generalization and specifics, and chronological order. ESL students should be made aware of the strong tendency in English for linear argumentation. Unlike many other languages, contiguous English sentences often imply causation or chronological sequence of events. Therefore, it is necessary to emphasize the arrangement of ideas as an important clue in deciphering the overall meaning of a text. We must also take pains to point out the styles which generally accompany certain types of writing. Discourse work lacks the rigor of vocabulary and syntax because the system of organizing larger-than-sentence language units is not rigid and because writers are not always as careful in organizing their ideas as they are in checking their grammar and word usage. Although discourse work cannot be reduced to formulas as easily as our vocabulary and syntax lessons, it is nevertheless imperative to help students develop an awareness of the conceptual presuppositions that native-speaker writers and readers apply to the organization of a text. In addition to increasing the ability to make predictions based on syntax and semantics, students should be developing an ability to predict content on the basis of textual organization.

Sample Lesson Plan

In the preceding pages we have attempted to show how a psycholinguistic perspective of reading might affect the learning environment, teacher behavior, and the preparation of L2 reading materials. We will narrow the focus now to describe a week's sequence of events in an intermediate or advanced ESL reading class (see the Sample Five-Day Lesson Plan below).

A few general comments apply to all lesson plan preparation. First, although lessons are planned painstakingly, we must also allow for maximum flexibility. On the one hand, we should plan carefully, establishing loose time limits for each task. On the other hand, it is assumed that teachers will take advantage of any situation which may arise, abandoning prepared tasks for activities which spark student interest. This does not mean that reinforcement in a particular skill will be forfeited; our constant efforts to systematically reinforce and recycle all skills work throughout the semester allow us flexibility on a day-to-day basis. Approximate time limits are established in advance for each activity so that the teacher realizes, for example, that a successful activity is being continued at the expense of another. This type of flexibility in the classroom—spontaneously extending the time allotted for one activity so that not enough time remains for a second planned activity—may leave teachers with time on their hands at the end of the hour. In an effort to avoid this problem, more than enough work is planned for each day. If we have extra exercises ready to use, we are less likely to push forward with a task which is boring, too difficult, or too long.

Second, while we acknowledge the value of such nonreading activities as discussion, writing, and focused grammar or vocabulary work, we are committed to the view that one learns by doing: in a reading class, students should read. Furthermore, as much as possible, students should work with conceptually complete reading tasks. Focused work on words, sentences, and paragraphs is tolerated because a teacher can thereby deal more effectively with specific language problems which have caused comprehension difficulties in longer readings.

Finally, because our ultimate goal is to make students independent of our guidance, we should allow for consistently greater student participation in determining the appropriate strategies for particular readings. As the semester progresses, it is hoped that the class will gradually develop into a group of people working together to increase their reading skills.

A few comments are necessary concerning the lesson plan presented here. The activities outlined would be appropriate for intermediate or advanced students who have worked together for several weeks. This is important for two reasons. First, we hope that a nonthreatening atmosphere has been established in which people feel free to volunteer opinions and make guesses without fear of ridicule or censure. Second, we can assume that by now students recognize the importance of a skills-based reading program and that they are working with the teacher to improve those skills using a variety of readings and exercises. That is, they have been introduced to all of the skill exercise types and are working toward that ultimate goal of complete independence.

The lesson plan is meant only as an example of how goals might be translated into practice. We do not imply that a particular presentation is the only one possible for a given reading activity or that the exercises presented here are the only activities possible to achieve our goals.

These lessons, planned for 50-minute, ESL reading classes, are ambitious; we have chosen to provide more than enough work in the belief that it is better to err in the direction of too much rather than too little. Approximate time limits for each activity are indicated. Below each exercise heading appear possible sources of materials and a brief description of how the exercise type might be used.

A close examination of the sample lesson plan reveals several important characteristics to be found in any successful teaching situation. First, and most importantly, the plan represents a skills approach to the teaching of ESL reading. The students do more than merely read passages and answer questions; the type of reading that the students are asked to perform varies from task to task. They scan the train schedule and newspaper, skim the longer reading, and read it and several other selections carefully. The vocabulary and syntax work is presented as a tool for comprehension, appropriate for helping students solve persistent reading problems.

Second, within a single week a great variety of activities is presented. In the course of any single lesson the tempo and task change several times. Monday, for example, begins with a scanning exercise, followed by paragraph work, concluding with a vocabulary and skimming introduction to the longer reading which will not be due until Wednesday. In the course of the week, virtually all language and reading skills are reinforced in a variety of contexts and with a variety of materials.

Of course, the classroom dynamics change to fit the task. The train schedule and poem are treated as a class activity, the teacher encouraging students to volunteer answers and opinions. The paragraph work on Monday, as well as the vocabulary and structure exercises on Tuesday and Thursday, might be organized as workshop sessions, giving students the chance to work at their own pace and providing the teacher with the opportunity to assist individuals. For such lessons it is necessary to provide either a great number of exercise items or several worksheets, so that faster students are challenged either by the quantity or difficulty of the material. We have had great success having students discuss reading comprehension questions in small groups. Students choose a chairperson who is responsible for seeing that everyone talks, that all comprehension problems are resolved, and that consensus is reached on each exercise item. Students are forced to defend their choices with portions of the text. This process encourages student autonomy and responsibility and minimizes teacher intervention.

The role of the teacher also changes from activity to activity. During vocabulary and structure work, the teacher is a teacher, providing help and encouragement as students work to solve language problems. The teacher is a facilitator during the poetry and short passage readings, intervening only in the event that linguistic expertise is needed to keep discussion going. In the analysis of news events and discussions of how readings relate to the "real world," the teacher is primarily a participant on equal terms with the students in exploring a mutually interesting topic. Of course, the role and behavior of the teacher can change a number of times in the course of one session to suit the situation. It is hoped, however, that, as the semester progresses, the teacher as teacher will gradually be replaced by the teacher as facilitator and participant.

A third important feature of this lesson plan is the opportunity to encourage students to choose their own reading strategies and to apply the skills dictated by the strategy chosen. It should be noted that the longer reading is introduced by the teacher through vocabulary work and discussion, followed by skimming. It is often the case that students are discouraged by long readings and should therefore be given as much of this kind of support as necessary in attacking a long selection. It is hoped that the procedure used by the teacher will be repeated by the student when similar readings are attacked in the future. Later in the week, students are encouraged to choose their own strategies for attacking Thursday's short selection and to be able to defend their approaches. Often the teacher will want to simulate a "real life" situation, give the students a task, and ask them how they would approach it. One's approach to a newspaper editorial, for example, might be quite different depending on whether one is reading the selection for pleasure or for a university political science course.

Throughout the semester, students are taught to shift gears, to vary their reading strategies according to their goals for the selection at hand. As they become more proficient readers, we expect them to determine for themselves what they read, why they read it, and how they read it.

SAMPLE FIVE-DAY LESSON PLAN
Day 1
Non-prose reading (15 min) (train schedule, menu, map, graph, etc.)
—Students are given teacher-prepared questions and told to scan to find the answers.

—The questions should reflect "real life" situations.

—The work is fast-paced and oral, students working individually or in small groups.

Paragraph work (20 min) (paragraphs from Baudoin et al., Harris, SRA, or teacher-prepared)

—As an introduction, a paragraph is read by the teacher, and the students are given time to answer the questions. Discussion follows, with students defending answers using vocabulary and syntax analysis. Students are then given the opportunity to work individually.

—Students read silently and answer questions.

—Discussion follows with the class as a whole, in small groups, or in pairs. Intensive work is done on determining the main idea, drawing inferences, as well as sentence and discourse work.

—If students aren't able to finish in the allotted time or if problems arise, the work can be continued as homework.

Introduction to longer reading (15 min) (ESL textbook reading of over 2000 words found, for example, in Baudoin et al., and Baumwoll and Saitz)

—Reading is introduced by a discussion relating the topic to students' experiences, followed by an introduction of potentially difficult vocabulary from the reading.

—The teacher reads the first few paragraphs orally to introduce the students to the reading. Discussion follows on the topic and on potential vocabulary and syntax problems.

—If time permits, students skim the selection to answer general questions posed by the teacher.

Assignment

—Read longer reading, answer comprehension questions for Day 3.

—Finish paragraph work, if necessary.

Day 2

Paragraph work (10 min)

—Finish paragraph work begun on Day 1.

Vocabulary work (15 min) (vocabulary from context, stem/affix, or dictionary: exercises taken from Baudoin et al., Harris, Yorkey, or other skills textbook or are teacher-prepared)

—Intensive oral skill work in which students are pushed at fast pace. Focus is on skills, not on learning new vocabulary.

—Teacher-prepared exercises can be used to introduce vocabulary from the next reading selection.

Short passage (25 min) (ESL textbook such as Baudoin et al., Saitz and Carr, Markstein and Hirasawa, or teacher-prepared activity; reading of 500-1000 words)

—Students do intensive forced reading for a particular purpose. (The reading determines what you do with it.)

—The teacher: (a) reads the passage orally to the students while they read silently forcing them to read quickly, or (b) sets a time limit for silent reading.

—The reading is followed by comprehension questions to be done orally, or in writing if true/false, multiple-choice format is used.

—Discussion of questions can take place with the class as a whole, in small groups or in pairs.

Assignment

—Reminder from Day 1 to read longer reading and answer comprehension questions.

Day 3

Longer reading (50 min)

—Vocabulary exercises are answered orally and quickly.

—Comprehension questions are discussed, flipping back and forth from questions to passage to scan for answers when difficulties arise. This can be done by the class as a whole, in small groups or in pairs.

—Teacher pulls out sentences and vocabulary items for explanation and discussion as problems arise. Care is taken to build bridges between this and previous syntax and vocabulary skill work.

—The passage is discussed using text and teacher-prepared questions.

—Teacher can act as facilitator: keeping discussion moving, encouraging all students to contribute, or small groups can elect a chairperson from among the students. Discussion focuses on evaluations arising from critical reading.

—Teacher moves students through a variety of activities so that, although the content is the same for fifty minutes, the pace and focus keep everyone interested in the work.

Assignment

—Vocabulary review exercises or possibly a composition based on the reading passage. The assignment should allow students to capitalize on vocabulary and syntax work which accompanied the lesson.

Day 4

—Go over homework.

Structure work (15 min) (worksheets from Quirk and Greenbaum, Rutherford, Praninskas, or teacher-prepared).

—Work should be done orally or, if in writing, in a workshop setting where the teacher moves from student to student. Discussion occurs with class as a whole, in small groups, or in pairs.

—Teacher can provide work on structures which have caused reading comprehension problems in previous reading. This might include work on problems uncovered in Wednesday's work.

—Extra work can be assigned as homework as needed.

Short passage (20 min) (ESL textbook or teacher-prepared reading of approximately 500 words with comprehension, vocabulary, and syntax exercises as appropriate)

—Reading can be on a topic seen earlier, or a new content area can be introduced.

—Students can be asked to determine the proper goals and strategies for the task. A time limit is agreed upon.

—The passage is read and exercises are completed in class.

—Discussion follows reading, guided by comprehension questions.

Realia (15 min)

—Discussion of current news which students are likely to know about from TV or radio, and which the teacher can predict will appear in newspapers daily.

—Teacher and students discuss topic; the teacher provides cultural, vocabulary information, as needed.

Assignment

—Buy the same English language newspaper that evening and scan to find all articles on "realia" topic. Read the articles. Answer teacher-prepared questions the preparation of which requires only a general knowledge of the kinds of information available daily on the "realia" topic e.g., "Who is Mr. X?" "What arguments are used by opponents of the proposed project?" Bring newspaper to class on Day 5.

Day 5

Realia (35 min)

—Students discuss the articles which treat Thursday's "realia" topic. Teacher will have read the articles and prepared appropriate exercises.

—Students do intensive oral work with the newspaper. Tasks are realistic: comparison shopping with classified ads, analysis of news reports, etc. Work can be done as a class, in small groups, or in pairs.

Poetry (15 min) (teacher-prepared exercises)

—This kind of activity is done for a change of pace. Teacher should emphasize that poetry requires the same skills as other reading selections.

—Poetry is especially good for reinforcing vocabulary from context skills, using syntax clues and for drawing inferences.

CHAPTER 6

A Model Program for Teaching Advanced Reading to Students of English as a Foreign Language

David E. Eskey
University of Southern California

For many advanced students of English as a foreign language—university students in the United States, for example—reading is the most important skill to master. The student who speaks the language fluently but cannot read or write well is much more likely to find himself in trouble than the student who speaks with a heavy foreign accent but understands what he reads and writes acceptable papers. Consider Henry Kissinger. Yet most programs for teaching English to foreign students concentrate on *spoken* English—reading and writing play a supplementary role described in our Skinneresque jargon as "reinforcement." There are reasons for this, some good, some not so good, but they apply with diminishing force as students work their way up the language-learning ladder. No one doubts that it is easier to teach someone to read a language he can speak, and that therefore beginners must concentrate on spoken English. At this level it seems reasonable to talk of reinforcing what the students have learned to hear and say by asking them to read and write the same or very similar material. In programs at most schools in the United States, however, the average foreign student is not a beginner. The majority are likely to know a good deal of English and may need, to return to my original point, more help with reading than with any other skill.

A curious thing about our programs is that they stick to a kind of beginner's model, no matter what the student's level really is, instead of tailoring each level to meet the student's needs. The source of this

First published in *Language Learning*, Vol. 23, No. 2, 1973. Reprinted by permission of the editor of that journal and the author.

devotion to a single approach is almost certainly the dogma that "language is speech," but we ought to know better than that by now. The first major premise of my argument is thus that *for advanced foreign students reading and writing must be considered at least as important as, and largely independent of, listening and speaking.* Following Ted Plaister, I have loosely defined "advanced students" elsewhere as "students who can already converse with native speakers, understand and give directions, order a meal or buy a ticket, employ simple patterns correctly in writing, and most important for my purposes here, read simplified or simple English prose at a reasonable rate with good comprehension" (Eskey 1970, see also Plaister 1968). By *largely independent of* I merely mean to underscore the fact that the spoken and written languages differ and that the latter, despite the old structuralist saw, is not a "secondary representation" of the former.

I am not of course denying the obvious and important interrelation among the four basic skills or attacking the so-called "integrated" approach. There is no reason not to cover some of the same ground both orally and in writing, but written materials appropriate to the needs of advanced foreign students must not be limited to or determined by the students' aural-oral abilities or needs. At this level the reading/writing relation is much closer, although there are situations which call for greater stress on one or the other. At most overseas universities, for example, the students must read English but may never have to write it. Virginia French Allen has recently noted a growing tendency to make the most of the reading/writing relationship by "having students practice *writing* the kinds of English prose which they will need to *read.* In composition courses for native speakers of English, most teachers have traditionally stressed the "reader-writer contract" and the close relationship between the way something is written and the way it is to be read. But it seems to me that today we are finding renewed emphasis on composition as training for reading" (1973). This paper deals with reading only, but I certainly support a mutually enlightening reading/writing trade-off wherever it might reasonably be achieved. (For further discussion see Carr 1967.)

There is, however, no need at all to work laboriously through an oral introduction to a kind of English the like of which was never *heard* anywhere in the English-speaking world. Here, for example, is a sentence from Hans Zinsser's popular little curio *Rats, Lice and History:*

When all is said and done, we have no satisfactory explanation for the disappearance of plague epidemics from the Western countries, and we must assume that in spite of the infectiousness of the plague bacillus, the plentifulness of rats, their occasional infection with plague, and their invariable infestation with fleas, the evolution of an epidemic requires a delicate adjustment of many conditions which have, fortunately, failed to eventuate in Western Europe and America during the last century.

The sentence is 77 words long. By the most conservative estimate, in transformational terms it contains at least 11 deep structure sentences— the two conjoined independent clauses, the introductory dependent clause, one relative clause, and seven complex nominalizations. There are several discontinuous constituents, including one factive nominal in which the clause marker *that* is separated from the following subject *the evolution of an epidemic* by a 24-word prepositional phrase *in spite of . . . fleas*. And yet the sentence is not especially difficult to read, although it seems safe to say that no one talks like this. Of course anything that can be said can be written and vice versa, but in practice the English we ordinarily hear and the English we ordinarily read are quite different.

Given a separate and equal reading component, how do we go about improving our students' reading? The major problem here is that although we do know a great many interesting things about reading, no one knows exactly what reading is or how anybody learns to do it. Despite a library-sized bibliography devoted to reading and the teaching of reading, the only brief description of the process itself that I find at all convincing is Kenneth Goodman's "Reading: A Psycholinguistic Guessing Game" (1967) reprinted in Gunderson (1970). (For a more complete discussion of the reading process see Smith 1971. See also Goodman 1968, Goodman and Fleming 1969, Levin and Williams 1970 and Smith 1973.) As the title suggests, Goodman takes exception to the common-sense notion that a reader proceeds by decoding a series of verbal units in sequence and, ideally, in perfect detail. This he maintains is much too simple a model for what is in fact a complex performance involving many different kinds of skills. Goodman's typical reader responds to "graphic cues, guided by constraints set up through prior choices, his language knowledge, his cognitive styles, and strategies he has learned" in forming "a perceptual image." The image is "partly what he sees and partly what he expected to see," and on this basis "he makes a guess or tentative choice" as to what the words he is reading mean (Gunderson 1970:117). As far as it goes, this is an honest and largely valid description of the complex reading process as a whole. But it does beg the crucial questions of how a skillful reader can draw on so many different kinds of skills at once and why some readers are so much better than others at guessing right. Surely "guessing game" is only a metaphor for achieving the kind of successful mix that the skillful reader habitually does achieve. Good reading must be something more systematic than guessing.

One clue to the process that we *can* be sure of is the relatively high redundancy level typical of natural human languages. Because of it, every successful reader quickly learns to respond to a limited number of critical signals at increasingly higher levels of abstraction; he soon learns, that is, to get by without reading, first, every letter, then every word, and eventually even larger chunks of the text. Frank Smith has in fact defined the "fluent reader" as "a person who can make optimal use of all the redundancy in a piece of text" (1970). In his introduction to the recent MIT reprinting of Edmund Burke Huey's "The Psychology and Pedagogy of Reading," Paul Kolers notes that "the skilled reader can work with vestiges of an array, with only parts of words and phrases from the page, which he uses to build the message he is constructing in his own mind. The less skilled reader needs more of the immediate visual input, and may actually thereby be restricted to a simpler cognitive construction. Seeing the trees only, he may miss the forest they form; concentrating upon letters or words only, he may miss the information in the message and, even more, be unable to see beyond the information given to its implications and its relevance to other matters" (Kolers 1968). This suggests that the process might best be described not as haphazard guessing, but as a kind of prediction based on very poorly understood rapid-fire sampling techniques of some kind.

In this as in every higher use of language we might as well admit, however, that we are up against a major mystery. No one knows how the human mind effects the kind of creative synthesis that puts the best of our current computers to shame, as the failure of machine translation attests. If we knew that we might, in Tennyson's phrase, "know what God and man is." But for the moment we must face the disquieting truth that the fundamental systems of human thought may be not only unknown but unknowable.

The fact remains that all we know about the reading process now is some of the kinds of skills that go into good reading, which brings me to my second major premise: Since we do not know how successful readers can draw on several kinds of skills at once, but do know that they can, and do know what the skills are, within limits, *the best reading program at this particular time would be composed of instruction in the critical skills and plenty of practice in various kinds of reading.* Such a program might in fact be as close as we can come to a means of teaching students to read with skill. Reading is an art and great readers, like great athletes, may be born and not made, although the average student can learn to do a passing job.

As in so many other kinds of teaching and learning, we have almost certainly underestimated the contribution of the learner to learning to read. It seems clear that for reading as for all of the higher-level language functions, the human mind must be innately programmed, and that the job of the teacher is to activate, not to create, the program. Teaching a skill as complex as reading is mainly a matter of getting the student moving in the right direction and providing him with feedback as he develops that skill to the best of his largely innate ability. Thus there is no real reason to suppose that future reading programs will be radically different from the best of what we can do today. According to Smith: "The current instructional methods are probably not much inferior to the methods we shall develop as we learn more about learning to read. So many instructional methods have been tried, and so many succeed (in some instances at least), that further permutations in the game of instructional roulette are unlikely to produce any great gain, either by chance or design. What will make a difference is an understanding of the reading process" (1971).

What skills does successful reading entail? Of those Goodman mentions, at least one—the elementary ability to decipher "graphic cues"—may be discarded for the great majority of advanced foreign students. Individual students, especially those who originally learned to read in something other than left-to-right roman script, may continue to have their residual problems, but these should be treated individually. No matter what his background or his aural-oral skills, the student with widespread phoneme-grapheme problems, that is, problems of simple word identification (not to be confused with pronunciation problems in reading aloud), cannot by my definition be considered advanced. Two skills remain for the advanced student: "language knowledge," which in functional terms means the ability to decode the syntactical and lexical signals of English, and a much neglected skill, the ability to follow a given line of argument, subdivided by Goodman into "cognitive styles" and any "strategies" the reader has learned to employ. To a surprising degree the latter skill is culture-bound and constitutes a major problem for many foreign students.

Notice that these are *active* skills. As Ronald Wardhaugh has noted: "Reading is not a passive process, in which a reader takes something out of the text without any effort or merely recognizes what is in the text. Nor does it appear to be a process in which he first recognizes what is on the page and then interprets it, a process in which a stage of decoding

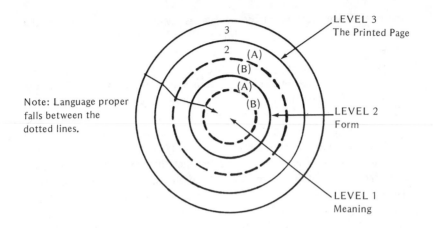

Note: Language proper
falls between the
dotted lines.

LEVEL 3
The Printed Page

LEVEL 2
Form

LEVEL 1
Meaning

LEVEL 3
A written product of the culture: a novel, journal, textbook, etc.

LEVEL 2
(A)   Rhetorical form: the structure of the text

(B)   Linguistic form: the structure of sentences, phrases, words

LEVEL 1
(A)   Linguistic meaning: the meaning of sentences, phrases, words

(B)   Meaning: the meaning of the text

Figure 1.   The reading problem

precedes a stage of involvement with meaning. There is little reason to
suppose that there are two such discrete, non-overlapping stages. Reading
is instead an active process, in which the reader must make an active
contribution by drawing upon and using concurrently various abilities
that he has acquired" (1969).

Before turning to a more detailed discussion of these skills and of
the kind of reading program they seem to imply, it might be useful to
define the reader's problem—that is, *any* reader's problem—as precisely as
I can. Consider Figure 1. The concentric circles cut by an inward-
pointing arrow depict the typical reader's journey from printed page to
discourse. As the diagram suggests, he must process information at three
levels simultaneously. There is first the outer layer of the printed page
itself, the bundles of letters to be deciphered; then, at one remove, there
is the level of abstract form, which in the case of reading includes both
rhetorical form, the structure of the text, and linguistic form, the
structure of the sentences, phrases, words; and there is finally the inner
level of meaning, both the meanings of the separate linguistic forms and

the cumulative meaning of the passage as a whole. This is, of course, the language-typical situation, the simultaneous apprehension and linking of physical signal and abstract message; the reader's eyes read letters, the reader's brain reads forms, the reader's mind reads meanings. As noted, the skillful advanced reader works from a different kind of mix than the beginner; he depends much less on the outer layer letter-and-word-level clues and much more on higher-level syntactic and semantic expectations. Such a reader can in a pinch make use of lower-level "mediated reading methods," but as Smith points out, he "uses mediated reading techniques as little as possible, and the fact that he does so requires no elaborate explanation. Immediate comprehension is synonymous with facile and interesting reading. But mediated reading is hard work. The rate of progress is slower, there is a greater burden on memory, and the rewards, in terms of comprehension, are less. If we cannot read with immediate comprehension, we soon feel tired and bored" (1971). The advanced reading teacher must be mainly concerned with rhetorical and complex syntactical structure, with advanced vocabulary in context, and with potentially confusing cultural assumptions.

To summarize: In the ideal language program for advanced foreign students, the reading component: (1) will not be an adjunct to the teaching of oral skills (since reading may be the most important skill to master) but will instead concentrate on reading for its own sake; (2) will not attempt to teach the reading skill directly (since no one really knows what reading is or how readers do it) but will instead provide instruction in the various kinds of skills required at each level of the reading process and plenty of practice in reading itself.

With reference to constructing a language program, my *approach* (Anthony 1963) is inevitably eclectic, because reading involves so many different kinds of skills and because we know so little about the process as a whole. My *method* is reciprocal intensive/extensive, a moving back and forth between close in-class analysis and the synthesis that reading in quantity provides. With one notable exception (cloze procedure), this chapter avoids discussion of particular *techniques* since these largely depend on particular situations. (For an excellent introduction to the teaching of reading to foreign-language students, and a survey of such techniques, see Rivers 1964 and 1968, and Norris 1970.)

The "ideal" language program mentioned above might look like the one in Figure 2. The whole subdivides into complementary halves, an intensive program, comprising in-class instruction, and an extensive program, which is mainly outside reading.

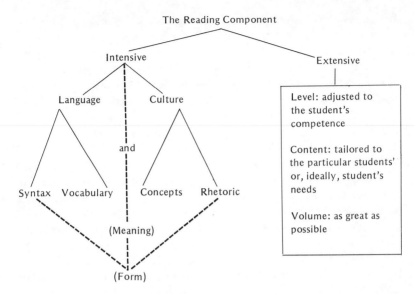

Figure 2.   A model reading program.

About the latter there are three major points to make. First, the level of difficulty should be carefully controlled. Ideally the material will strike a perfect balance between too easy and too hard—challenging but not frustrating the student's reading competence. However, too easy material is considerably better than too hard, since the object is not translation, but rapid silent reading. Second, the content should be tailored to the particular students' needs, ideally to the particular student's needs. Victorian novels will not do for biochemists. Third and most important, there must be plenty of it, perhaps a book or a series of articles a week. For many foreign students, the problem is not only to learn to read English but to develop a reading habit for the first time in their lives.

The one major exception to the rule is speed reading, a kind of extensive reading to which some class time should be devoted. In general I subscribe to the Noss principle that most foreign student readers are unsafe at any speed (Eskey 1970), but the student who cannot read at a reasonable rate will be limited both in the volume of reading he can do and in his overall comprehension, both critical factors in higher-level reading, especially at the university level. Two hundred words a minute or better might be a goal for the advanced foreign student. No student can be pushed beyond his real capacity, but the foreign student frequently suffers from a kind of mental block in his reading of English, a conviction that he must correctly process every word if he is to understand anything at all. Since good reading entails doing precisely the opposite, no student can make normal progress in this way. The ideal reading program thus includes brief but regular work on increasing reading speed, partly for its own sake and partly as a means of demonstrating to the students that they can read faster with acceptable comprehension. (Two useful texts for this particular purpose are Harris 1965 and Fry 1963.)

As frequent references to the individual student's needs suggest, I fully support the recent shift in emphasis from language teaching to language learning and the subsequent development of individualized instruction. (For discussion and illustration see Johnson 1973, Gougher 1972, and two volumes of readings: Altman and Politzer 1971 and Harris and Smith 1972.) Since reading, like writing, is individualized by definition, the reading program provides a fertile field for this approach. Among individualized materials for teaching reading the SRA reading labs are perhaps the best known; there are many of these kits (though none specifically designed for the nonnative speaker), now including an international series. Similar effects may be achieved on a more ambitious scale by establishing a genuine reading lab, a collection of graded readers shelved in one convenient place, e.g., the Longman series or the Ladder editions, dealing with many different subjects at various levels of difficulty.

I have argued that the intensive program should be devoted to teaching those skills that contribute to good reading. These include both strictly linguistic skills and several kinds of culturally determined techniques. The two are not, of course, really separable (as the dotted *and* line is meant to suggest) but one or another may be emphasized at particular times in particular classes. The recent work of Lackstrom, Selinker, and Trimble provides an interesting glimpse of a possible better future. (See, for example, Lackstrom et al. 1970 and 1973.) Starting from the assumptions that the paragraph, not the sentence, is the basic unit of discourse in English and that context and rhetorical organization largely determine correct grammatical choices, this team is exploring the complex relationship between rhetorical form and syntactical form. They are thus in my terms attempting to fill in the lower dotted line in Figure 2. Should they and others like them succeed in working out a major part of this relationship, we may someday be able to approach the formal aspect of the advanced reader's problem (Level 2 as defined in my discussion of Figure 1) not as rhetoric *and* syntax but as an integrated whole.

At the level of decoding there is first of all the problem of syntactic structure, some more complex, some even different in kind, from the syntax of everyday English speech. No reader who translates word by word has any real chance of learning to read unsimplified English, and every foreign reader must eventually learn to see the various groups of words, the intricate and often unmarked linguistic forms, of which every English sentence is composed. Most advanced readers have already mastered at least the basics of English grammar. Obvious exceptions are articles and prepositions, but these are more production than reading problems. There are certain constructions more common, or even peculiar, to written English that are probably best handled in the reading class. Examples include complex nominalizations, nonrestrictive relative clauses, participials, and the closely related absolutes. (For a more detailed discussion of these problem constructions see Eskey 1971. See also Pierce 1973 and Wilson 1973.)

To complement his skill in reading by structures, every good reader must also have mastered a considerable number of English words. Most TESOL specialists have underrated the importance of acquiring a large vocabulary. Here again the beginner's model prevails in teaching basic patterns, the teacher does best to limit the words to be manipulated to a small set that the students already know. This restriction should gradually be relaxed as the students' control of the language increases. For advanced foreign students, vocabulary is crucial and probably should not be left to whatever turns up in the readings a particular teacher assigns. Words come in various systems and subsystems and may be directly and systematically taught. (See for discussion Lado 1955, Scherer 1964, Yorio 1971, and Twaddell 1973.) Since teaching materials for this purpose are becoming increasingly available, the language subcomponent should now include the teaching of selected vocabulary items, again selected with the students' special needs in mind. Two examples of these materials are Barnard's "Advanced English Vocabulary" (1971/1972) and Part Two of Kenneth Croft's older but still reliable "Reading and Word Study" (1960).

By isolating and contrasting key vocabulary items, such materials can provide a kind of head start for the hard-pressed foreign student. There is, however, only one means of acquiring control of an adequate English vocabulary, and that is reading itself. As Kolers has observed,

word meanings do not exist in isolation in the reader's mind like so many entries in a dictionary. What a word means to the reader depends upon what he is reading and what he expects to read, the phrase, clause, or sentence in which the words appear. The meaning of a word, that is to say, depends upon the thought that it is being used to express and the context of its expression. Whether one reads *unionize* as a verb in chemistry or a verb in labor relations depends on many things other than its spelling and its symbol-sound relations. Indeed, a very large number of words in a dictionary have multiple meanings, and for some words the definitions are contradictory For example, *scan* means to glance at quickly *and* to read in detail, and *cleave* to join and to separate. The reader, clearly, must construct a representation of what he is reading *about* if he is to appreciate the meaning of what he is reading. This paradox runs through a great deal of the psychology of perception, for very often we must know what we are looking at in order to recognize what it is we are seeing (1968:xxx).

Taken together, these two language skills—the abilities to interpret syntax and lexis—provide the reader with the keys to both the forms and meanings of language per se, obviously a major aspect of reading. Traditionally grammar has concerned itself with forms, vocabulary with meanings, but each of these studies involves the other since the meaning of any word is partly a function of its syntactical context. This in turn is nothing more than a formal arrangement of appropriate words which convey, to complete the cycle, a meaning.

If reading is to lead to understanding, the reader must have at least a minimum access to the writer's underlying assumptions about his subject and, perhaps, the larger world of which that subject forms a part. To provide it, the cultural subcomponent must include a good deal of cross-cultural information, more specifically information about the writer's conceptual universe—what he questions, what he values, and what he takes for granted. As anyone who has worked with foreign students knows, these things vary widely from culture to culture. Here again the relevant concepts depend on the cultural background of the students themselves and on their interest and needs. The more unlike the cultures, the more likely it is that cultural misunderstandings will occur.

There may of course be some irreducible base, the conceptual equivalent of a universal grammar. I like to think that there is, but that kind of thinking is not likely to lead to anything an ESOL specialist can use. Whatever the deep structure (if it exists) situation, there are interesting problems at the level of surface structure (which is after all the level at which our students must begin) involving both rhetorical and syntactical presuppositions. The writer of English not only assumes a particular world view and a knowledge of certain "logical" ways of organizing a piece of writing which may have syntactic consequences: he also assumes a perfect mastery of the system of ellipsis peculiar to English syntax. A basic transformational principle is that anything which can be deleted must be recoverable (I want to go = I want *for me* to go). But the nonnative speaker may not always share the full set of grammatical presuppositions which account for the native speaker's skill in handling ellipsis, in reading, that is, what is not really there. Such problems suggest that one reader's road to meaning may be another's blind alley.

Finally there is the largely formal problem of what is coming to be known as contrastive rhetoric. (As the lower dotted lines suggest in Figure 2, we have moved from linguistic form to meaning and from cultural meaning back to another kind of form, a cycle isomorphic with the circles in Figure 1.) The pioneering work in this somewhat esoteric corner of research is that of Robert B. Kaplan. (See, for example, Cultural thought patterns in intercultural education 1966, "The Anatomy of Rhetoric" 1972. See also Horn 1969, Kaplan 1963, and Bander 1971.) Many a reading teacher has had the maddening experience of having a student who appears to understand every sentence and yet cannot answer the simplest question about a passage as a whole—Does the author like it? Is he for or against? Why does he prefer this course of action to that one? Broad comprehension problems like this, and a number of similar smaller problems, usually follow from one of two causes: a straightforward cultural conflict of some kind (the writer's message is either inconceivable or totally unacceptable to the reader) or the reader is simply missing, and thus failing to respond to, the writer's rhetorical orientation. Under normal conditions this last provides an area of shared expectations. But rhetoric also varies from culture to culture. The foreign reader of English, no matter how advanced, may miss or misinterpret the rhetorical signals which, for example, establish the writer's purpose (to inform, to persuade, to entertain), his attitude toward his subject (committed, scientifically detached, ironic), and the logical strategy (induction, deduction, comparison, and contrast) by which he structures his text. For some foreign students, the trickiest job of all is to develop an ability to read critically, to weigh and judge an author's work on the basis of its merits as opposed to preconceptions about the author himself or the alleged infallibility of anything in print. Since the ultimate goal of reading is understanding, some time must be devoted to the study of these things.

There is one technique for both teaching and testing which draws on all four of these critical skills in a way which nevertheless allows for close, intensive in-class analysis. This is cloze procedure, a simple technique whereby students are presented with a text from which words have been systematically deleted, and asked to replace the missing words on the basis of any relevant clues (lexical, syntactic, stylistic, or contextual). Originally developed by W. L. Taylor as a more scientific means of achieving a reliable measure of readability, the technique has proved invaluable in both placement testing and achievement testing. "The principal attraction of cloze procedure," according to Jonathan Anderson, "is its ease of use by the classroom teacher. It is certainly far simpler for the teacher to construct his own cloze tests than to construct the usual comprehension tests where questions are asked about the passage read, and research has shown that cloze tests work at least as well. The teacher requires no training in test construction. Nor does he need to compute any complex calculations beyond simple percentages and averages. Furthermore, the teacher may construct cloze tests of readability as they are called at any time using the reading materials in the classroom" (1971a). (See also Anderson 1971b, Oller et al. 1971 and Oller 1972. One text which employs cloze procedure for teaching is Newmark et al. 1964.) Much of this applies equally to the use of cloze procedure as a teaching device in which use it has several additional virtues. It forces the hesitant student to think, to attack his reading problems actively by drawing on his several kinds of knowledge about English. There is also the important pedagogical virtue of its gamelike appeal: cloze procedure generates a series of puzzles which the restless student mind finds it hard to resist. (Ted Plaister tells the story of introducing cloze materials by means of a lecture on how to use them and why he had chosen to do so in the first place. About halfway through the lecture he suddenly noticed that no one was listening to a word he was saying—the students were too busy doing the exercises.) Best of all, perhaps, cloze procedure entails working with larger units of discourse and thus circumvents the natural tendency of teachers to focus on sentences in isolation when dealing with syntactical and lexical problems.

Having now assembled and displayed my model program, I conclude on a cheerful but skeptical note. The game of model building is exhilarating (creating order out of chaos has divine overtones) and models are undeniably useful. We all like to know what we are doing, or at least what we are trying to do. But a model program is not a program. The chances of any real reading program's succeeding may be enhanced by the structure a good model provides but depend in the long run on human variables—the talent and dedication of its teachers, the ability and motivation of its students, and the number of hours both are willing to devote to mastering the difficult art of reading.

CHAPTER 7

Teaching the Information-Gathering Skills

Ronald Mackay
Concordia University, Montreal

In many parts of the world where English is not the mother tongue, students are expected to extract information from spoken or written texts in the English language as part of their postschool training.

From having studied English as a subject in the school syllabus, they are now required to use English as an instrument of learning. In many cases their efforts to do so meet with a decided lack of success which may have a prejudicial effect on their vocational or academic progress.

The purpose of this chapter is to suggest that there are areas of linguistic knowledge which we have tended to neglect or even omit from our teaching in the intermediate and advanced comprehension class but which are essential for the successful comprehension of either spoken or written texts. The word *text* will be used throughout this chapter to cover both spoken and written manifestations of the language.

While it is acknowledged that the skills of listening and reading are not identical, they may be discussed together under the term "information-gathering skills." Both are comprehension skills involving the perception and interpretation of all the linguistic signals which make up the text. Moreover, the use of magnetic tape in the classroom has eliminated one of the greatest differences between spoken discourse and written texts, namely, the ephemeral nature of the former. Thus a student presented with either listening or reading materials can take his

First published in *RELC Journal*, Vol. 4, No. 2, 1974. Reprinted by permission of the Regional Language Centre, Singapore.

own time over them in the sense that he can regress as often as he finds is necessary. He has no "author" present and therefore has to cope with an immutable permanent text. Neither does he have any source of extra- or paralinguistic clues, unless, of course, illustrations are provided to supplement the text. We will focus our discussion upon texts which do not incorporate illustrations or figures. After all, many lectures, tutorials, or discussions which students or trainees are required to listen to do not involve visual aids, nor do their textbooks include many illustrations. We are concerned, then, in this chapter with texts in which all the information is marked linguistically—either graphically on paper or orally on magnetic tape.

In discussing the information-gathering skills we must distinguish between the skills which can be exhibited as a result of comprehension and the linguistic knowledge which the learner is required to have in order to exhibit the comprehension skills. The distinction is an important one not only for materials development but also for syllabus planning and for testing.

A typical taxonomy of comprehension skills would include, for example, the ability to extract the literal meaning from the text, to identify the main ideas or facts supporting details and the relationships between ideas or facts, and to identify longer units of text which convey "thought units" or "units of information" essential to the development of the information. They are a description of successful comprehension in terms of the skills the student can demonstrate to have mastered. But they tell us nothing about the kind or amount of linguistic knowledge a student requires in order to master them. They are behavioral goals; as teachers and course planners we require additional information, namely, a clear specification of the language items we have to teach our students in order to develop each of these skills.

To ask a student to demonstrate a skill may indicate whether or not he has mastered it, but it may teach the student nothing. If our purpose is not to *test* comprehension but to teach it, then our materials should provide the student with linguistic information about how a text conveys meaning so that he can use that information in order to understand not only the text under scrutiny, but any text his studies may require him to cope with.

The successful demonstration of a comprehension skill implies knowledge of the language system in question and an operational knowledge of how that system is used to convey meaning. All information in a text is signaled linguistically. The successful demonstration of the skill must therefore depend upon a correct interpretation of the linguistic signals in the text.

In order to illustrate what is meant by "linguistic knowledge," consider the following example. Imagine you did not hear or see part of the last word of the following sentence (based on Smith 1971, p. 20):

"The captain ordered the sailors to haul up the an_____." What kinds of knowledge do we call upon to complete the sentence ourselves? "None" may initially appear to be an appropriate answer to some; the last word is "obviously" anchor. The most likely word is, of course, *anchor,* but how did we arrive at that decision? We have called upon one or several kinds of knowledge about the English language although we may have done so unconsciously. We may have made use of:

(i) *Knowledge of the spelling or phonological system of English.*
    If the word is an English word, it must correspond to the spelling or pronunciation rules of English and so cannot be continued using b, f, h, j, m, p, q, r, w, or z.

(ii) *Knowledge of the grammatical system of English*
    The word is almost certain to be a noun. After "the" a pronoun or a verb cannot follow and, as the word completes the sentence, it cannot in this instance be an adjective or an adverb.

(iii) *Semantic knowledge*
    While words like *anger, anchovy,* and *anarchist* satisfy the requirements of the system outlined in (i) and (ii), our knowledge of the world tells us that they are either impossible or unlikely in the context. A verb like *haul up* must have a concrete object; thus an abstract noun like *anger* is unacceptable. Moreover the concrete object of *haul up* must also be heavy, and so, although *anchovy* has the right association in the context, it too must be ruled out. The word *anarchist* is merely unlikely in the context; it does not obviously collocate with *captain* and *sailors.* Only the context in which the entire sentence appears could provide the information necessary to accept or reject it. *Anchor* seems to be the most acceptable; it satisfies the requirements in (i) and (ii), it is a heavy concrete object which would require to be *hauled up* by more than one man, and it collocates satisfactorily with *captain* and *sailors* and fits into our understanding of the duties of the crew of a sailing ship.

Of course we did not *consciously* go through the procedures described in (i), (ii), and (iii) in deciding that the word was *anchor,* yet in solving the problem we made use of our knowledge of the graphological, phonological, and grammatical system of English. An inadequate competence would have resulted in an inadequate performance in the problem. In other words, we have used specified "linguistic knowledge" in order to solve a problem of comprehension.

The linguistic knowledge we drew upon in this example was knowledge of what makes a sentence a sentence. When we are dealing with the comprehension of longer stretches of language, we must make use not only of the linguistic knowledge of what makes a sentence a sentence, but also of what makes a text a text.

Consider the difference in the linguistic knowledge required in order to answer questions 1 and 2 below:

> Over the past century pollutants have been released into the air in mounting quantities. In recent years a good deal of attention has been given to the possibility that these may affect the climate of the earth as a whole.

Question 1   What have been released into the air in mounting quantities over the past century?
                   Answer: Pollutants.

Question 2   What may affect the climate of the earth?
                   Answer: (Mounting quantities of) pollutants.

To answer question 1 correctly requires a knowledge of sentence grammar only. The "What" of the question deletes the immediate constituent "pollutants" of the first sentence. To answer question 2 correctly requires a knowledge of one kind of intersentence cohesive tie. The "What" of the question deletes the word "these" in the second sentence whose referent is "pollutants" in the first sentence. The word "these" is an anaphoric tie syntactically linking the two sentences to make a short text.

While adequate grammatical descriptions of sentence structure in English exist, there is correspondingly little in the way of descriptions of the syntactic features which contribute to the cohesion of text. Since most teaching materials are based on one or other of the various descriptions of sentence grammar, the materials we use for teaching comprehension at the higher stages tend to be linguistically uninformed. Our students lack *instruction* in the grammar of text, and the grammar of sentence structure is generally assumed to have been mastered at the more elementary level. What they do learn about textual cohesion is the by-product rather than the direct result of systematic teaching.

In teaching the information-gathering skills, we need to be able to identify those linguistic features of text which *hinder* comprehension, if they are unfamiliar and which *facilitate* comprehension, once their role is properly understood. Since the grammar book has traditionally been concerned with sentence grammar, the kind of linguistic information we need is often missing from traditional grammars. The recent volume, "A Grammar of Contemporary English" (Quirk et al.), is a notable exception.

Let us examine a short text in order to try to identify some of the kinds of cohesive features of text we have in mind.

Sample Text

1. The dumping of massive and durable pieces of junk, like the hulks
2. of old vehicles and abandoned kitchen equipment, has become a
3. nuisance. This debris is a menace to the farmer, destroys amenities,
4. and costs money to the individuals or the local authorities who have
5. to clean it up. Hence this problem cannot be allowed to expand in
6. parallel with growth in the number of vehicles in service or with the
7. increase in the total amount of household equipment produced.
8. Dumping of waste by people in this way is already illegal and
9. prosecutions are brought from time to time. Moreover, all local
10. authorities have established and advertised the existence of tips to
11. which those who are not prepared to incur the cost of a special
12. collection can bring bulky objects for disposal. Therefore, the solution
13. appears to be in the further development of the current threefold
14. approach of legislative penalty, improved public services, and increased
15. public awareness.

We recognize "intuitively" that the above paragraph is a text and not just a collection of unrelated sentences; there are identifiable and describable linguistic relationships of various kinds set up between the sentences which contribute to the overall cohesion of the text. Let us consider these in more detail.

First there are *lexical relationships*. The phrase "massive and durable pieces of junk" (line 1) is repeated as "debris" (line 3) and as "waste" (line 8). The relationship here is one of "inclusion" or hyponomy, which can be illustrated thus

general   waste
↑   ↑
specific   debris
                       ↑
                  massive and durable pieces of junk.

The introduction of a specific term which is later introduced as a more general term is characteristic of texts; e.g., *wolf* can be repeated later in the text as the more general *animal* or as the even more general *creature; Rolls Royce* can be repeated as *car* or as *vehicle*. Consider the unacceptability of working from the general term to the specific:

Last night a construction (1) was gutted by fire in the dock area of Singapore. Firemen fought the blaze for six hours but were unable to save the building (2). Early this morning what was left of the eight-story warehouse (3) was declared a public hazard and the authorities have granted permission for its demolition.

The most specific *eight-story warehouse* must be used at (1) and the hierarchically dominant, i.e., more general, term *construction* must be placed at (3).

There is also another kind of lexical relationship within the sample text—that of equivalence or synonymy. *Massive and durable pieces of junk* (line 1) is repeated as the textual equivalent *bulky objects for disposal* (line 13); likewise *nuisance* (line 3), *menace* (line 3), and *problem* (line 6) are used as synonyms or near synonyms in the text.

It is clear then, that vocabulary difficulties are a matter of not just the meanings of unknown words, but also the relationships holding between lexical items in a given text. I believe that the responsibility for the solution of the difficulties encountered by unknown words at the advanced level lies with the learner rather than with the teacher. The student must make the same effort as the native speaker when faced with a new field involving a new vocabulary, that is, guess intelligently, use an appropriate dictionary, and develop the memory sufficiently to allow recognition of the word when it is met subsequently. However, the relationships of hyponymy and synonymy into which lexical items may fit and thereby provide textual cohesion can be usefully pointed out and practiced in the class. For example, consider an exercise like the following, where the student is required to fill in the blanks in the text from the words supplied:

Experience has proved that _____ are of great value in the protection of crops and livestock. Most _____ in use were developed in the past 30 years and demand for new _____ continues to grow.

        (*a*)   products
        (*b*)   ones
        (*c*)   pesticides

But it is well known that the good effects of _____ can be offset by dangers to the natural environment. An advisory committee on pesticides and other toxic chemicals made a thorough investigation of _____ such as _____ and _____

(*a*)   organochlorine insecticides
(*b*)   pesticides
(*c*)   dieldrin
(*d*)   DDT

The committee found that the persistence of these _____ may cause harm to beneficial _____ such as _____, to fish, birds, and other wild life.

(*a*)   substances
(*b*)   bees
(*c*)   insects

Once the student has been taught the nature of the lexical relationships to be found in text and has had experience of how they operate, he will be more capable of interpreting the value of the vocabulary items he meets in new texts. Of course, to some extent he will have to rely upon the knowledge of his subject to help determine the relationship between, for example, "organochlorine insecticides" and "pesticides," recognizing that the latter includes the former. It is relationships and how they contribute to textual cohesion that are being taught.

Second, there are *syntactic relationships* holding between sentences. The most obvious are those signaling anaphoric reference. Referring back to the sample text, the demonstrative "this" (line 3) refers back to "massive and durable pieces of junk" (line 1). The demonstrative "this" (line 5) has a more general reference function referring back to the fact, presented in the first sentence, that dumping has become a nuisance; the phrase "in this way" (line 8) likewise has no single word or phrase as its referent but refers to the dumping of waste in such a way that it has become a problem—the content of sentences 1, 2, and 3. The pronoun "it" (line 5), on the other hand, has a single word referent—"debris" in line 3 and "those" (line 11) refers back to people in line 8.

The use of pronominals and demonstratives are only two of the ways in which a text is made to cohere syntactically. Other syntactic devices of anaphoric reference follow.

Comparison.   When we find expressions of similarity or difference, we may have to look back in the text in order to find the basis of the comparison, e.g.,

> Aung scored 80% in the examination. Both Ting and Fong got the *same* mark but Chan scored more than 10% *less.*

> In 1970 there were approximately 16 million motor vehicles in Great Britain. This was 3 million *more* than in 1965 and 6½ million *more* than in 1960. However it is 4 million *fewer* than the estimate for 1975.

In order to answer the questions:

1.   How many motor vehicles were there in Great Britain in (*a*) 1965 (*b*) 1960?
2.   What is the estimated figure for 1975?

the point of reference must be taken from the first sentence.

Nominal and Verbal Substitution.

1.   I'd like a vehicle which is self-propelled, has no running costs, does not depreciate, and travels at up to 50 mph.
2.   I'd like *one* too.
3.   *So* would I.

Summary Words.   These are words which are used to summarize a stretch of text, e.g.,

> First she boiled the water in a small pot. Then she added a lot of sugar and after that, the coffee. She let it almost boil over three times before she was satisfied that it was ready. The whole *process* took about 15 minutes.

Other common summary words are *case/affair/problem/idea/ business.*

The student's attention can be directed to such syntactic features of cohesion by asking him to read or listen to a piece of text and asking a question which focuses upon the feature. For example:

(Tape)   And then finally, stage four, a true horse, with only one huge toe on each foot, an animal made to run really fast—as it had to, to keep alive, in a land of sabre-tooth tigers!

(Workbook)   as *it had to*
             (*a*)   To what does *it* refer?
                     Answer _____

(*b*)   What did it have to do?
Answer _____

(Tape)   Well now, back to our question. How? The horse didn't decide to change its toes and its legs and its teeth—but it did change. It did evolve. Well, this is how it happens.

(Workbook)   Well this is how *it* happens.
(*a*)   To what does *it* here refer?
Answer: It refers to _____

(Tape)   Almost every plant and animal is the result of the mating of a female with a male. She has the eggs or seed—he has the sperm or the pollen. The two come together and make a cell which will eventually grow into a new living thing.

(Workbook)   The *two* come together and make a cell.
The *two* refers to:
(*a*)   she and he
(*b*)   the sperm and the pollen
(*c*)   the egg and the sperm

The above examples are taken from a listening comprehension course (Morrison 1974), which uses live discussions on tape as the teaching text. In the eight units, features of cohesion are focused upon where they occur naturally in the text. The set of texts were selected on the basis of the breadth of coverage it provided.

Third, there are *logical relationships* holding between sentences or stretches of text, marked by the use of logical connectors. In the sample text "Hence" (line 5) introduces a deduction which may be deduced logically from the information which precedes it. "Moreover" (line 10) introduces additional information reinforcing the information given in the previous sentence. "Therefore" (line 14) introduces the logical conclusion to be drawn from the information presented so far.

It is clear, at this point, that we are now dealing with a different kind of cohesion from the lexical and syntactic relations we discussed above. In considering the logical or meaningful relationships holding between sentences or larger units, we are not now primarily concerned with the linguistic properties of the excerpt as text but with "the communicative function of the sample as discourse" (Widdowson 1974). That is, in addition to reacting to the formal devices used to combine sentences into continuous text, we are now reacting to the linguistic signals, or "discourse markers" (Wijasuriya 1971), which tell us whether to interpret a stretch of text as an observation, a reinforcement, a conclusion, or some other act of communication.

These discourse markers, usually adverbs or prepositional phrases, can be grouped in notional or semantic categories in the following way:

TYPES OF DISCOURSE MARKERS

Notional Category/Meaning	Marker
1. *Enumerative.* Introduce the order in which points are to be made or the time sequence in which actions or processes took place.	first(ly), second(ly), third(ly), one, two three / a, b, c, next, then, finally, last(ly), in the first / second place, for one thing / for another thing, to begin with, subsequently, eventually, finally, in the end, to conclude.
2. *Additive*	
2.1 Reinforcing. Introduces a reinforcement or confirmation of what has preceded.	again, then again, also, moreover, furthermore, in addition, above all, what is more.
2.2 Similarity. Introduces a statement of similarity with what has preceded.	equally, likewise, similarly, correspondingly, in the same way.
2.3 Transition. Introduces a new stage in the sequence of presentation of information.	now, well, incidentally, by the way, O.K., fine.
3. *Logical Sequence*	
3.1 Summative. Introduces a summary of what has preceded.	so, so far, altogether, overall, then, thus, therefore, in short, to sum up, to conclude, to summarize.
3.2 Resultative. Introduces an expression of the result or consequence of what preceded (and includes inductive and deductive acts).	so, as a result, consequently, hence, now, therefore, thus, as a consequence, in consequence.
4. *Explicative.* Introduces an explanation or reformulation of what preceded.	namely, in other words, that is to say, better, rather, by (this) we mean.
5. *Illustrative.* Introduces an illustration or example of what preceded.	for example, for instance.
6. *Contrastive*	
6.1 Replacive. Introduces an alternative to what preceded.	alternatively, (or) again, (or) rather, (but) then, on the other hand.
6.2 Antithetic. Introduces information in opposition to what preceded.	conversely, instead, then, on the contrary, by contrast, on the other hand.
6.3 Concessive. Introduces information which is unexpected in view of what preceded.	anyway, anyhow, however, nevertheless, nonetheless, notwithstanding, still, though, yet, for all that, in spite of (that), at the same time, all the same.

The student's attention should be focused upon these discourse markers, and the meanings they introduce can be explained whenever they occur. Once they have been taught, multiple-choice questions can be used to make the student focus on the meaning. For example:

Student reads or hears:
The first thing that one has to realize about a robot is that man is God for the robot—he creates the robot. Therefore, its good qualities and its bad qualities are his fault, either way.

Workbook:
Question: The word *Therefore* here means:
   (a)   Because this is the first thing one must realize about a robot.
   (b)   Because man is the one who creates the robot.

Alternatively, suitable passages can be retyped omitting the discourse marker and the student asked to fill in the blanks from a list of alternatives. For example:

The digestibility and therefore the feeding value of grass falls rapidly after an emergence. _____ (1) silage made from overmature grass will reflect this reduced feeding value. _____ (2) cuts for silage, particularly first cuts, have to be made over a short period if uniformly good silage with a high feeding value is to result. _____ (3) efficient organization of labor and machinery is one of the most important aspects of good silage making. _____ (4) it will help to minimize the effect of unsettled weather if this occurs at the critical time.

In the blanks above, supply the most appropriate marker from the list:

1.   for example, in spite of that, again, alternatively
2.   again, similarly, therefore, incidentally
3.   likewise, finally, hence, however
4.   nevertheless, moreover, for example, on the other hand

It is also a useful procedure to have the students formally recognize the kind of communicative acts being performed in the discourse. Once they have been made familiar with the notional categories into which acts can fall, they can be asked to reorder a given list of acts to conform to the pattern exhibited in the passage.

The above discussion has attempted to illustrate that the adequate comprehension of texts from which information has to be extracted requires the reader to make use of a different kind of linguistic knowledge than sentence grammar provides. Of course, there is no suggestion whatsoever that "text grammar" is a *substitute* for sentence grammar; mastery of the former depends upon mastery of the latter. The implication which can be drawn is that the features which make up the grammatical cohesion of text and the communicative cohesion of discourse (Allen and Widdowson 1978) must be taught to the student at the intermediate and advanced stages in a systematic and purposeful way, just as sentence grammar was taught systematically in the elementary stage. Much of what passes for "advanced comprehension teaching" consists of little more than asking the student to perform a skill which he has not the competence to perform because he has never been formally taught the linguistic knowledge required for the performance of the skill.

Conclusion

In this chapter features of continuous spoken and written language which are seldom systematically taught to the intermediate and advanced learner have been discussed. These features of lexical inclusion and equivalence, anaphoric reference and intersentential connection form part of the linguistic system of all texts, and since the information in a text is signaled linguistically, an inadequate mastery of these features must hinder comprehension. If the student knows only part of what he needs to know in order to understand a text, he will be a poor information gatherer, and where professional or vocational success depends upon gathering information from English texts he will fall below the required standards.

Successful teaching of the information-gathering skills depends upon:

1. The teacher being able to identify in linguistic (phonological, grammatical, or lexical) terms the knowledge a student must possess in order to understand a given level or kind of text.
2. The teacher systematically teaching that knowledge to his students.
3. The teacher providing his students with the opportunities for practicing that knowledge.

Testing a student's comprehension only tells us if he possesses the necessary linguistic knowledge for comprehension; systematic teaching provides the necessary knowledge and exercises it. When "teaching comprehension" the teacher should always be able to answer the question "What kind of language knowledge does this text or this question on the text require?" Focusing on the appropriate language knowledge required for comprehension guarantees that we are indeed *teaching* comprehension, and not testing it.

CHAPTER 8

Reading in the Foreign Language Teaching Program

Sheila Been
Tel Aviv University, Israel

As a member of the team which plans the course of study in English for Israel Instructional Television, I have been concerned for some time with what is known as the "reading gap." This refers to the fact that on reaching the "advanced level," that is, the last two years of an eight-year course of study, Israeli high school students have difficulty in coping with the literature curriculum of the compulsory school-leaving examination. These reading requirements comprise original works by modern writers such as Arthur Miller, Tennessee Williams, Philip Roth, Stephen Crane, and James Joyce. Students have difficulty in understanding the texts because they suffer from paucity of vocabulary, they are not used to reading independently, and they do not have the appropriate mental set, in the sense of a special kind of reading readiness, to be able to cope with the demands made of them.

In this chapter I describe the reading program in Israel in general, offer some explanations as to why the "reading gap" arises, and then put forward some ideas which might contribute to solving it.

There is such an abundance of psycholinguistic and educational literature on "reading" that it is clear the problem is not only a local one; I hope therefore that the suggestions made below will be found relevant to foreign language teachers in other countries as well.

First published in *TESOL Quarterly*, Vol. 9, No. 3, 1975. Copyright 1975 by Teachers of English to Speakers of Other Languages. Reprinted by permission of the publisher and Sheila Been.

Aims

Under the influence of the structuralist school of linguistics with its emphasis on the spoken language, the audio-lingual method became the vogue for some decades. As so often happens, the enthusiasm for the new approach caused a loss of perspective as to the long-term objectives of the program, and the teaching of reading as a goal in itself fell by the way. This was a serious omission, for English remains the language of international communication (written as well as oral), and most students in universities and adult education programs are required to read English-language texts. As Saville-Troike (1973; p. 25, this volume) says: "The audio-lingual method has placed a high priority, and rightly, on oral communication, and *good* audio-lingual programs have succeeded in producing fluent speakers of English and other languages. But these programs must additionally recognize reading as a skill in and of itself instead of merely reinforcement for orally introduced structures and vocabulary if they are to produce fluent readers as well."

With the emergence of the theories of transformational grammarians, new insights were gained regarding the nature of language and language acquisition which were adopted to some extent by those involved in language pedagogy in the form of what has come to be known as the "cognitive code view" of language learning. Thus today, while an emphasis on speech is maintained in our courses in Israel, the general approach focuses on the apprehension of the *system* of the language, and priority is awarded to the teaching of syntactic structures. The 4 to 5 hour a week schedule, geared as it is to "grammar," leaves very little time throughout the elementary and intermediate levels for much concentration on the teaching of reading as an objective in its own right.

Psycholinguists such as Bever and Bower (1970) and Smith (1971) have made significant contributions to our understanding of the reading process; yet there seems to be little application of this to current classroom practices.

Current Classroom Practices

In the typical Israeli classroom situation, the first two years of English (grades 5 and 6) are devoted mainly to the study of the "mechanics of reading." The orthography is taught, and students learn the reading and writing skills more or less simultaneously. Left to right directionality is emphasized, as Hebrew script proceeds from right to left. Thereafter a combination of a phonic and global approach is adopted for the identification of words and phrases. This can be characterized as the "learning to read" stage.

In the third year of English the emphasis changes slightly, and what we might call the "reading to learn" stage is introduced. At this point reading is viewed largely as a vehicle for vocabulary enrichment. New words are usually introduced orally by the teacher through a variety of techniques, the students being required to understand the word (in one particular context), pronounce it, and recognize its visual shape before being exposed to the word in a reading passage. The first reading is usually done aloud by the teacher; this is followed either by reading aloud around the class or in response to comprehension questions, the answers to which can be lifted directly from the text. By the fifth year of English, teachers are encouraged to allow more silent reading, but only after the students have been thoroughly prepared for all the new words, lexical loading generally being carefully controlled. Questions following the reading passages generally aim at literal comprehension with a minimum of high-order questions (inferential, evaluative, etc.).

Analysis of Procedures in Teaching Reading

In the light of analysis of the "reading process' by psycholinguists, procedures such as the above seem to undermine the development of fluent reading (reading for meaning) rather than to further this objective. The problem can be explained in terms of a conflict of interests between the strategies required in reading per se, and the skills involved in learning to read a foreign language. In other words, an activity which might make a positive contribution to the learning of a foreign language (such as reading aloud) might also inhibit the promotion of fluent reading in that language.

Reading Aloud

Once the "mechanics" of reading are achieved, any reading aloud—including the first reading by the teacher—should be discouraged, for it treats reading as a linear activity; the pupils follow the words as they are read, and therefore read every word (albeit subvocally), and follow the text linearly. Smith cites research which shows that a fluent reader's eye fixations are placed where they are likely to yield optimum information; this means that the reader's eyes may move down, across, up and back (Smith 1971, p. 204). Thus empirical evidence does not support the premise that learners should be trained to read linearly. Nonetheless reading aloud by the teacher and to a lesser extent by the pupil can serve valuable functions in terms of foreign language learning; for example, it demonstrates the correct pronunciation of new words, as well as meaningfulness, by words being in sense groups with appropriate phonological and syntactic correlates. Thus there is a conflict of interests here of the type noted earlier.

Furthermore, if we accept the theory of transformational grammar (which seems to offer the most plausible explanation to date as to how a speaker of a language perceives, interprets, forms, and produces an utterance in one way rather than another), we accept the hypothesis that meaning is related to deep structure and is not directly available from surface forms. It thus seems logical that a reader needs to perceive whole sentences in order to apprehend the deep structure (and hence the meaning); since deep structures are abstractions, they do not proceed linearly. Saville-Troike (1973, p. 25, this volume) supports the view that the good reader is not limited by linear sequencing.

Reading aloud requires that every word be apprehended not only by its visual configuration but also by its oral counterpart. This leads to mediated word identification which necessarily slows down the pace of reading. Smith (1971, pp. 90-94) argues that in order to apprehend meaning, reading must be fast, and the reader must perceive as large a chunk of visual information as possible. Smith's claims are supported by Bever and Bower (1970, p. 306), who state that visual readers comprehend written material better and faster than auditory readers. Ferguson (1973, pp. 30-34) likewise supports the view that fast reading contributes to the apprehension of meaning. For instance, in slow reading the overall picture may be lost owing to attention to detail, while unfamiliar vocabulary may frighten the student into not reading.

The Teaching of Vocabulary

The teaching of vocabulary is an essential element of foreign language study, and one which can be best taught through contextualized material. Yet the tendency to teach reading mainly for the purpose of teaching vocabulary likewise conflicts with the more general aims of reading for understanding. Overemphasis on understanding individual words perpetuates the misconception that understanding is entirely dependent on a knowledge of the individual words. Twaddell (1973, p.

61) describes research in the frequency distribution of words. He says: "It is a near impossibility to teach the learner what he will need [in terms of vocabulary resources] for the next page he will read or the next 60 seconds of lecture or conversation that he will hear. If we try to prepare him in advance for specific vocabulary needs for any real reading or listening we are sure to fail, and he is sure to be frustrated and discouraged." Thus the practice of ensuring that all words are familiar before the learner is confronted with a reading passage in fact fosters nonproductive attitudes. The learner begins to feel that it is essential to have an explicit understanding of every word if he is to apprehend meaning, and he is immediately at a loss if his expectations are not met. Furthermore, he has not been given the chance to develop the skill of intelligent guessing, nor has he learned to proceed beyond the word or sentence which causes difficulty. Smith (1971, p. 24) notes: "Whether an object is perceived depends less on the clarity than on the attitude of the observer. . . . Signal detection theory shows that in identification tasks (such as reading) a proportion of correct responses can be selected by the perceiver, but that the cost of increasing the correct responses is an increase in the number of errors; in other words, the more you want to be right, the more you must tolerate being wrong."

This has important pedagogical implications: if the objective is to encourage a reader to rely on less information in order to make decisions, it follows that the reader is likely to make more errors. The teacher (or the reading text) must be very sensitive to the amount of information which is given to the pupil in order to strike a balance between encouraging this decision making on the one hand, and frustrating him (if his decisions are wrong) on the other. The teacher's attitude toward wrong decisions is also important—he must recognize that the errors are the result of cognitive activity in the right direction, and appreciate them as positive responses. The teacher's role (together with appropriate textbook material) is twofold:

1. To help the student utilize whatever resources he has to make up for information that he is lacking, thus building up his confidence.

2. To help the learner exploit the redundancies in the language, by demonstrating how information is supplied from more than one source—conversely, that the same information can be obtained from less data. This will help the learner to understand that in the reading process it is more important to see the trees than the forest.

Comprehension Questions

Emphasis has usually been on literal-type questions. Such questions may be a valuable foreign language teaching device because they test the ability to identify the visual configurations of strings of words and to recognize grammatical function and they offer opportunities to focus on particular lexical items. Yet from the point of view of reading for meaning they seem to accomplish very little. Consider, for instance, the following sentence:

> Mrs. Tse-Ling flies to the Occident twice a year to buy fashionable clothes.

A literal comprehension question would be *Where does Mrs. Tse-Ling go twice a year?* Most pupils would be able to answer this question from the grammatical clues supplied; however, a correct answer would give no indication as to whether the meaning of the word *Occident* is understood or not.

High-order questions (inferential, evaluative, applicative, etc.) encourage the student to search for meaning, and they can and should be introduced at the earliest level possible—as long as they are framed so that answers are within the productive competence of the learner. Yes/no questions and multiple-choice questions can be oriented toward these high-order cognitive activities. For instance:

Inferential:
  Yes/No Questions
    1. Does Mrs. Tse-Ling live in a western country?
    2. Does Mrs. Tse-Ling have a lot of money?
  Multiple Choice
    1. Mrs. Tse-Ling lives in America/Africa/Asia.
    2. Mrs. Tse-Ling is interested in traveling/clothes/flying.
Evaluative
  Pretend you have a lot of money. Would you
    1. spend it on clothes and pleasures?
    2. save it for the future?
    3. give it to people who need it?

The learner must be brought to an awareness that in acquiring the skill of reading he needs to bring to bear all the cognitive abilities with which he is endowed.

Introduction to the Text

Teachers usually prepare students before the text is presented by first teaching the new lexical items. This procedure, too, is entirely valid if the primary objective is to enrich vocabulary; it ensures that the student will understand the passage with less effort and will also give him exposure to new words. However, it is unrealistic in terms of what he will be required to do in later reading activities—when he will meet words that are not familiar and that he cannot pronounce. In teaching "reading for meaning," it would be preferable to stress the general content of the passage. This approach would be on the lines of what Seliger (1972, p. 54) calls "directed reading" and what Morris (1973, p. 190) calls "context support." Here the intention is "to ensure that the message of the text is already alive in some form in the mind of the reader, so that when the reader identifies words he does so within a context that has already been given." Morris (1973, p. 190) In other words, the reading activity should be directed; the reader should know what to look for. Thus, in introducing a new piece of fiction, one or more of the following could be used:

1. A brief summary of the story
2. A brief outline of *where, when,* and *with whom*
3. Dwelling on the title—and then talking about what the text will deal with
4. Using key words to give an outline of the text in contexts directly related to the contents of the text
5. Giving a brief background introduction to the topic of thē text, again using key words.

This kind of introduction not only facilitates the reading activity but also provides motivation—in the final analysis probably the largest single factor in promoting proficient reading.

Proposal: "Reading for Language" and "Reading for Meaning"

Against the above background, I propose that the teaching of reading in the foreign language teaching program be conducted along two parameters:

A. Teaching "reading for language" as one of the means of teaching the language. This would include activities such as reading aloud, teaching new vocabulary before presentation of a reading passage, literal comprehension questions, and all the other activities usually considered part of the "reading lesson."

B.   Teaching "reading for meaning." As soon as the "learning to read" stage is accomplished, a program should be inaugurated which teaches strategies of "reading for meaning." This program would contain two elements:

1.   The reader would be given "context support" by means of questions which precede the text; these would direct the reader to search for specific information. Only one or two questions would be asked before each reading, and the questions might elicit only the main idea. Before a second reading the questions might require inferences .based on particular sentences or parts of the text.

2.   The reader would be given *cues* which lead him to ignore linearity, help him to exploit redundancies, and demonstrate that meaning can be apprehended even though he does not understand every word. These cues would be provided by means of different kinds of print: for example, in some exercises key words would be in larger type face so that they stand out, and the reader's attention would be attracted toward these words; in other exercises, some of the words or phrases would be in very small print so that the reader would realize that these can be glossed over; in other exercises there might be a combination of regular print, large print, and small print, thus encouraging the reader to combine the strategies of ordinary linear reading (in the regular print), to focus particularly on the key words (in the larger print), and to ignore the redundancies (in the smaller print).

Thus the reading program would consist of two sections, each with different objectives, and the textbook would include both kinds of activities, the objectives for each being clearly stated. The remainder of this chapter presents samples of materials intended to demonstrate the "reading for meaning" program.

Specimen "Reading for Meaning" Materials

These samples represent no more than the germ of an idea. Full-scale experimentation would clearly have to be carried out over a fairly long-term period in order to discover whether this approach can in fact help students to overcome the reading gap.

SAMPLE 1

Assumptions: Key words are familiar.

Aims: To discourage linear reading and to encourage searching for specific information (i.e., to train the learner to ignore anything which is not directly relevant to the question).

Question: First reading.
Which room is described in the following passage?

The lights are **bright**. It is painted **white** and is very **airy**. The lights are situated over the **stove** and the **sink** as well as over the ceiling. There is a lot of cupboard space and several **electric outlets**. The **working surfaces** are just the right height. There is constant **hot water**. The Russell's kitchen is one of the best planned that I have ever seen.

Question: Second reading.
Do you think the kitchen is easy to work in?

The lights are bright. It is painted white and is very airy. The lights are situated over the stove and the sink as well as over the ceiling. There is a lot of cupboard space and several electric outlets. There is constant hot water. **The Russell's kitchen is one of the best planned that I have ever seen.**

SAMPLE 2

Assumptions: Structures are known.
Content words following connectives are unknown.

Aims: To train the reader to make use of contextual clues to compensate for lack of understanding of words, i.e., utilizing redundancies (in the text below, it is assumed that students are familiar with the connectives in bold type but not with the vocabulary in the small type).

Read the passage in order to answer the following questions:
1. Did the trip go smoothly on the second day?
2. Did the boys worry as soon as things went wrong?
3. Did the boys get help quickly?
4. Did the boys give up hope?

We had an exciting holiday. We decided to go on a walking trip. On the first day everything was fine, **but** *then mishaps began to befall us—Bill tripped and injured the muscles in his thigh.* We had enough food and water **so** *we assumed that our plight was not acute.* John went off to look for help, **but** *he did not achieve his objective.* We waited and waited for many hours **and soon** *desperation began to overcome us.* **However,** *we managed to keep up our spirits by recounting famous stories of rescue operations.* **At last** a helicopter saw us and help soon arrived.

SAMPLE 3

     Assumptions: Structures and lexical items are known.

     Aims: To train the reader to skim over information which can be inferred.

Read the passage in order to answer the question.

     What do you know about John?

The two brothers Bob and John were quite different. Bob was tall, fair, and slim; John *was short, fat, and dark.* Bob was never happier than when he had something practical to do; John, *on the other hand, was always clumsy when using his hands.* Bob rarely spoke to other people if he didn't have to, but John *was always the center of a group.* In fact, it was hard to believe that they were brothers.

SAMPLE 4

     The following mini-unit is more conventional than the three preceding samples, since it does not involve varieties of type face, and appears to be a blank filler exercise to which students are accustomed. Note, however, that it does not follow a *cloze* technique since only content words are omitted, they are not omitted at regular intervals, and no test of grammatical function is intended.

EXERCISE A

     Assumption: The words represented by blanks are unknown.

     Aims: To train in context reading, i.e., apprehending the main ideas by making use of redundancies and guessing at the general idea of words which are unknown.

     Questions: Choose the correct answer in the sentences below on the basis of the following passage; the numbered blanks in the passage stand for missing words.

  1.   Brighton is known as a business center/industrial area/holiday town/fashionable suburb.

2. The weather in summer is pleasant/unpleasant.
3. The people are unfriendly/friendly.
4. Brighton is most suitable for old people/young people/ young and old people.

BRIGHTON

Brighton is a small ___1__ on the south __2__   1. _____
of England. Many people spend their holidays there.   2. _____
In the summer the weather is ___3__ , with clear   3. _____
skies and long hours of daylight. Even in the evenings it is possible to wear summer clothes with a
thin sweater.

Every season it is ___4___ with people of all   4. _____
kinds. There is always a very ___5__ atmosphere;   5. _____
people are ready to talk to strangers and many
new friendships are started. In fact, the formality
of the big city is completely forgotten here.

People spent their time according to their
own tastes. Young people generally ___6__ on the   6. _____
beaches, older people usually prefer to ___7__ along   7. _____
the __8__ . Young and old usually enjoy __9__   8. _____
on the machines in the amusement __10__ , or   9. _____
visiting the __11__ called "The Lanes" where there   10. _____
are a lot of little shops selling different sorts of   11. _____
__12__ which they can take home for friends and   12. _____
relatives. Many people enjoy riding on the little
electric railway which is a special __13__ of   13. _____
Brighton.

EXERCISE B

Assumption: The missing words are unfamiliar to the students.

Aim: To train the student to guess any word which has a suitable connotation in terms of the context of the sentence, without concern for its correct grammatical form.

(The pupils are invited to place their suggestions in the column on the right-hand side rather than in the blank space within the sentences; this is done in order to prevent the formation of an ungrammatical sentence.)

Instructions: Read the passage again. Fill in the spaces provided in the column with words that might suit the meaning of that sentence.

EXERCISE C

This offers several additional questions which require the student to scan the passage again for specific information.

Assumption: All ideas are understood.

Aim: To train in scanning for specific information.

Instructions: Look through the passage again in order to answer the following questions:

1. How many items of information are there relating to the weather?
2. How many items of information are there relating to the general atmosphere?
3. How many items of information are there relating to "things to do" in Brighton?

SECTION III

PRACTICE

In this section, the theoretical assumptions and organizational principles which are related to reading a second language are applied to the description of specific sets of teaching materials and different types of written language. Detailed descriptions of teaching techniques show how current knowledge and beliefs about reading a second language can be implemented in classrooms.

In Chapter 9, Mackay and Mountford provide helpful information for teachers of English for special purposes concerning text selection and techniques for analyzing special subject areas, an overview of the linguistic information necessary to advanced reading comprehension, and some illustrations of methods and materials for practicing reading comprehension skills.

As a first step toward familiarizing himself with the learners' areas of interest, the authors suggest that the teacher examine the table of contents of basic textbooks dealing with those fields. This provides the English for special purposes teacher with the basic specialized vocabulary of each area as well as some idea of the scope and the various subdivisions of these specialties. Consultation with subject-matter specialists is also recommended as an invaluable aid to the often scientifically naïve second language instructor.

In addition to the linguistic information needed for understanding individual sentences, such as word meanings, recognition of syntactic patterns, and affixation, the authors point out the necessity for instruction in the linguistic devices which signal the semantic links among the sentences of a text (cohesion) and which help identify the logical and rhetorical relations in a given piece of writing (discourse markers). Many examples of such linguistic signals are given, along with suggested exercises for teaching and practicing them. Mackay and Mountford note that materials may be chosen from existing sources with no modifications, modified from such sources, or created especially for the English course. All materials are to be selected after careful consideration of the learners' specific needs and interests and of their current state of knowledge or stage of development with respect to their specialty. Materials that are suitable for second year undergraduates are not likely to be so for postdoctoral scholars or laymen with an interest in the same specialty. Modified or created materials are designed to draw the learners' attention to specific language points or to simplify in some sense the learning tasks.

In Chapter 10, Munby defines intensive reading as "a close examination of the text to get the full meaning." The successful reader must be able to understand literal and implied meanings of sentences, paragraphs, and larger textual units, and to relate the meanings of the text to his prior knowledge and experience. Effective training in intensive reading skills can be provided through the use of multiple-choice questions which require learners to exercise the linguistic and intellectual abilities involved in reading comprehension.

The author provides a set of multiple-choice questions based on a sample text, with a detailed analysis of the categories of comprehension error which the learner must avoid if he is to choose the correct alternative from the choices offered. Munby then presents and illustrates a classroom procedure, involving group selection and class discussion of each alternative, designed to provide feedback and explanation of the required skills. While multiple-choice questions are best for factual and implicational information, Munby thinks that free-response questions are more suitable for summarizing or relating the comprehension passage to the learner's experience.

Chapter 11 is an introduction to the basic rhetorical units of nonfiction, with emphasis on the kinds of linguistic forms which signal these structures and the meanings of extended texts. Pierce's principal assumption is that students can better arrive at valid semantic interpretations of texts if they are aware of rhetorical structures and of how these are represented in English. This awareness is commonly lacking, even among advanced learners of English, who appear to consider all parts of a text as bearing an equal semantic burden.

The author points out that the most typical structure of a book is paragraph, chapter, and the book as a whole, and she suggests that students be taught to use the table of contents as a guide to the extended context in which readers conduct their search for ideas. An idea, according to Pierce, is an author's judgment or conclusion about an array of facts. Ideas have the rhetorical status of topic at the paragraph level. A set of ideas, represented in a series of paragraphs or chapters, has the status of theme, and the themes of the book are said to constitute an area of study. Descriptive rules and examples are used to illustrate this hierarchical structure.

Pierce gives many illustrations of the uses of connecting words and phrases, the position of sentences in a paragraph, summary words, transitional expressions, and other cohesive and discourse markers in the presentation and development of ideas. Redundancy is viewed as "a set of environmental signals which provide clues for identifying ideas" rather than in its usual linguistic or informational sense.

This chapter points up the fact that the same message can be communicated in a great many different ways and that quite different messages can be communicated by formally similar sets of language events.

In Chapter 12, Berman proposes to teach students an awareness of grammatical and rhetorical structures, through a technique she calls analytic syntax. This is "the use of *structural paraphrase,* where phrases and whole sentences are reworded and juggled about with a minimum of change in lexical content and hence in lexical load." A series of nine types of grammatical structures from a college-level reading passage, including fairly difficult nominalizations and negation, are used to illustrate the technique. Berman advises against using more than two or three grammatical areas per reading passage. This chapter contains practical suggestions and classroom techniques as well as explanations of how each structure presented contributes to overall reading comprehension.

In the final chapter, Ibrahim states that the ESL reading teacher's role is to give students advance knowledge of the overall organization of the reading passage to be studied. Citing Ausubel, she claims that "optimal anchorage" is thereby provided.

The author describes a program she developed for teaching Arabic-speaking students how to read English social science texts more effectively. She first lists the common patterns of exposition in social science textbooks. She then provides an extended analysis of a reading passage. Finally, a detailed lesson plan for teaching the analyzed passage is given. This chapter provides a convincing illustration that structural, semantic, and organizational relationships must all be taken into account in the preparation of advanced second language materials.

CHAPTER 9

Reading for Information

Ronald Mackay and Alan Mountford
Concordia University
and The British Council

Introduction and Aims

Of methods of teaching reading it has been said that the best, whether traditional or new, are those "of which it can truly be said that

1. They teach children to read more effectively by enabling them to enquire more effectively.
2. They focus the attention of both pupils and teachers upon the specific goals sought.
3. They are related to the pupils' state of readiness for reading at any given stage.
4. They arouse interest and inspire effort.
5. They are sufficiently flexible to permit of such modification as may be justified by the research and experience of others." (Macmillan 1965)

We do not claim that what we present in this chapter can stand up to such rigorous requirements, but it is with these criteria in mind that

First published in E. Anthony and J. C. Richards (eds.). 1976. "Reading: Insights and Approaches." RELC and Singapore University Press. Reprinted by permission of the Regional Language Centre, Singapore.

we offer this contribution to current thinking on the teaching of intensive reading comprehension to advanced students of English. By "advanced" students we mean students who have already studied English, probably as a subject in school, who can comprehend simplified readers, and who now require to read original texts in their special fields of study.

Our principal aims are practical and threefold:

1. To offer advice which will help teachers of English for special purposes to orient themselves to the specialist fields of study of the students they teach and provide them with practical criteria for text selection.

2. To discuss what kind of linguistic knowledge appears to be necessary in order to master the skill of advanced reading comprehension.

3. To suggest materials for and methods of exercising these skills in the learner.

The Students

It cannot be assumed that all students learning English are interested in either the language itself or its literary manifestations. Many students regard English merely as the vehicle of a body of scientific or technological information which they need for their undergraduate or postgraduate studies, and the skill of reading English as the essential means of access to this information without which their professional studies would be impaired. Such a utilitarian attitude to English is clearly justified by the fact that in many universities throughout the world reading lists for undergraduate courses in the sciences, applied sciences, agriculture, and medicine necessarily include textbooks written in English because translations into the vernacular do not exist. Postgraduates are faced by the fact that over 50 percent of the world's scientific literature is in English, though not necessarily produced in English-speaking countries! Table 1 illustrates the position clearly. The table is from Wood (1967). Although the intention of Wood's report is to indicate how much literature is not originally published in English, it is the corollary which is most striking for teachers of EST—namely, that well over half the world's scientific and technological literature is published in English and that the other 40 percent is split unevenly among other languages.

Table 1   Percentage of Scientific and Technological Literature in English (from Six Major English-Language Abstracting and Indexing Publications)

Chemical Abstracts	50.3%
Biological Abstracts	75%
Physics Abstracts	73%
Engineering Index	82.3%
Index Medicus	51.2%
Mathematical Reviews	54.8%

The Teachers

The teachers of English to such students are generally employed in a language services department and are themselves usually the products of an arts training, with most of their attention and effort having been to English language and literature during their undergraduate studies. They may feel they have no special aptitude for or even interest in the areas of study which preoccupy their students. They may, possibly unconsciously, convey their feelings of ignorance and alienation from their students' fields of study by an inappropriate selection of materials or even, in a few extreme cases, an overt rejection of all that is scientific and technological.

Such attitudes, we feel, result from the fact that most training courses for English language teachers concentrate on the first two or three years of "general English" language instruction for which materials abound, and neglect instruction on how to cope with the learning problems of the advanced adult student who may require English for a very specific purpose, rather than from any real inability of the teacher to face the language learning problems presented by texts from any branch of science or technology, were these problems to be made explicit.

Orienting the Teacher

Although some would argue that the teaching of English to specialists in the various branches of science and technology is most effectively done by an appropriately qualified scientist or technologist who also has some skill in or experience of language teaching, there is no evidence to support such a view. Neither does a realistic appraisal of the question suggest that this is practicable. While it is unquestionable that a specialist subject can be taught through the medium of English and in the process the student can learn a great deal about both his science and the language used to cope with it, the teaching inevitably either stresses the scientific insight being imparted or highlights the characteristics of the language by means of which they are expressed, but it does not do both together, and unless the teacher is dually qualified, it cannot do both together. Scientists, who are trained at considerable expense, naturally enough are particularly interested in their science, and it is exceptional if one chooses to refocus his interest upon the mechanisms of the language. The English language teacher, on the other hand, *is* professionally concerned with the mechanisms of language and how they convey meaning, and can focus his expertise on any corpus of language from creative literature, which has received a great deal of attention, to the literature of science and technology, which has received less attention than its importance merits.

Although it is by no means necessary for the teacher of English to scientists and technologists to be also a specialist in the field of study with which his students are involved, it is necessary for him to master some principal points of reference which permit him to become familiar with the dimensions of the branch of science concerned, and how it relates to the broader body of science of which it forms a part. This can be done without difficulty or great effort by scanning the table of contents of one or two basic textbooks introducing the science concerned. In order to avoid miscomprehensions and to supply explanations which the English teacher will certainly require, the cooperation of a sympathetic and patient scientist is invaluable.

Let us imagine that our students are concerned with tropical agriculture. We may assume that we know what agriculture is from our general knowledge—food production and animals and things like that—or we may disclaim any interest in knowing as the easy alternative to what we imagine must be the time- and energy-consuming effort of finding out.

However, an examination of the tables of contents of one or two basic textbooks in tropical agriculture will provide us with a fairly clear idea of the scope of the field and into what principal branches it can be divided up. Tables 2 and 3 illustrate the "dimensions" of the field of tropical agriculture as presented in the contents pages of two basic textbooks on the subject.

Table 2 Tropical Agriculture*

I *The Tropical Background*	II *Agricultural Practice in the Tropics*	III *Economic Considerations*
1. Climate and Vegetational Factors	1. Soil Conservation	1. Marketing and Transport
2. Tropical	2. Cropping Sequences and Agricultural Systems	2. Land Tenure and Use
3. Types of Agriculture suited to the Tropics	3. Fertilizers	3. Finance and Credit
4. Development of Tropical Agriculture	4. Cultivation and Weed Control	
5. Agricultural Research	5. Irrigation and Drainage	
	6. Crop Improvement	
	7. Pests and Diseases	
	8. Grassland and Fodder Production	
	9. Animal Husbandry	
	10. Processing Tropical Soils	
	11. Storage of Crop Products	

Each of these subheadings is itself subdivided, e.g.:

1. *Climatic and Vegetational Factors*	1. *Soil Conservation*	1. *Marketing and Transport*
Temperature — Rainfall and Atmospheric Humidity — Wind — Humidity — Vernalization and Photoperiodism — Influence of Vegetation on Climate — Penetration of Rainfall in the Soil — Ecoclimatic Conditions — General Conclusions.	Cause and Effects of Erosion — Factors Influencing Erosion — Erosion in Relation to Cultivation and Grazing — Effects of Erosion on Water Supplies and Climate — Control of Erosion and Methods of Soil Conservation — Mechanical Methods of Soil Conservation — Gullies — Erosion Occasioned by Livestock — Special Aspects of Erosion Control — Policy and Administration in Soil Conservation	Marketing Plantation Produce — Government Intervention in Marketing — Produce Restriction Schemes Conclusions Regarding Restriction Schemes — — Marketing Peasant Produce — Official Price Declaration — Effects of Wartime Conditions on Marketing — Developments in Africa — Effects of the Second World War on Produce Marketing in West Africa — Cooperative Marketing — Transport of Agricultural Produce

*Drawn from the contents pages of H. Tempany and D. H. Grist, 1958. "An Introduction to Tropical Agriculture." London: Longmans Green & Co.

Table 3   Tropical and Subtropical Agriculture*

I *General*	II *Crops*
1. Climate and Physiography	1. Bananas and Citrus
2. Formation of Soil	2. Other Fruit Crops
3. Chemical and Physical Properties of Soil and Soil Organic Matter	3. Spices
4. Soil Fertility	4. Beverages — Coffee, Cocoa, Tea
5. Soil Management	5. Rubber and Cinchona
6. Cultural Practices, Crop Improvement, Economic and Conditions and Food Value of Tropical Products	6. Oil Crops
	7. Fiber Crops
	8. Sugar Cane and Other Field Crops

Each of these subheadings is itself subdivided, e.g.:

2. *Formation of Soil*	8. *Sugar Cane and Other Field Crops*
Mineral constituents of rocks	(i) Sugar cane
Pedogenic influences	(ii) Rice
Weathering	(iii) Maize
Mineral constituents of soils	(iv) Sorghum
Development of the soil profile	(v) Tobacco
The great soil groups.	all of which are dealt with under the subheadings:
	Botany and botanical description
	Breeding and selection
	Varieties
	Climatic and soil requirements
	Culture
	Cultural practices in relation to disease and nematode control
	Harvesting and processing
	Diseases
	Pests
	Shipment and marketing

*Drawn from the contents pages of J. J. Ochse et al. 1961. "Tropical and Subtropical Agriculture." New York: Macmillan.

Besides providing us with the general dimensions of a whole field of study, this simple approach gives us a manageable picture of the ramifications of what we might originally have assumed was a simple subject. In addition, we can acquire an essential basic vocabulary for the entire field. This approach can be repeated with all specialist fields of study, and while it in no way implies that we "know" the science or technology involved, it provides us with a certain confidence which does not remain undetected by our students. Students quickly lose respect for the English teacher who constantly proclaims "Of course I don't know anything about agriculture/chemistry/medicine/mathematics" and whose tone implies that his state of ignorance is to be commended rather than remedied.

This we suggest is an essential step the EST teacher must take in order to be fair to both himself and his students and one which we hope most teachers take as a matter of course. Failure to take this step results in the teacher's unfamiliarity with the scope of the field and ignorance of the basic vocabulary associated with the principal branches contained within it. This basic lack may lead the teacher to ascribe unnecessarily to the field seemingly insurmountable difficulties which he may use as an excuse to remain aloof and uninvolved with his students' interests.

The Skill of Comprehension

Reading is not a single skill but a process comprising a complex set of interrelated skills. These involve:

1. Word recognition and the mastery of basic vocabulary and such technical or specialized vocabulary as may from time to time be required.
2. The ability to see in the material the structures of the sentences, paragraphs, and longer passages that constitute the thought units.
3. The intelligence necessary to follow the thought development thus presented and make any relevant deductions, inferences, or critical assessments.
4. The ability to concentrate on the reading task. (Macmillan 1965)

There have been numerous attempts to list the skills involved in reading comprehension both before and after the appearance of Macmillan's in 1965. We feel, however, that most lists consist largely of alternative formulations of the same skills. Our purpose at this point is not so much to select the most detailed list but to find one which provides an appropriate starting point for considering means within the teacher's power of giving the student practice in the use of these skills.

If we neglect from Macmillan's list those factors over which the teacher has no control—intelligence and ability to concentrate—we are left with a list of skills which can be taught:

1. To recognize English words and to build up an appropriate vocabulary.
2. To identify sentence patterns.
3. To react to typographic conventions.
4. To identify the "longer passages that constitute thought units."
5. To follow and evaluate the development of the information being presented.

The first three of these skills are those traditionally taught in the elementary stages of reading instruction with which we are all familiar. Moreover the units used to teach these skills of recognition and structuring correspond more or less exactly to the units used by linguists to describe the language, and their order of introduction in most courses parallels the linguist's hierarchically ordered list of speech sound or letter, morpheme, word, group, phrase, clause, and sentence. We teach the rules by which the units of the language are put together to form the variety of sentence structures permitted in English, in the not erroneous belief that this knowledge makes it possible for the reader with an adequate and appropriate vocabulary to understand the meanings of English sentences. There appears, however, to be little research to support any claim that the units used by linguists to describe the language actually represent the units by which a learner in fact acquires proficiency in its use. But until more is known about the process of language acquisition the linguists' units of description remain the most convenient upon which to base textbooks and materials.

Since such pedagogic steps we as teachers have for developing reading in the early stages depend almost entirely upon the units the linguist uses to describe the language, it is not surprising that the teaching of the last two skills in the list—the identification of longer passages which constitute "thought units" and the ability to follow the development of a theme—are not provided for in instructional materials. Although it is likely that they may be tested, they are not exercised; but the distinction between testing materials and exercises or practice materials will be discussed later. Traditionally, the sentence has been the highest unit of linguistic description. The grammarian, having described and illustrated the range of possibilities English permits in sentence constituents, has seen his task as over. Likewise, teaching materials have concentrated on the efficient mastery of sentence production and comprehension. The teacher's confidence in "what to teach" falters once he has taken his students through the range of possible sentence patterns in the grammar book. The materials writer is likewise confounded. The proliferation of texts and courses for elementary and intermediate students and the dearth of materials for advanced students bear this fact out.

This obsession with the sentence as the linguistic unit upon which almost all teaching has been and still to a great extent is based has had two principal effects on teaching methods and materials for students who have "come to the end of the syllabus." The first is that once sentence grammar has been "covered," usually by the end of secondary school, pedagogic help is either withdrawn or seen as an essentially "remedial" activity. The good student may be encouraged to believe that in order to improve his command of English he must "absorb it through his pores" in an English-speaking country. Unfortunately there is no theory of language acquisition which includes human pores, nor is there a dermatological branch of linguistics. The poorer student may be subjected to a high-speed version of the syllabus already covered at school in the hope that whatever had not been learned the first time round may somehow be retained the second time. There is little evidence to support this optimism, although such a program is almost certainly guaranteed to result in student boredom.

It would appear, then, that we need to find some describable linguistic unit or units which will correspond to the tantalizing and intuitively satisfying idea of the existence of structures larger than the sentence, and some kind of linguistic markers which interrelate these units and make it possible for the reader to follow the argument or the development of the way the author is treating the points under discussion.

Reading Problems

There is both a danger and a misconception in assuming that once we have listed the skills which make up reading comprehension and have been provided with a description of linguistic units beyond the sentence, we have identified the problems involved in learning to read English for information. The misconception arises out of a failure to differentiate among the skills and abilities used in reading, the linguistic knowledge required to read, and the difficulties inherent in acquiring the necessary skills and knowledge. The danger lies in the inference that no further steps need be taken in order to identify reading problems and present them in a hierarchy of difficulty. In fact, to establish that there exists a relationship among the presence of certain skills, familiarity with linguistic features of discourse, and successful reading comprehension would require elaborate research and extensive testing. Little has been done along these lines, but what research there is indicates that it is an exacting and time-consuming activity.

Sim (1973) also points to a relationship between a knowledge of formal devices of textual cohesion—in particular anaphoric devices and sentence connectors—and effective reading comprehension for nonnative speakers. While acknowledging the value and importance of research in establishing the exact nature of reading problems, as practicing teachers we must also be pragmatic and make intelligent guesses on the basis of our own experience as to what the learner needs to know in order to read with increasing understanding, where research is either lacking or inconclusive. Hence we may operate on two assumptions:

1. That the writer of a textbook, paper, report, etc., has an "intuitive" knowledge of at least some of the comprehension problems his intended readership may experience and that he does his best to cater to these problems in his writing;
2. That just as a knowledge of sentence grammar appears to contribute to comprehension, so familiarity with the linguistic features which bind a text together will help to extend and amplify comprehension of the whole.

Understanding the Writer's Problems:
An Approach to Advanced Reading

In using the phrase "units of thought," Macmillan highlights the agency behind the text, the author's conscious process of organizing information on paper for a reader or group of readers. The fact that the reader is inevitably always the perceiver or recipient of a written communication means that any problems he may have in comprehending it have been preceded by the writer's difficulties in producing it for him. Although it is not being suggested that the problems of the reader and those of the writer are identical, the fact that the principal aim of the scientific writer is to record information for a reader or readers to understand and in the way which will cause fewest problems indicates that the writer has "reading problems" uppermost in his mind. This would suggest that an examination of the kind of problems taken into consideration by the author who composes the text and a close study of the solutions he finds to overcome such problems might throw light on the kind of knowledge required to read and comprehend the text. It would not be reasonable to assume, therefore, that the advice offered to writers of scientific or technical reports, papers, books, etc., in a manual on the craft of effective writing might provide the teacher with an approach to the principles which go into the production of texts and that principles of writing are in fact principles of comprehension. Once uncovered, these principles might provide the basis for strategies which the student might adopt in order to read for information in the most efficient way.

Clear and precise written communication depends to a large extent upon the author's skill at presenting information in a way in which it is appropriately perceived by the intended readership. Most scientific journals require authors to write to a standard format laid down rigorously in their "Instructions to Authors." This format is as standard as is punctuation and serves much the same purpose as do full stops, capital letters, and indented paragraphs, namely, that of providing the reader with "chunks" of text which contain related information. However, whereas full stops and capital letters perform an explicitly linguistic function, "sections" of texts such as those marked Introduction, Methods and Materials, Results, Discussion, etc., serve a "logical" function. They break the information up into logically manageable pieces of varying length. The question we as teachers must constantly bear in mind while examining a writer's manual is "Are these logical 'chunks' of information marked linguistically?" If they are, and if we can identify the markers, we will be well on the way to providing some means of coping with units larger than sentences in texts and thereby coping with the problems of advanced reading.

The writer's manual which deals most profoundly with the organization of language and offers the writer most help with transferring his information into writing in order to minimize reading problems is that by Daniel Marder (1960). Marder draws together scientific method and logical presentation under the three principles of rhetoric—unity, coherence, and emphasis. A piece of written communication has unity when the parts of the whole together add up in a meaningful way; coherence provides the framework for that unification of meaning— "Unity concerns the relation of materials to the subject; coherence concerns the matter of relating, of organizing the materials to give a continuous development of the subject." Emphasis ensures that the information has been put together in such a way as to give to each of the constituent elements their intended scale of importance—"The less important detail is subordinated to the more important (and) items of equal importance receive equal treatment." The stated purpose of the writing manual is to provide the writer with the "techniques of organization and style" which are "methods of solving various writing problems so that unity, coherence and emphasis are maintained throughout the communication."

The violation of these principles is what makes the otherwise grammatically correct written work of advanced students "un-English." Their lack of linguistic explicitness is what makes the principles difficult to teach, or even discourages an attempt to deal with them at all, and encourages both teacher and student to believe that good scientific writers are born and not made.

Techniques of scientific exposition are basically ways of coping, in writing, with the questions implicit in scientific inquiry. Scientific inquiry involves certain activities:

Observation
Description
Analysis
Classification
Identification, etc.

and asks some or all of the questions: What happened? How did it happen? Why did it happen? What was the purpose of the happening? What was the reason for the happening? What was the significance of the happening? What is it? How does it work? What are its parts? What are its attributes? How or why does it exist? In what ways is it similar to or different from other occurrences of the phenomena? Where does it belong? How is it put together? What is it like? What are its characteristics? What happens when we observe it? What does it look like?

Now this simple description of scientific method may provide a framework for the teacher who is not scientifically trained or inclined within which he can begin to see the professional work and points of reference of his students. It should be borne in mind, however, that not all, or even many, exemplify all the characteristics or stages of what is called "the scientific method." The vast majority of textbooks used by undergraduates appear to be taxonomic descriptions of the field rather than accounts of scientific inquiry.

The techniques of exposition which are used by the writer to cope with the questions asked and answered by scientific inquiry are, according to Marder, basically:

Technical Definition   Technical Description
  Classification   Technical Narration
  Analysis   Illustration

The first of these expository techniques, of central importance since "identifying" is an essential activity in science and "naming" a primary though by no means the only function of teaching, can be further subdivided into formal and expanded definitions. A formal definition is realized in English by a number of structures conforming to the pattern:

Term (species) = class (genus) + sum of differences
     part of the verb   (differentia)
Article Noun be class noun which clause(s)

An expanded definition consists of a formal definition plus one or more additional expository techniques from the list:

Explication   Contrast
Analysis of Division Analogy
Description   Elimination
Illustration   Origins, Causes and Effects
Comparison   Derivations

which may be necessary in order to ensure that the definition is adequate.

Ideally we would have a "grammar of expository techniques" with all the possible linguistic realizations of each category listed and some indication of the criteria determining the use of one rather than another. We tend to feel, however, that even if the practical and theoretical problems of compiling such a "grammar" were to be overcome, the resulting description would have more application to the teaching of scientific writing than to reading. Our experience indicates that readers can learn, without difficulty, to identify the *notional* categories to which rhetorical or expository techniques belong with the minimum of syntactic cues to aid them and to appreciate their role in and contribution to the flow of communication.

Our method of teaching this kind of sensitivity to text has been to create exercises on extended definitions taken from the Penguin specialist dictionaries most relevant to the students' field of study. (The advantages of using the Penguin specialist dictionaries are that they are cheap and usually easily available and are of course also useful reference books in their own right. Groups of students from various fields of studies can carry out these exercises using the most appropriate dictionary and so feel that the effort is to their immediate and direct benefit. Examples of individual expository techniques, taken at random, would either be impossible to find or would lose their rhetorical significance by being dissociated from the discourse within which they occurred. Expanded definitions in the specialist dictionaries illustrate a wide range of expository techniques and constitute in themselves complete "mini-texts.") The teacher teaches the various expository techniques by assigning of parts of the discourse to one or other of the notional categories and suggests why the author chose to use the categories he did in order to expand the definition and the significance of the particular order in which they appear. Once this procedure has been repeated several times, the entire range of expository techniques has been illustrated in context and a number of markers will have been seen to recur, associated with a particular category.

The students themselves, either orally or as a written exercise, can read other selected definitions and examine their composition. The written result of one such exercise might be:

RAINFALL. The total amount of rain deposited on a given area during a given time, as measured by a rain gauge.	formal definition
Melted snow and hail are included with the rain, and this precipitation from the clouds constitutes most of the rainfall; very small additions are made for dew, hoar frost, and rime.	
Three different types of rainfall are generally recognized, depending on the process by which the clouds were formed: orographic, cyclonic, convectional.	classification (+ explicit criterion).
The comparatively heavy rainfall received on the mountains of western Scotland is largely orographic; cyclonic rainfall, due to depressions, provides much of the rain of the eastern half of the British Isles and Continental Europe;	illustration i. illustration ii.
convectional rain is typical of the Equatorial regions.	illustration iii.
The rainfall of a place is very largely dependent upon the prevailing winds; it varies seasonally in many regions according to the movement of the sun and the accompanying movement of the rain belts.	description

A variation on the same exercise is to offer the students a list of sentences in random order which together make up an expanded definition. They are then asked to rearrange the sentences in the way which produces the most cohesive text. This type of exercise may require the teacher to "loosen up" the original text, by simplifying complex sentences, e.g.:

1. Three different types of rainfall are generally recognized, depending on the process by which the clouds were formed.
2. The rainfall of a place is very largely dependent upon the prevailing winds. It varies seasonally in many regions according to the movement of the sun and the accompanying movement of the rain belts.
3. Convectional rain is typical of the Equatorial regions.
4. Very small additions are made for dew, hoar frost, and rime.
5. Cyclonic rainfall, due to depressions, provides much of the rain of the eastern half of the British Isles and Continental Europe.
6. The total amount of rain deposited on a given area during a given time, as measured by a rain gauge, is known as "rainfall."
7. The comparatively heavy rainfall received on the mountains of western Scotland is largely orographic.
8. Melted snow and hail are included with the rain, and this precipitation from the clouds constitutes most of the rainfall.
9. These are orographic, cyclonic, and convectional.

The most appropriate ordering would be 6, 8, 4, 1, 9, 7, 5, 3, 2.

The total amount of rain deposited on a given area during a given time, as measured by a rain gauge, is known as *rainfall*. Melted snow and hail are included with the rain and this precipitation from the clouds constitutes most of the rainfall. Very small additions are made for dew, hoar frost, and rime. Three different types of rainfall are generally recognized, depending on the process by which the clouds were formed. These are orographic, cyclonic, and convectional. The comparatively heavy rainfall received on the mountains of western Scotland is largely orographic. Cyclonic rainfall, due to depressions, provides much of the rain of the eastern half of the British Isles and Continental Europe. Convectional rain is typical of the Equatorial regions. The rainfall of a place is very largely dependent upon the prevailing winds. It varies seasonally in many regions according to the movement of the sun and the accompanying movement of the rain belts.

The changes that have been made to the text for the purpose of this exercise can be seen by comparing it with the original dictionary entry in the first example.

Selection of Reading Texts

Reading texts can be (1) selected from appropriate sources without alteration, (2) modified versions of such texts, or (3) specially written from scratch. We will discuss the first of these procedures in detail, since it is the one most EST teachers follow, and besides it is the simplest and least time-consuming.

Unmodified Texts

The most appropriate selection of reading texts increases motivation. Familiarity with the dimensions of the field of study involved will make that choice less of a hit-or-miss affair.

Reading texts chosen for use in the English language class must represent the kind of text which the students are required to read for information in the course of their studies. This means that they must meet certain requirements. First, they should provide motivation by virtue of the information they contain being seen to be *relevant* to their specialist studies. Just because our students study agriculture will not ensure the relevancy of an article on irrigation methods we happen to come across in the course of our reading if the students are concerned with grazing systems in arid regions. The text should be taken from that specific area of the field upon which the students are engaged if we have a homogeneous group. Second, the text chosen should be one aimed at neither a broader nor a more narrow readership than our students represent. A research paper on grazing systems will be just as irrelevant to undergraduates as will an article on the same subject taken from a journal such as *Scientific American.* In the former, aimed at the author's peers, themselves agriculturalists engaged in research, a great deal will be taken for granted as understood; the style of the latter—in terms of sentence structure and vocabulary—will bear little resemblance to that of the textbooks on the students' reading lists. The intended readership places constraints on the author which will affect the choice of detail included (or excluded), the focus of attention, and the language used to convey the information.

Table 4   Writing Situations

Readership	Type of Publication
Postgraduate	Scientific report for supervisor
	Paper for specialist scientific journal
	Advanced textbook
	Basic textbook
Undergraduate	
	General survey type textbook
General scientific readership	"House Journals," e.g.,
	Endeavour (ICI)
	Shell Magazine
Nontechnical readership with	Popular scientific journals, e.g.,
some interest in science and	*Scientific American*
technology	*New Scientist*
	The Ecologist

Third and last, the text, having been selected from that specific area of the field upon which the students are engaged, should be no more advanced than their knowledge of the area. Clearly, textbooks teach as they go along, and all the undergraduate textbooks we have examined are organized in such a way that each chapter or even subchapter relies for complete understanding upon the previous one having been read and learned. For example, an adequate understanding of the sentence which might at first glance appear to satisfy the criteria of relevancy and appropriateness:

Regulated ley systems, which are widespread in the subtropics of the northern and southern hemisphere, are rare in the tropics.

depends upon explanation of the term "regulated ley system" having been read in the previous subchapter, which in turn depends for its comprehension on an earlier explanation of "ley system" and an appreciation of the exact geographical area referred to by the word "tropics" having been explained in the introduction to the book. The task of the English teacher is to teach English language skills, not the specialty of the student. He must therefore rely upon the students' specialist knowledge contributing to the comprehension of the text. In order to ensure this, he should avoid selecting texts so advanced that the students are confounded by both the language *and* the complexity of the information itself.

Failure to observe any of these three criteria results in problems in the classroom. Either the students find the text irrelevant and so lose interest, or else they find it so full of lexical problems that they think learning to read English is coterminous with learning vocabulary lists, and never in fact learn to "read" as a communicative skill. There is more to the advanced skill of reading for information than merely "mapping on" specialist lexical items to an existing knowledge of "general English," though a sound grounding in English grammar as imparted by the many standard course books for elementary and intermediate students is essential. Perren (1963) suggests that the difficulties often associated with the technical vocabularies which characterize different fields of study may reflect the English teacher's reaction to such words rather than that of the foreign scientist. He points out that specialist terms have limited and defined meanings and that "the high-frequency words like put, to, from, take, have, etc., which constitute the 'vast, shifting ill-defined mass' of common words and structures cause the real problems for the foreign scientist." In his paper, Perren discusses other problems of interest to the teacher of EST/ESP (mostly still unsolved even though the paper appeared over ten years ago!).

Modified Texts

Texts taken from one or other of the types of publication listed in Table 4 can be modified in order to highlight a point or points of linguistic interest or to reduce reading difficulty by simplifying certain structures. Complex nominal groups can be expanded into clauses or even sentences, compound and complex sentences can be divided up, and logical connectors, discourse markers, and anaphoric expressions can be introduced and the students' attention drawn to these devices of textual cohesion.

Specially Written Texts

This method of providing suitable texts is time-consuming and assumes a knowledge of the subject on the part of the teacher. The pedagogic advantages accruing from investing time and energy in this way will not be discussed here, but those interested should examine Tom McArthur's "A Rapid Course in English for Students of Economics" (OUP 1973) and James Herbert's "The Structure of Technical English" (Longman 1965). The texts contained in both these books were written either by or on the instructions of the author to provide contextualized illustrations of what were regarded as important teaching points.

So far, we have been concerned with an intuitive approach to the way in which information is organized for the reader. In the process of discussing this we have suggested ways in which the nonscientific teacher can be wooed to an appreciation of the aims and methods of science and the problems facing the scientific writer. In addition we have provided practical suggestions for the classroom and a set of criteria according to which the texts most appropriate for particular groups of students can be selected. Now we will be more linguistically explicit and discuss what kind of knowledge appears to be useful for the advanced reader to possess and how this knowledge might be taught and practiced.

Testing or Teaching?

The traditional pedagogic procedure of asking questions on a text may, in fact, test the student's comprehension rather than teach him strategies which he can use to improve his understanding. As teachers, we are first of all concerned with teaching and only secondarily concerned with testing. Tests measure how much has been understood; exercises practice techniques for understanding. How can we give a linguistic account of these strategies and how can these be taught to and practiced by our students?

We have said that we will assume that the pedagogic material we use to teach the elementary and intermediate stages of English based on the grammarians' description of what makes a sentence are effective for their purpose. Thus we can extend the assumption and surmise that materials for the advanced stages of English learning, based on a description of what makes a text a text, will likewise be effective.

Text and Discourse

It will be helpful at this point to distinguish between features of textual cohesion, that is, the grammatical ways by means of which "sentences which are structurally independent one of another may be linked together so as to determine their interpretation" (Hasan 1968) and discourse markers, that is, "all those words, phrases and sentences which mark out particular parts of the discourse as important or unimportant, or as being examples, glosses, corrections, reformulations, and repetitions" (Wijasuriya 1971). Allen and Widdowson (1978) make the following distinction: "Textual cohesion includes those formal devices which are used to combine sentences in creating continuous passages of prose." Units of discourse are identified by the way in which "sentences are used in the performance of acts or communication." Several useful ways of exercising these two kinds of knowledge are described in their paper.

In what follows, we will deal particularly with methods of practicing a knowledge of how reference, word equivalence, intersentence connectors, and rhetorical structure contribute to how the text coheres and functions as a meaningful whole. These features have been selected on the grounds that they are little dealt with in traditional courses, and since they are likely to be met frequently in the kinds of texts encountered by undergraduates and postgraduates, it might reasonably be assumed that lack of familiarity with them might adversely affect comprehension.

Table 5   The Relation Between the Constituents of Text and Discourse

	Meaning	*Intrasentential*	*Intersentential*
Text	Lexical	Word meanings	Word equivalence
	Grammatical	Conjunction Clause structure Word order and thematization	Reference
Discourse			Connection
	Rhetorical	Expository techniques and sequencing of expository techniques (Speech arts/Rhetorical acts)	

Reference

This feature of text has been traditionally left untaught and unquestioned in comprehension exercises. In order to understand a text, it is essential to know what words like *this, that, these, those, it,* and *them* refer to. The selection of the wrong referent for one of these items may lead to a grave misinterpretation of what the writer has said. These words are most frequently used in order to refer back to a word, phrase, clause, sentence, or longer stretch of text which appeared earlier. Frequently they are marked by "summary words," e.g., *this type, that fact, these cases, those factors.* Occasionally, even a native speaker is forced to stop at such anaphoric ties and identify the referent. Foreign learners need to be taught these points which can be dealt with using either a multiple-choice format, e.g.,

Does "this case" in line x refer to (1) _____

(2) _____

or

(3) _____

Or an alternative method: Ask the student to identify the referent, e.g.,

What does "these points" refer to in the sentence "Foreign learners need to be taught these points . . . "?

Most pronouns are used anaphorically, and students can be trained in the habit of accurate identification of their referents by means of the exercises described above.

Items other than the demonstratives and pronominals mentioned which can be practiced in this way are the definite article "the" and implied comparatives. The usual treatment of the articles is to claim they indicate "definiteness" or "indefiniteness"; a more appropriate and effective way might be to make the distinction between "previously mentioned in the text" and "not previously mentioned in the text."

Implied comparisons require the student to supply the half of the comparison which is missing in order to understand the half supplied, e.g.,

Animals treated in this way are healthier and put on weight faster.

Question: (1) What does "this way" in line x refer to?

(2) Line x "Animals . . . are healthier and put on weight faster."

healthier than what?

put on weight faster than what?

Over and above the value of training the student in the perception of the cohesive ties binding the text together, questions on anaphoric devices refer the student back to the close scrutiny of the text. This in itself justifies the inclusion of questions the answers to which might appear "self-evident."

Equivalence

Learning how lexical equivalence is used to establish textual cohesion is one important element in the broader problem of "vocabulary." Equivalence is a matter of lexical patterning; in most texts there are words, phrases, and even entire sentences which have essentially the same meaning or are used by the author with the same meaning in a particular text (see Mackay et al. 1978).

Paraphrases and Summaries

Words or phrases may be paraphrased for the purposes of clarification or in order to offer a summary of what has been said. This can be marked overtly by the use of "i.e.," "this is," "that is to say," "or ...," "in other words," "otherwise known as ... ," "in short," etc., for example:

> In subsistence farming, that is, a system in which agricultural products are raised with the main purpose of covering only the needs of the household, selling is limited to surpluses of these products.

> Rice growers in Thailand make use of the treading of animals; i.e., a large number of cattle are driven across the moist field until it becomes a mire ready for planting.

Both these examples show how texts may "teach" new lexical items. Most undergraduate textbooks use this technique constantly when a new technical term or concept is introduced. The great bogey of vocabulary difficulty may be to some extent a function of the teacher's unfamiliarity with the subject of text selection from an inappropriate level and of a basic unawareness of the techniques textbook writers employ to explain new terms. It may also be due, in part, to the dearth of strategies for coping with new words on the part of the student. Expectation, intelligent guessing, and "reading on" to discover whether the writer explains a new term are all techniques which should be encouraged over and above dictionary use.

However, there is a covert variety of equivalence which has to be systematically taught to students. This variety involves the hyponymic or synonymic relationships in which expressions may stand to each other, for example:

Holdings may be regarded as organized, economic units in which plant and animal products are produced for the purposes of gain. In larger holdings market production and profits are the main objectives whereas for the smallholder—and most of the tropical land is farmed by smallholders—the farm and the family are closely connected.

In the above example it is important for the student to recognize that the words "holding," "unit," and "farm" are being used synonymously in the text.

In the example, "Shifting cultivation in the rain forest is still occasionally practiced without cultivation implements; after burning off, seed is sown in the ashes. The axe and the machete are the main tools. Where the ground is prepared, as is usually the case, tools for cultivation are required," the student must recognize that tool and implement are being used synonymously and axe and machete are two distinct members of the class "tool" or "implement," and so bear a relation of hyponymy to these two words.

The student must be taught these kinds of relationships if he is to develop a technique for understanding texts for himself as opposed to mastering one or two individual texts. His attention can be drawn to relationships of synonymy and hyponymy by paraphrase-type questions, e.g.,

Instead of saying that shifting cultivation is still occasionally carried out without tools for cultivation the writer says that it is carried out without . . .

This kind of treatment of vocabulary items which are judged to be difficult or new avoids the danger of the student's selecting the wrong word from the dictionary where there are alternatives. It concentrates on getting him to read complete sentences and see words in context which are exercises of reading ability. The alternatives, that of dictionary use or the provision of a paraphrase, have the disadvantage of concentrating on the isolated word.

Intersentential Connection

Intersentential relationships have to do with the way in which sentences and groups of sentences combine to form units of discourse. The communicative value of such units may be explicitly marked by means of a connective (or conjunct). On the other hand, there may be no such explicit marker. Earlier, when we discussed ways of identifying expository techniques, we saw that it was possible to understand the communicative function of a sentence or groups of sentences by means of "key words" such as "for example" or "can be classified according to," etc., or by other means which we made no attempt to define rigorously but which satisfied us intuitively.

A great deal of work still has to be done on the "illocutionary force" of sentences (Austin 1962, Searle 1969). We will first of all direct our attention therefore to an examination of markers which have been well described (Greenbaum 1969, Winter 1971) and which can provide us with a framework upon which to base teaching materials. Here is a categorization of these intersentential markers:

Types of Intersentential Relationships

Note: Those with an asterisk occur in initial position only.

Type of relationship		Meaning	Connectives
1. *Enumerative*			
1.1	Listing	What follows outlines the order in which things are to be said	first, second, etc., one, to begin with, next, then, finally, last(ly), etc.
1.2	Time sequence	What follows outlines the time sequence in which things happen.	first(ly), in the beginning, next, then, subsequently, eventually, finally, in the end, etc.
2. *Additive*			
2.1	Reinforcing	What follows suggests a reinforcement of what has been said.	and, again*, also*, moreover, furthermore, in addition, etc.
2.2	Similarity	What follows is similar to what has been said before.	equally*, likewise, similarly*, etc.
3. *Logical Sequence*			
3.1	Summative	What follows summarizes what has been said before.	so, altogether*, overall*, then, thus, therefore, in short, etc.
3.2	Resultative	What follows is a result of what has been said before.	so, as a result, consequently
3.3	Deductive	What follows is an observation which may be deduced logically from the generalization that has preceded it.	so, therefore, hence*, thus, consequently

Type of relationship	Meaning	Connectives
3.4 Inductive	What follows is a generalization based on observations that have gone before.	therefore, hence*, thus, so, this shows/indicates that, etc.
4. Explicative		
	What follows explains or glosses what has been said before.	namely, thus, in other words, that is (to say)*, by (this) we mean*
5. Illustrative		
	What follows is an illustration or an example of what has been said before.	for example, for instance
6. Contrastive		
6.1 Substitutive	What follows is a preferred rewording of what has been said before.	better*, rather*, in other words, etc.
6.2 Replacive	What follows is a replacement of what has been said before.	alternatively, instead, (but) then, rather, etc.
6.3 Antithetic	What follows is in complete opposition to what has been said before.	conversely, on the other hand, oppositely, etc.
6.4 Concessive	What has been said before is conceded as true or correct, but what follows is, in contrast, also true or correct.	but, however, nevertheless, still*, nonetheless, notwithstanding, etc.

Although these words may not be omitted from traditional English courses, if they are taught, their grammatical/structural function is generally stressed and their semantic value taken little or no notice of at all. Questions must be devised to exercise the students' ability to comprehend the meaning of the relationships which these words bear. Three ways are suggested:

Substitution

The text which the students are going to study may be scanned for occurrences of such intersentential connectives. The most frequent links are *additive, contrastive* and *logical sequence,* expressed by *moreover, however,* and words like *therefore* and *consequently* to express the various aspects of logical sequence. Occurrences of these words may then be replaced in the text by more general connectives such as *and, also, but,* and *so.* The exercise would be to substitute the more specific connectives. Other types of connectives can be substituted in a similar manner, e.g., *similarly* for *in the same way, thus* for *in this way.* The point of the exercise is to get the student to perceive more clearly the relationship, and to note the various linguistic means available to make it explicit.

Insertion

Texts written by and for native speakers frequently *omit* connectives. Indeed, invariably they *can* be omitted from the text without too seriously affecting the flow of intelligibility *for a native speaker;* an advanced reader is, for the most part, intuitively aware of the expository or rhetorical force or function of different parts of the text. For the foreign student this is much more difficult; indeed, it is the skill to be mastered. However, by asking the student to *insert* connectives, possibly from a list to encourage discrimination, this connection between parts of the text can be made explicit. A blank space can be left in the text indicating where a word is to be inserted. Moreover, it is preferable if the semantic value of the connectives supplied has been previously taught. Otherwise, there is little basis for choice, and the task is more guesswork than practice of acquired knowledge. Substitution and insertion can, of course, be combined in one exercise. Here is an example.

Text: (1) For a given type of soil the amount of water which is required varies with the type of crop. (2) It depends mainly on the plant species and the growing season. (3) And, the irrigation requirement of a crop is not the same throughout its growing period. (4) Most plants require larger quantities of water during the later stages than in the earlier stages. (5) Sugar cane needs heavier irrigation or more frequent irrigation from about the sixth or seventh month onward. (6) In the same way, grain crops require their maximum irrigation during the time earheads are forming. (7) Most annual crops do not need to be irrigated when they are maturing. (8) In the case of many fruit trees irrigation has to be stopped during the resting period.

Exercise: Substitute or insert the following words in the sentences indicated. Make any other changes in word order necessary. (3) moreover; (5) for example; (6) similarly; (7) on the other hand; (8) indeed.

        This exercise can of course, be redesigned using a multiple-choice format to introduce a "testing" element.

Reordering Jumbled Sentences

A third way of exercising understanding of connectives does not involve any production. The sentences of a text may be presented in a jumbled form and the student is required to reorder them correctly using his knowledge of connectives and clues provided by other cohesive ties. This is similar to the exercise illustrated during our earlier discussion of expository devices but depends more on recognizing and understanding explicit clues and less on "intuition." A variation of this exercise is to present a paragraph structure indicated by connectives, and then from a jumbled series of sentences (or groups of sentences) "compose" the paragraph. Part of the exercise above can be presented in this way.

Place the sentences below in the correct sequence A to E.

The irrigation requirement of a crop is not the same throughout its growing period. A. For example, B. Similarly, C. On the other hand, D. Indeed, E.

1. Most annual crops do not need to be irrigated when they are maturing.
2. Sugar cane needs heavier irrigation or more frequent irrigation from about the sixth or seventh month onward.
3. Most plants require larger quantities of water during the later stages than in the earlier stages.
4. In the case of many fruit trees irrigation has to be stopped during the resting period.
5. In the same way, grain crops require their maximum irrigation during the time earheads are forming.

It should be noted that *A. For example B* can be either sentences 3 and 2 or 1 and 4, but that C, sentence 5, *must* follow sentence 2. The correct order is therefore 3, 2, 5, 1, 4.

Knowledge of Rhetorical Structure

The distinction between the lexico-grammatical features of textual cohesion and the semantic or communicative function of sentences which we earlier identified intuitively using Marder's "expository techniques" has not, so far, been made as precisely as we would desire. Our "way in" to the interpretation of text was to examine the techniques of communication employed by the scientific and technical writer. As we have proceeded we have attempted to relate these techniques to identifiable features of language upon which we could base teaching materials.

Marder's "expository techniques" were ways of organizing language into chunks—as "a series of answers to a series of related questions about a subject" with the communicative value of "definition, classification, analysis, description, narration, and illustration." We saw that in the expanded definitions, certain meaning relationships held between the constituent sentences. It is these relationships which we now want to discuss.

These relationships form the rhetorical structure of a text—that is, what sentences or combinations of sentences count as in the flow of communication. A sentence may act as a definition, a classification, an illustration, etc., in a text, and the choice of these "rhetorical acts" or speech acts is the writer's and is dependent upon his purpose and the nature of the subject matter he is writing about.

There is no adequate reference for "rhetorical acts," but there are language textbooks which exhibit awareness of communicative criteria in their organization. In listing "Various Concepts and How to Express Them" (Hornby 1954), sentences are being organized according to similarity of communicative function with no regard to structural similarity. Similarly organized, but presented as a classroom text rather than a reference book, is Binham's "How to Say It" (1968).

For the teacher of ESP/EST, Herbert's "The Structure of Technical English" (1965) provides the most useful framework organized according to the communicative or rhetorical value of sentences. His examples also provide clues which we might look for in the texts we use with our students in order to identify the rhetorical function of a particular sentence or series of sentences. Despite this lack of isomorphism there are often indications in the text which signal how a sentence is to be interpreted. For example:

> Soil conservation in its widest sense means the maintenance of soil fertility. Soil conservation measures can be classified under three heads, viz.: (i) mechanical methods, (ii) choice of agricultural system, (iii) administrative measures. The object of mechanical methods is to reduce quality and velocity of runoff and the effects of wind. Terraces are the oldest example of all mechanical methods of soil conservation. They are frequently employed on steeply sloping land in the tropics. In the Far East, for example, they are extensively used in cultivating "wet" rice on hillsides. There, the

primary purpose is retention and collection of water, but they also serve to check erosion.

In the first sentence the word "means" indicates that the sentence is essentially an informal definition or paraphrase; "can be classified" in sentence two marks the rhetorical act of classification, etc. In cases where there is no overt signal of rhetorical function, the sequence of the sentences may provide the clue. For example:

> Malleability is the property of a metal which enables it to be shaped by hammering without cracking. Wrought iron is malleable. If a wrought iron bar is heated to bright red and hammered into shape, it will spread out without cracking.

This exemplifies the frequent and regular pattern:

Definition + Illustration + Observation
(+ Prediction).

Here are three ways in which knowledge of rhetorical structure can be exercised:

1. Students are asked to identify particular rhetorical acts in a text, e.g., in the previous example,
    (a)   Which sentence acts as a definition?
    (b)   Which sentence acts as an observation?
2. Students may be asked to insert rhetorical markers such as "may be classified" or "for example" or "it can be predicted that" at appropriate points in a text. The previous example could produce a text with the following markers inserted:

    Malleability *may be defined as* the property of a metal which enables it to be shaped by hammering without cracking. *For example*, wrought iron is malleable. *Therefore*, if a wrought iron bar is heated to bright red and hammered into shape, it can be predicted that it will spread without cracking.
3. A.   Arrange the following sentences in the sequence:

    Definition + Classification + Generalization
    + Restriction

    (1)   The majority of collectors also hunt and fish.
    (2)   Collecting is a primitive agricultural practice which involves cropping without cultivating.

(3)   Whereas in prehistoric times these activities were a source of food supply, today they tend to provide additions to the subsistence food gained from organized production in arable farming and animal husbandry.

(4)   It can include either regular or irregular harvesting of uncultivated plants.

B.   Now insert the following expressions where you think most appropriate:

        could be defined as, however.

It is suggested that the exercises described in this chapter are used not in place of but in addition to the usual types of comprehension questions involving multiple-choice techniques, true/false statements, yes/no questions, and questions on implications which can be deduced from the text.

In conclusion we should note that a knowledge of reference, equivalence, and connectives together appears to make up the overt grammatical cohesion of text. A knowledge of connectives plus a knowledge of expository techniques or rhetorical acts make up what we may call the rhetorical coherence of discourse. Together, when mastered by practice, they provide the advanced student with a strategy of comprehension which he can apply to any text he is required to read for information.

Appendix A

The following is an extract from materials for students of Agricultural Marketing in the University of Newcastle upon Tyne.

The text was taken, as it stands, from an article in a journal which the students are expected to read regularly. The text and that in the following unit make up an extended informal definition based on analysis. (The reading text and questions, as well as providing practice in comprehension techniques, are also intended to form the basis for oral work. In this unit, during the very simple activity of formulating questions, e.g., What is marketing/a supermarket? or What is involved in processing/market research? and of giving the appropriate responses, it had been observed that few of the students were able to ask their tutor questions in an acceptable way. Being able to ask questions about the material being studied is an essential tool in learning. Hence the apparently basic oral teaching point.)

Unit 2
MARKETING FUNCTIONS

What is marketing? The comparatively elementary consideration of marketing functions tells us, better than any definition or discussion of theory, what marketing is, or how utility is added by the marketing system.

In agricultural marketing there are three principal functions. These are (1) assembly, (2) processing, (3) dispersion. Assembly is in many ways a special characteristic of agricultural marketing, arising out of the large numbers of scattered small farm businesses. Examples are numerous and obvious. Milk is collected by dairies in small quantities, from large numbers of farms. Less obviously, when auction sales take place these are as useful in providing centers for assembly as vehicles for price formation. Again, cattle being delivered to abattoirs are being assembled into bulk rather than being distributed, even though this is the first link in the chain of distribution. It is a necessary process to bring together the product in sufficient economic quantity to attract buyers or allow economies of scale in processing. It is partly because assembly is almost peculiar to agricultural marketing that possibilities of direct selling from farm to processors or retailers or, alternatively, increasing the size of farm units are now being considered in many countries. It is an additional cost forced on agricultural marketing by the small-scale structure of farming.

Processing can vary from quite simple operations such as pasteurizing milk or cleaning eggs or potatoes to complicated production processes requiring heavy investment and often leading to virtually a complete change in the form of the product. Carding and spinning wool, making and maturing cheese, and slaughtering fat animals together with aging and cutting of carcasses are examples.

Dispersion is the final function of marketing by which the product is placed in the hands of the consumer. It may obviously pass through several hands, secondary wholesalers, food brokers, and retailers on the way. You will note that the three principal marketing functions have been mentioned and discussed without any reference to selling. Indeed, most marketing specialists would include this with a number of secondary or facilitating functions or, as indeed they are, services. It is not, in a sense, possible to distinguish any one of these as being more important than others, as assembly, processing, and distribution could not be undertaken at all without most and probably not efficiently without at least some of them being performed. These secondary or facilitating functions include (1) packaging, (2) grading and quality control, (3) transporting, (4) storing, (5) price determination or price discovery, (6) risk bearing, (7) financing, (8) buying, (9) selling, (10) demand creation, (11) provision and use of market information.

A   *Paraphrase*

6.   Instead of saying that auction sales are useful places where goods are gathered together, he says that they _____ centers for _____

7.   Instead of saying that auction sales are useful places where prices can be discovered, he says they are _____ for price _____

12.   Instead of saying that the need for agricultural assembly is caused by the fact that farms are small and so produce small quantities of goods, he says it is caused by the _____ _____ of farming.

B   *Implication*

In Exercise A we were concerned with what the writer actually said or stated. In this exercise we are concerned with what he *implied*. Give reasons for your answer.

1.   Does the writer imply that marketing is a difficult concept to define clearly?

2.   Does he imply that marketing involves more than three functions?

4.   Does he imply that farms produce goods on a small scale?

C   *True or False*

Write TRUE or FALSE after these statements.
If false, write out the statement you believe to be correct.

1.   A useful approach to the study of marketing is a consideration of its functions.

2.   Agricultural marketing involves three functions.

3.   Assembly is common to all types of marketing.

D   *Cohesion*

1.   What does *these* (line 6) refer to?

2.   "Examples are numerous . . ." (line 9)—Examples of what?

5.   "It is a necessary process . . ." (line 16)—What is a necessary process?

6. "It is an additional cost . . ." (line 22)—What is an additional cost?

7. ". . . are examples" (line 30)—Examples of what?

E   *From your understanding of the text, fill in the blanks.*

_____ many farms produce goods in _____ quantities, it is _____ to bring together the product in sufficient _____ quantity to attract _____ or allow economies of scale in _____ . This activity is known as _____ and _____ is one of the _____ functions of _____. It results in _____ cost but unless farms are _____ in size or _____ goods are _____ direct from farms to _____ or _____ it is unavoidable. _____ alternatives are now being _____ in a _____ of countries.

F   *Structure of the text*

(i)   Expository technique: analysis
A writer uses analysis to answer the question "What are its parts?" or "What does it consist of?" The language patterns used to express this are:

A can be $\left\{\begin{array}{l}\text{divided}\\\text{analyzed}\\\text{split}\end{array}\right\}$ into n $\left\{\begin{array}{l}\text{branches}\\\text{parts}\\\text{constituent parts}\\\text{functions}\end{array}\right\}$ B, C, and D

or A $\left\{\begin{array}{l}\text{is made up of n}\\\text{consists of}\end{array}\right\}$ $\left\{\begin{array}{l}\text{parts}\\\text{etc.}\end{array}\right\}$ $\left\{\begin{array}{l}\text{(namely)}\\\text{(these are)}\end{array}\right\}$ B, C, and D

or in A there are n $\left\{\begin{array}{l}\text{(parts,}\\\text{etc.}\end{array}\right.$ $\begin{array}{l}\text{(namely)}\\\text{(these are)}\end{array}$ B, C, and D

Look at these examples:
In agricultural marketing there are three principal functions _____

Agricultural marketing is made up of three main activities _____

Agricultural marketing can be divided into three principal functions _____

(ii)   Write the following out in the alternative ways shown above.
(a)   Agriculture can be divided into nine major branches.

(iii) Write out in full, the alternative ways of expressing the following information:

(*a*)   Industry

  Manufacturing   Service
  Industry   Industry

(*b*) Agricultural Marketing
Three Principal Functions and Eleven Secondary Functions
1 2 3   1 2 3 4 5 6 7 8 9 10 11

Appendix B

The dumping of massive and durable pieces of junk, like the hulks of old vehicles and abandoned kitchen equipment, has become a nuisance. This debris is a menace to the farmer, destroys amenity, and costs money either to the individuals or the local authorities who have to clear it up. This problem cannot be allowed to expand in parallel with growth in the number of vehicles in service or increase in the total amount of household equipment produced. Dumping of waste in this way is already illegal and prosecutions are brought from time to time, while all local authorities have established and advertised the existence of tips to which people who are not prepared to incur the cost of a special collection can bring bulky objects for disposal. The solution appears to lie in the further development of the current threefold approach of legislative penalty, improved public services, and increased public awareness.

1. The strength of the relationship between comprehension and an ability to cope with the cohesive devices of anaphoric reference and lexical equivalence may be demonstrated by answering the (legitimate comprehension) questions:

    (1) What is the precise nature of the problem which must not be allowed to expand?

    (i.e., what does *this problem* in sentence (3) refer to?)

    (2) What sort of dumping constitutes an illegal act?

    (i.e., what does *in this way* in sentence (4) refer to?)

2. The lexical relationships in the passage may be identified as follows:

    Hyponymic relationships:

                        debris
               massive and durable
                  pieces of junk

    hulks of   abandoned
    old vehicles   kitchen equipment

Synonymic or near-synonymic relationships:
(i) debris: waste
(ii) nuisance: menace: problem
(iii) massive and durable pieces of junk: bulky objects for disposal

It should be emphasized that, especially in the social services and in journalistic-type texts, co-referential relationships may be valid only within the particular text itself; i.e., it is not the case that in *all* contexts, debris and waste, etc., will be, or can be, used as lexical equivalents.

Appendix C

1. Reorder the following sentences into a coherent passage:
   (i) Hence, efficient organization of labor and machinery is one of the most important aspects of good silage making.
   (ii) Silage made from overmature grass will reflect this reduced feeding value.
   (iii) Therefore, cuts for silage, particularly first cuts, have to be made over a short period if uniformly good silage with a high feeding value is to result.
   (iv) The digestibility and therefore the feeding value of grass falls rapidly after ear emergence.
   (v) It will also help to minimize the effect of unsettled weather if this occurs at the critical time.

2. Reorder the following acts to correspond to the reordered passage:
   (i) Example
   (ii) Deduction
   (iii) Reinforcement
   (iv) General observation
   (v) Deduction

3. Select the most suitable title for the passage:
   (i) The relative digestibility of grass.
   (ii) How to secure maximum nutritional value from grass.
   (iii) Efficiency of labor and machinery utilization.
   (iv) Grass harvesting methods.

4. (i) What effect does overmaturity have on the digestibility of grass?
   (ii) How would you recognize overmature grass?

5. Give reasons for your answers.
    (i)   Does the writer imply that ear emergence in grass occurs uniformly?
    (ii)   Does the writer imply that efficient farm organization contributes to the speed of the grass-cutting operation?
    (iii) Does the writer imply that unsettled weather will have a beneficial effect on grass being harvested?

6. (i)   "It" (5) refers to — uniformly good silage   (3)
                                efficient organization   (4)
                                to minimize   (5)
    (ii)   "this" (5) refers to — ear emergence   (1)
                                efficient organization   (4)
                                unsettled weather   (5)

7. (i)   What are the qualities of good silage?
    (ii)   At what point should grass be cut to produce the best silage?
    (iii) How does efficient use of men and machinery contribute to the quality of silage?

CHAPTER 10

Teaching
Intensive Reading Skills

John Munby
The British Council

The purpose of this chapter is to establish
what we mean by intensive reading skills, to discuss methods of teaching
these skills at the secondary school level, and to suggest a procedure for
each lesson. The discussion under Follow-up is particularly important.

Main Approaches

There are two main approaches to reading as a section of the secondary
school English syllabus: skills training and nonskills study. Skills training
is fundamental and functional in character; nonskills study is developed
and literary in character. The following diagram is an attempt not to be
exhaustive but to show the basic difference graphically:
Naturally these two approaches are not mutually exclusive—the one
supports the other—but where English is being taught other than as a
mother tongue, the reading section of the English program should
emphasize skills training. Even at this level, however, a start can be made
in nonskills study, in an elementary way, using a simplified reader like
"The Adventures of Tom Sawyer."

First published in J. Munby, "Read and Think: Training in Intensive Reading
Skills," Longman, 1968. Reprinted by permission of the Longman Group Limited,
United Kingdom.

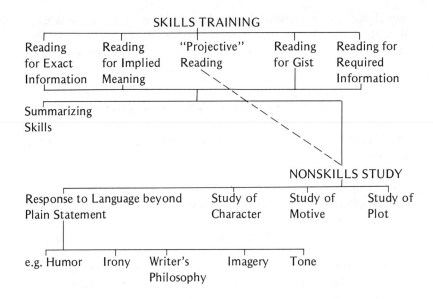

Intensive and Extensive Reading

The skills detailed above relate to both intensive and extensive reading. Although extensive reading is not our subject here, it is the other side of the same coin and so needs to be distinguished from intensive reading. The two, despite areas of overlap, involve different objectives and different skills. In extensive reading we want to develop the habit of reading, of reading for pleasure, which involves the ability to read quickly, since we are more likely to enjoy books when we do not have to struggle through them. This rapid silent reading is also essential for assignments which involve reference work, i.e., training in how to look for specific information which is required, where the answer does not lie conveniently in one book with a good index, and where a person does not have the time to read each line carefully as with intensive reading. Extensive reading skills, then, are not concerned with a detailed examination of the text but involve, for example, reading for some specially required information or to get the gist or general picture of the passage, chapter, or book (the latter being the first steps to skimming). Intensive reading, on the other hand, involves a close examination of the text to get the full meaning. Here we are concerned to train our pupils to respond to the plain sense of words and sentences, and to see their implications, to follow relationships of thought between sentences and paragraphs, and to integrate information in the text with their own experience and/or knowledge. The diagram above shows these skills as reading for exact information, reading for implied meaning, summarizing, and "projective" reading. These skills will be exemplified below. From now on, our discussion concerns only intensive reading.

Main Categories of Questions in Intensive Reading

Most questions to train these reading skills will belong to one of the following categories:

A. Plain sense (i.e., mainly factual, exact, surface meanings).
B. Implications (i.e., inference, deduced information, emotional suggestion, figurative usage, etc.).
C. Relationships of thought (i.e., between sentences/paragraphs, summarizing).
D. Projective (i.e., questions where the answers require integration of data from the text with the pupil's own knowledge and/or experience).

There is a subcategory which can be described as "grammatical relationships" (i.e., questions which demand a response to grammatical signals, e.g., structural words, word order for emphasis, subordination; relationship of time and tense). Questions of this type can help get the plain sense or implication, etc. In the analyses below, reference will be made to the question categories.

Training versus Testing

The first thing to get clear is that in most comprehension lessons we should be concerned in *helping* the pupil to understand the text, *not* in *finding out* if he has understood or not. Helping the pupil means enabling him to understand or giving him the skills necessary for understanding, whereas finding out is checking on the pupil's ability and is in the main only of use to you the teacher. In other words, we should be *training* the pupil to understand, *not testing* whether he has understood. It follows, therefore, that the text must always be *open* when we are training. Of course, at some stage in a lesson, or at intervals in a term, and always in an examination, we do want to test a pupil's comprehension. But, unless we have spent most of our time training the skills of comprehension, the testing will show no progress and the pupil who is weak at the beginning of the year will still be weak at the end of it. This means that whatever technique we use for questioning should facilitate the training of these vital comprehension skills. This is a matter, then, not only of the type of questioning but also of the way it is handled.

Free Response and Multiple-Choice Questioning

Two of the most widely used systems of questioning are known as "free response" and "multiple-choice." Of course, there are other ways of conducting question-and-answer work, but these two are still often the subject of heated debate, and comprehension-type textbooks usually use either or both. Free response questions are those where the answer involves the writing of words and where the answer is not given but is available from reading the passage. Multiple-choice questions are those where the answer is given among a list of alternatives and the answering is done by placing a tick against the alternative chosen or indicating in a similar way, usually without the writing of words. Used as testing techniques, free response questions can be either subjective or objective. When they are subjective in nature, the teacher or examiner will often have to decide on the accuracy or merit of the answer, whereas multiple-choice questioning is objective in that the examiner has no such decision to make. The advantages and disadvantages of each system for *testing* have been well expounded elsewhere and are not our main concern here, which is how to use them for *training*.

Training with Multiple-Choice Questioning

The thesis that multiple-choice questioning can be used effectively to *train* a person's ability to think is now being widely accepted wherever the subject comes up for discussion. This idea—certainly at least its implementation in a textbook—was first suggested in "Comprehension for School Certificate" by J. L. Munby, O. G. Thomas, and M. D. Cooper (Longmans 1966). It is developed here in much greater detail, with suggestions on implementation.

The criticism is sometimes heard that multiple-choice questioning is too simple and does not make the pupils think, since it is easy to pick out the answer among the given alternatives. This is invalid, since it is a criticism of the particular question or questions, not of the system. It is possible to set the distractors (the alternatives which are not acceptable as the best answer) so close that the pupil has to examine each alternative very carefully indeed before he can decide on the best answer. Notice we say "best" answer—not right answer, since it is perfectly valid to have distractors which are partly right or even more than one acceptable answer one of which, however, is the best. A bad multiple-choice question, in intensive reading, is one where the best answer is so obvious that the distractors do not attract more than a passing glance, or where the distractors are all very weak. Of course it is not possible, or indeed desirable, to have all distractors strong on every question. Each question should contain at least one distractor (preferably two) which will make the student think carefully, or else it is not intensive reading. Even the weakest distractor in an easy question should generally cause some students to pause before eliminating it.

When a person answers a comprehension question incorrectly, the reason for his error may be intellectual or linguistic or a mixture of the two. Such errors can be analyzed and then classified so that questioning can take account of these areas of difficulty. Here is an attempt at classifying the main areas of comprehension error:

1. Misunderstanding the plain sense.
2. Wrong inference.
3. Reading more into the text than is actually there, stated or implied.
4. Assumption, usually based on personal opinion.
5. Misplaced aesthetic response (i.e., falling for a "flashy" phrase).
6. Misinterpreting the tone (or emotional level) of the text.
7. Failing to understand figurative usage.
8. Failing to follow relationships of thought.
9. Failing to distinguish between the general idea (or main point) and supporting detail.
10. Failing to see the force of modifying words.
11. Failing to see the grammatical relationship between words or groups of words.
12. Failing to take in the grammatical meaning of words.

Distractors in multiple-choice work should, as far as possible, take account of these areas of error. Multiple-choice work has the advantage of the teacher or text writer taking the initiative in putting the pitfalls of faulty thinking, in the form of distractors, under the student's nose, so as to confront him with the mainly intellectual problem that you want solved. Subjective free response questions do not have this advantage, since the question is open-ended and the amount of training depends on the particular and fortuitous response of an individual student.

It should be realized that this process, being basically an intellectual one, is not the same as that for structure work, which involves training to produce automatic responses (habit formation). In structure teaching, we avoid confronting the student with error because we are trying to form correct habits, but in comprehension training we want him to recognize the areas of comprehension error (through the distractors) so that he learns to respond accurately and more maturely to what he reads.

Let us now analyze a text for its question category, the areas of error which the distractors exemplify, and the level of difficulty of each question. The following text is from "Things Fall Apart" by Chinua Achebe.

(*Note*: the questions are those asked in "Comprehension for School Certificate." Question 3 only has been altered in its stem.)

1. The drums and the dancing began again and reached fever heat. Darkness was around the corner, and the burial of Ezeudu was near. Guns fired the last salute and the cannon rent the sky. And then from the center of the delirious fury came a cry of agony and shouts of horror. It was as if a spell had been cast. All was silent. In the center of the crowd a boy lay in a pool of blood. It was the dead man's sixteen-year-old son, who with his brothers and half-brothers had been dancing the traditional farewell to their father. Okonkwo's gun had exploded and a piece of iron had pierced the boy's heart.

2. The confusion that followed was without parallel in the tradition of Umuofia. Violent deaths were frequent, but nothing like this had ever happened.

3. The only course open to Okonkwo was to flee from the clan. It was a crime against the earth goddess to kill a clansman, and a man who committed it must flee from the land. The crime was of two kinds, male and female. Okonkwo had committed the female, because it had been accidental. He could return to the clan after seven years.

4. That night he collected his most valuable belongings into headloads. His wives wept bitterly and their children wept with them without knowing why. Obierika and half a dozen other friends came to help and to console him. They each made nine or ten trips carrying

Okonkwo's yams to store in Obierika's barn. And before the cock crowed Okonkwo and his family were fleeing to his motherland. It was a little village called Mbanta, just beyond the borders of Mbaino.

5. As soon as the day broke, a large crowd of men from Ezeudu's quarter stormed Okonkwo's compound, dressed in garbs of war. They set fire to his houses, demolished his red walls, killed his animals, and destroyed his barn. It was the justice of the earth goddess, and they were merely her messengers. They had no hatred in their hearts against Okonkwo. His greatest friend, Obierika, was among them. They were merely cleansing the land which Okonkwo had polluted with the blood of a clansman.

6. Obierika was a man who thought about things. When the will of the goddess had been done, he sat down in his "obi" and mourned his friend's calamity. Why should a man suffer so grievously for an offense he had committed accidentally? But although he thought for a long time he found no answer. He was merely led into greater complexities. He remembered his wife's twin children, whom he had thrown away. What crime had they committed? The Earth had decreed that they were an offense on the land and must be destroyed. And if the clan did not exact punishment for an offense against the great goddess, her wrath was loosed on all the land and not just on the offender. As the elders said, if one finger brought oil it soiled the others.

QUESTIONS

1. The drums and dancing
   A. had begun before dark.
   B. had begun just before dark.
   C. began when darkness arrived.
   D. had been going on all day.
2. The people were beating drums and dancing because
   A. they enjoyed doing this.
   B. they were preparing for war, to avenge the dead man.
   C. this was a customary part of a funeral.
   D. they were chasing away evil spirits.
3. The first paragraph begins with an atmosphere of noise, then changes. The atmosphere changes to
   A. confusion.
   B. silence.

C.   agony.

D.   excitement.

4.   We can deduce from the text that the punishment for the male kind of the crime committed by Okonkwo was

A.   less severe than that for the female kind.

B.   more severe than that for the female kind.

C.   the same as that for the female kind.

D.   unknown, since the male kind of the crime had never been committed.

5.   The action of the men who attacked Okonkwo's compound can be described as

A.   cowardly, because Okonkwo was not there to defend his property.

B.   revengeful, because they came from Ezeudu's quarter.

C.   merciful, because they had waited until Okonkwo had departed.

D.   necessary, because the religious laws of their society demanded this.

6.   Okonkwo's calamity upset

A.   his own family only.

B.   friends as well as his family.

C.   Obierika, more than anyone else.

D.   the whole clan.

7.   Obierika

A.   did not understand why Okonkwo was being punished.

B.   understood why Okonkwo was being punished, but disapproved of the reason.

C.   did not accept the reason for Okonkwo's suffering until he thought of his own experience with his twins.

D.   found it difficult to understand the severity of the punishment system which they followed.

8.   From reading this passage it seems that the author

A.   is in favor of the tribal idea of crime and system of punishment.

B.   is against the tribal idea of crime and system of punishment.

C.   is not concerned with any argument but simply recording the events of a story.

D.   is disturbed by the tribal idea of crime and system of punishment.

ANALYSIS

Question	Alternative	Comment	Area of Error (ref. to numbers in list on p. 146)
1.	B:	this is ruled out by the word "again" in the text. Since it was just before dark when the drums and dancing began *again*, they could not have *begun* just before dark.	10
	C:	either misunderstanding the figurative use of "darkness was around the corner," or not taking in the fact that the verb "began" in the answer does not indicate the same time as "had begun."	7 or 12
	D:	unjustified assumption, based perhaps on the personal experience of the pupil who may have been to such a ceremony where the drums and dancing did go on all day.	4
	A:	best answer. Not specific, but correct. This is an example of question category B (see p. 144). The distractors require careful examination before elimination. Level of difficulty of this question = fairly hard.	
2.	A:	wrong inference caused by association of drums and dancing with enjoyment.	2
	B:	wrong inference caused by association of guns cannon with war.	2
	D:	a person who chooses this probably has an overvivid imagination!	3
	C:	best answer. Information ("burial," "dancing the traditional farewell to their father") in passage. This is an example of question category A. The best answer is relatively straightforward. Level of difficulty = easy.	
3.	A:	this misses out a stage (noise → silence → confusion).	8
	C:	"cry of agony"—this is part of "noise," so no change. This is an example of misunderstanding or not taking account of the language of the question—"noise" is mentioned in the question but not in the passage.	8

Question	Alternative	Comment	Area of Error (ref. to numbers in list on p. 146)
	D:	excitement of a general sort prevailed, so atmosphere could not change to it.	8 and 9
	B:	best answer. It is all noise till "All was silent."	
		This is an example of question category C. The distractors are of approximately equal strength—about medium. Level of difficulty = medium.	
4.	A:	misses the point of "accidental" in paragraph 3.	2
	C:	failed to see the implication of "male" and "female."	2
	D:	a person who chooses this has not attempted a *deduction*, as required by the question. Also it is going too far to say that the male kind of crime had *never* been committed.	2 or 3
	B:	best answer. Deduction: female = accidental; therefore, male = deliberate; deliberate is more serious than accidental; therefore, answer = B.	
		This is an example of question category B. There is one strong distractor, D. Level of difficulty = medium.	
5.	A B C }:	these are all, considered in isolation, possible answers, but not when read in the context of the second half of paragraph 5, beginning "It was the justice of the earth goddess, etc.," which shows D to be the best answer.	2
	D:	best answer.	
		This is an example of question category B. It also contains an element of C, in that the answer D is a kind of summary of paragraph 5.	
		The distractors are easily eliminated once a person sees the implication of the "justice of the earth goddess." Level of difficulty = easy.	
6.	A:	misses the force of "only."	10
	C:	inference from last paragraph, but this overlooks paragraph 4 (wives and children weeping).	2

Question	Alternative	Comment	Area of Error
	D:	goes too far. It is possible, but if this were the answer, it would not be based on this passage alone.	3
	B:	best answer. See paragraphs 4 and 6.	
		This is an example of question category A. There is one strong distractor, C. Level of difficulty = medium.	
7.	A:	misses the point of the modifying words "so grievously" in the last paragraph. Obierika *did* understand the *basic* reason.	10
	B:	the word "disapproved" is too strong. This is misinterpreting the "tone" of the last paragraph. Possibly the student is allowing his own feelings to influence the argument.	6 (?4)
	C:	remembering his own experience with his twins = the greater complexities in which he was led (see middle of last paragraph). This, therefore, cannot make him accept the reason for Okonkwo's suffering. The elders' rationalization (last part of last paragraph) is not necessarily his—probably not, in view of the connection of thought between "greater complexities" and the rest of the paragraph.	2 and 8
	D:	best answer. This is, in fact, an accurate summary of the last paragraph.	
		This is an example of question category C. All distractors are strong. Level of difficulty = hard.	
8.	A:	too definite one way.	6 and 2
	B:	too definite the other way.	6 and 2
	C:	suggests a completely objective stand. But such writing (objective, detached) would not include a paragraph like the last one.	6 and 2
	D:	best answer. Paragraph 6 suggests some personal involvement or concern of the writer without defining his stand. This kind of question sometimes provokes the objection that it is terribly difficult for students to see	

Teaching Intensive Reading Skills / 153

Question	Alternative	Comment	Area of Error
		what the author's "intention" is or to gauge the emotional level. But unless questions like this are asked (and it would be more uncomfortable as a free response question here), students will never attempt to interpret an author's involvement. Of course, such questions should be asked sparingly outside a "literature" class.	
		This is an example of question category B. There is one strong distractor, C. Level of difficulty = medium.	

From the above analysis, we can see that in this text (1) there are four questions of category B, two of A, and two of C; (2) the area of error which receives most attention here is 2, with a spread over most of the other areas. (3) The level of difficulty ranges from two "easy" through four "medium" to one "fairly hard" and one "hard." The questions show how, using the multiple-choice system, we can set our pupils the very problems which we want them to exercise their minds upon, using intensive reading skills. By setting carefully constructed distractors, we can train them to reason their way through the linguistic and intellectual problems posed by the text.

Follow-up.   Now that we have seen the kind of material that such a set of questions contains for an intensive reading lesson, it can also be seen that one way *not* to teach with this system of questions is the following:

> After the pupils have written down their choices, the teacher says: "Who got number 1(A)?"—(several raise their hands)—"All right, Juma, tell us why you chose A"—(Juma gives an acceptable explanation)—"Good. Now do you all see that? Right, next question."—(and so on through all the questions).

This completely wastes all the potential of the exercise for training the pupils in thinking. This potential should be utilized by thorough "follow-up" work. This involves getting the pupils to eliminate the distractors, not immediately trying to justify the best answer but arguing why they have not chosen the alternatives.

After the pupils have done the questions individually, collect their work for marking, since you may wish to keep a record of progress through the year. They should write down their answers (1B, 2C, etc.)

twice: (1) on slips of paper which the teacher collects for his own marking, and (2) in their exercise books, which are retained for the follow-up work. The follow-up discussion can first be done as group work, where the object is to arrive at a group answer. This gets pupils to argue, to try to convince each other. Each group should try to arrive at a unanimous decision, but majority verdicts will do. It is usually not possible, if the group work is to be done properly, for all questions to be discussed. The teacher should select questions likely to provide the most useful discussion and tell the groups to discuss only those. During this group work, the teacher should try to get around all the groups to prompt those who need help without actually telling them the answer, and to ensure that they are eliminating the distractors after due discussion, especially those groups who seem to be moving too quickly. Here are just two kinds of things to look for. The teacher finds on arrival in Group 3, for example, that they are on to their second question rather too quickly. On further enquiry, he finds that five out of six pupils chose B for Question 1. They have probably gone on to Question 2 without eliminating the distractors since all but one agreed immediately, and that one may have surrendered without a fight. The teacher should ask why they rejected a certain alternative, especially the main distractor. If they do not give a satisfactory answer, he could leave them to continue the investigation while he turns to another group, returning to them a little later.

A different situation is where a group has been arguing for a while without reaching agreement. The teacher may discover that they were evenly divided at the outset, e.g., three for A and three for C. Here, assuming A to be the best answer, he should ask the supporters of C a question which directs their attention toward the crucial point without actually telling them. In this kind of situation, pupils may well ask for the teacher's intervention without waiting for him to arrive.

Whatever the situation, the teacher should concentrate on getting the pupils to ask each other why a distractor is not acceptable—the elimination of alternatives must be a reasoned rejection. To facilitate this, the teacher should constantly use the kind of language essential to a proper functioning of the follow-up stage so that the pupils learn to use it themselves to each other. Examples of this, in question form, are: "Doesn't that answer go too far? Isn't that your personal opinion? Do you see how that modifying word affects our answer (modifying words like "may," "would," "perhaps," "however," "all," "some," "only")? That is possible, but can you be certain? What has he overlooked?" From this we move on to: "Does the passage actually state that? If it is implied by the text, which words/sentences contain the implication? What conclusion/inference can we draw from that? Does that necessarily follow? What is the connection between this line and that one/this paragraph and that one? Isn't that simply a detail—what is the main point or general idea that it supports? Are you sure that is what the writer thinks—don't those words suggest that he is angry/serious, sad/laughing, in favor/against/unconcerned?"

The next stage after the group work is the class discussion of group answers. The teacher directs this carefully. Let me illustrate how this class follow-up is done, using Question 6 of "Things Fall Apart" (above) as an example. This is how it might go:

Teacher:	Which group chose A? (The secretary of Group 6 raises his hand.) Why did you choose A, Juma?
Juma:	Because it says in paragraph 4 that "his wives wept bitterly and their children wept with them without knowing why."
Teacher:	(asking another pupil, from Group 4, who have not chosen A—notice the teacher does *not* immediately tell that group why they are wrong.) Do you agree with him, Saidi?
Saidi:	No.
Teacher:	Why not?
Saidi:	Because other people were also upset, for example, Obierika.
Teacher:	Do you agree, Group 3? (Answer: "Yes.") Good, Saidi's reason is correct. Group 6, notice the word "only" in the answer you chose. This word rules out A as the answer. Don't overlook such modifying words. Now, which group chose D? (Group 2 indicates that it has.) Right, Mary, your group, 1, does not seem to have chosen D. Tell us why you eliminated D?
Mary:	Well, we did not choose D because we all agreed on C.
Teacher:	That won't do. You have to tell us why you think D is not acceptable or we may think you have merely guessed your answer. Did anyone in that group have a good reason for rejecting D? (No answer. You will not find much of this unacceptable approach if you get around during the group discussion and check those who have reached a conclusion without sufficient consideration of distractors.) All right, why did *your* group not choose D, Hilda?
Hilda:	The text does not mention how the whole clan feels.
Teacher:	What do you say to that, Emmanuel (whose group, 2, chose D)?

Emmanuel:	Well, it's implied in the passage. Paragraph 5 suggests that Okonkwo was probably a popular man, so everyone would be upset by his calamity.
Teacher:	Does that necessarily follow? Can you be sure that there were not even a few people who did not like him? Yes, Hilda.
Hilda:	D is quite possible, but we cannot be certain.
Teacher:	Yes, that's right. D is going too far. Now, who chose C? (The secretaries of Groups 1 and 5 raise their hands.) Right, please explain why, Ezekiel.
Ezekiel:	(rather bright pupil in Group 1). The last paragraph says that Obierika "mourned his friend's calamity." As we are also told that he was Okonkwo's best friend, and is a thoughtful man, we can conclude that he was more affected by what had happened than other people.
Teacher:	That sounds interesting. Ezekiel's group thinks that C is inferred from paragraph 6. Do you agree, Mwajuma (pupil in Group 3 who has not chosen C and therefore chosen B)?
Mwajuma:	That would be an acceptable reason if we were not also told, in paragraph 4, that his family wept, and friends, including Obierika, came to help and console them. They have overlooked paragraph 4.
Teacher:	Good, do you agree that this is the reason, Group 4? (Chorus of assent!) Right, this is not a question of inference—we are told directly, in paragraphs 4 and 6, though not in the same words, that his family and friends were upset by his calamity. So the best answer is B. Groups 3 and 4 are right—well done.

The next question, No. 7, is a hard one, and you would probably find it desirable to give some helpful hints during the group work, such as "Have you considered the connection between those two sentences?"—pointing at the middle of paragraph 6 (see analysis of Question 7C , above). But, whatever the level of difficulty, try to get the *pupils* to tell you, not the other way round, if possible.

Free response questions on the same passage.   If you want to ask questions on a passage where the answer is fairly straightforward, then free response questioning is probably preferable, for example, "Who had Okonkwo killed?" Of the questions in category A asked above, Question 2 would become "Why were the people beating drums and dancing?"

This is at least as good as when framed as a multiple-choice question. But Question 6 is probably better as a multiple-choice question since the possibility of useful follow-up is greater.

For questions of category B, multiple-choice is especially suitable. For example, Question 8, if asked as a free response question, would be something like "What is the author's attitude toward this tribe's idea of crime and punishment?" This would be tricky at a level other than advanced. That question, however, framed as a multiple-choice question, is more likely to prove a useful or good question, certainly from the point of view of training this particular kind of response. Notice, also, that you cannot ask so effectively questions like numbers 4 and 1 above by free response. It is, once again, the ability of multiple-choice questioning to confront the student with the whole of the problem to be solved which is its strong point.

For questions of category C, both systems have much to offer. Question 3 and Question 7 here are possibly better asked as multiple-choice questions, but see also the summary-type questions asked by free response below.

For questions of category D, not hitherto mentioned, we use free response, which is much better suited to its nature. Examples on this passage could be (1) "How do you think a modern court of law would deal with Okonkwo's crime?" (2) "In paragraph 4, why do you think the children wept?" (3) "In paragraph 5, the men were simply carrying out the justice of the earth goddess. What do you imagine they might have had to do if Okonkwo's "crime" had been of the male kind? How would you react if you were called on to be such a messenger of justice?"

"Projective" questioning. "Projective" questions have been defined as the kind where the answers require the integration of information from the text with the pupil's own knowledge and/or experience. That is, he may be required to link something in the text with something which is not in the text, to project himself into a situation suggested by the text, or to give his opinion on something connected with the text but where there is no single answer since the matter is entirely subjective. In each case, he is usually expected to draw on his own knowledge and/or experience of life in general or that subject in particular in order to provide an answer.

It must be made clear to the class what is expected of them in such questions, which must be sharply differentiated from the multiple-choice work which requires answers based upon what is either stated or implied in the text. Unless the pupils are informed of this difference, there may be some confusion.

Summary questions.   It will now be generally appreciated that the traditional form of summary (or précis writing), with its mechanical rules and arbitrary insistence on reducing any passage to one-third of its original is no longer in favor. Teaching the old form of précis has in fact been discontinued in countries where the School Certificate English examination asks for the skills of summarizing to be shown in a different way (e.g., as in the new Cambridge Overseas School Certificate examination—East Africa). The basic well-known principles involved in summary work still apply, of course, but this is not the same as following a set of rather artificial rules in order to reduce a whole passage of some five hundred words to a fraction, one-third, which may or may not be significant. Different kinds of passage are capable of different degrees of reduction and the whole question of what is an important point and how it should be stated depends on what or who the summary is for. The comprehensive question, therefore, which demands that a whole passage be reduced to one-third of its original length may be a complex, indeed skillful, exercise in the meaningless. The skills of summarizing should be trained by asking pupils to make a selective extraction of information to answer a specific question. The ability to summarize a whole passage has value when we want a brief idea of what the text is about, but the question must be phrased to elicit such a brief idea, e.g., a framework with cues provided. The type of questioning, therefore, is very important. It is also essential that the summary question should not be done until after the follow-up work on the multiple-choice questions has been done.

Summary of pattern of work/procedure for lessons.   Assuming that most teachers have two periods a week (at least), the following lesson pattern is suggested:

Lesson 1
(a) Pupils read text and record answers to multiple-choice questions only.
N.B. Teacher collects books or papers before group work.
(b) Group work. Group secretaries record group answers. Teacher moves among groups, listening and intervening to help where necessary (without actually telling) or to check that distractors are being eliminated properly.

Lesson 2
(a) Class discussion of group answers, directed by the teacher.
(b) Class does free response questions.
N.B. The follow-up work on the summary question will probably have to be done as part of a composition lesson because of the time factor.

CHAPTER 11

Teaching the Use of Formal Redundancy in Reading for Ideas

Mary Eleanor Pierce

Introduction

Advanced reading, particularly at the college level, requires the ability to recognize and relate a series of ideas. Recognition of vocabulary and sentence structures is not enough. ESL students need some guidelines for differentiating ideas and determining relationships. One approach is to teach them to look for clues within the composition forms.

The native English speaker who has progressed to reading advanced exposition has already acquired a reasonable grasp of paragraph structure, continuity, and the thematic character of a chapter. He recognizes the forms as vehicles for conveying ideas as well as facts, in a logical sequence. Although he may not always identify the ideas correctly, he has learned that they do not correspond to individual sentences, or necessarily to individual paragraphs. As he reads, he automatically uses formal clues.

The ESL student, on the other hand, is probably still absorbing the rules of form in composition class while he is looking for ideas in advanced reading. He may have learned that a topic sentence is a general statement which expresses the "main idea" of a paragraph, but this does not mean that he understands what a main idea is, or how it is related to

First published in *TESOL Quarterly*, Vol. 9, No. 3, 1975. Copyright 1975 by Teachers of English to Speakers of Other Languages. Reprinted by permission of the publisher and Mary Eleanor Pierce.

its environment. Even if his native language employs the same composition forms, which is not necessarily so, he may be unable to translate an automatic response to clues in one language into a conscious awareness of similar clues in another. With no clear concept of what he is looking for or how he should go about it, he reads paragraph by paragraph or even sentence by sentence, giving equal weight to everything that might be an idea.

This chapter offers some suggestions for teaching relationships between ideas and the formal environment. Specifically, it considers clues provided by redundancy in the forms.

Context and Formal Redundancy

Context is needed for understanding any statement, but it is particularly important when the material is centered around ideas. A fact taken out of context is still the same fact. An idea taken out of context can be a disaster, as any politician will attest.

Formal redundancy provides clues for identifying ideas within the context. Although emphasis is on form, any form necessarily includes semantic as well as structural clues. We can say

This is a sailor

and determine structurally that the sentence form is *S linking-V C*. But when Robert Louis Stevenson says

Home is the sailor

how can we know structurally that the form is *Adv V S*?

In the wider context, paragraphs are structured around a topic or a topic sentence. But paragraph form can only be recognized through semantic content. Therefore, for present purposes, formal redundancy may be defined simply as a set of environmental signals which provide clues for identifying ideas.

No attempt will be made to present specific teaching procedures. The rules and examples which follow are designed to answer three basic questions:

What is meant by "reading for ideas"?
What clues are present in the formal environment?
What clues signal the *development* of ideas?

Reading for Ideas
General Rules

1. Ideas are thoughts. In nonfiction, such as a textbook, they are the thoughts that put facts together. An author collects a set of facts. Then he forms a conclusion, or a judgment about them. When he writes, he puts his conclusion into a statement of *what he believes the facts show*, and presents the facts to support it. Reading for ideas means looking for the author's conclusions. The facts are important, but they are important only because they show how he reached those conclusions.

Example

Facts: Steve holds his book close to his face when he reads.
          He cannot read easy sentences from the blackboard.
          He often does not recognize his friends when he meets them in the hall.

Idea: Steve probably needs glasses.

2. The idea is presented in a general statement, which is supported by statements giving the facts. The general statement is not the idea; it is a sentence which contains the idea. The same idea may be stated in different ways, and it may come before or after the facts.

Examples

a.   *We think that Steve needs glasses.* He holds his book close to his face when he reads, and he cannot read easy sentences from the blackboard. He often does not recognize his friends when he meets them in the hall.

b.   Steve holds his book close to his face when he reads, and he cannot read easy sentences from the blackboard. He often does not recognize his friends when he meets them in the hall. *From this, it appears that he needs glasses.*

3. An idea shows what the author thinks about a situation. A fact shows what the situation is. The situation may be stated in various ways, but the basic fact remains the same.

Example

Statements of fact: a. The adult population of Wide Road, Oklahoma consists of 80 men and 40 women.

                       b. Wide Road, Oklahoma has an adult population of 120.

                       c. There are twice as many men as women in Wide Road, Oklahoma.

4. The same fact may support very different ideas. The statement that contains the fact fits the idea that it supports.

Examples

a. Statement of idea: Small town life still exists in the United States.

   Statement of fact: For example, Wide Road, Oklahoma has an adult population of only 120.

b. Statement of idea: Wide Road, Oklahoma needs more women.

   Statement of fact: At the present time, there are 80 men to 40 women, or a ratio of 2 to 1.

5. A supporting statement may contain a comment about a particular fact. This may look like a new idea. It can be recognized as a supporting statement because it relates only to that particular fact.

Example

Statement of idea: Light-skinned people should use caution if they want to get a suntan safely.

Statements of facts: Sunburn is produced by ultraviolet light rays from the sun.

White skin absorbs about 90 to 95 percent of these rays.

Severe sunburn damages the skin.

Since the skin usually does not turn red for at least an hour after burning, *reddening is not a good guide.*

Gradual exposure to the sun allows the skin to build up protective pigment.

6. A supporting statement may contain a comment about the idea. This may look like a new idea. It can be recognized as a supporting statement because it just repeats or expands the stated idea.

Example

Statement of idea: Bright children need an extended curriculum for developing their abilities.

Statements of facts: They become bored with material that is too easy for them.

They stop paying attention in class because the material does not hold their interest.

In some cases, they learn less than slower learners who concentrate on the lesson.

Expansion of idea: *Additional activities must be provided to remedy the situation.*

Ideas and Composition Form

In order to show different ways that ideas can be presented and supported, the students may be given a list of varied general statements and asked to suggest possible supporting facts. No mention is made of paragraphs and topic sentences unless the students bring the subject up themselves. Following this exercise, the connection is made quite easily by pointing out that they have been building paragraphs around topic sentences. In other words, the relationship between an idea and its supporting facts fits into a composition form.

"Backing into" the form in this way helps to clarify paragraph structure. It does not show the value of form in reading forward. Once the students know what kind of ideas they are looking for, they need to learn how to find them.

The redundancy approach does not change the basic rules of composition. However, it requires a change in emphasis in stating them. The following sections present the rules and suggestions for their application.

Clues in the Formal Environment

Redundancy in the Paragraph Environment

Rules: a. A paragraph usually has a topic sentence. The topic sentence contains the author's idea, but a sentence cannot *be* an idea. It is a general statement that is related to all the other sentences in the paragraph.
   b. The other sentences in the paragraph give information that supports the topic.

1. Ideas and their supporting facts are presented in paragraphs. Paragraph form contains clues for finding the idea in any paragraph.

2. The rules are especially important in advanced reading, because facts are often summarized in general statements.

Example
Wide Road, Oklahoma covers
an area of one square mile.

The adult population consists   *Wide Road, Oklahoma is a very*
of 80 men and 40 women.   *small town.*

3. After an author has gathered a set of facts, he can combine them in one of two ways.
   a. He can state them to support a topic sentence that puts the facts together in a conclusion.
   b. He can summarize them in a supporting statement for a *different* topic sentence.

Since a topic sentence is a general statement about all the information in the paragraph, it is also a kind of summary. Sometimes the only way to identify the topic sentence is to apply the rules.

Examples

a. Kansas is known as a farming state. It is particularly noted for the production of wheat, but it also produces corn, oats, soybeans, and numerous other food crops. In addition, it is a large producer of dairy and poultry products.

b. Kansas is known as a farming state. Its mineral resources are not so well known, but its oil wells are becoming increasingly important in the national economy. Before long, the stereotype of the Kansas farmer may be replaced by that of the supplier of much-needed fuel.

In paragraph (a), the first sentence is the topic sentence. It is supported by facts which show why "Kansas is known as a farming state." In paragraph (b), the first sentence summarizes the facts in paragraph (a). It is the same as the topic sentence of paragraph (a), but now it is a supporting statement for the *last* sentence in the paragraph. Application of the rules shows that:

1. Every sentence in paragraph (b) does not give information about the first sentence. The second sentence is about mineral resources, not farming.
2. The last sentence is related to both the first and second sentences, which give information to support it.

Redundancy in the Extended Formal Environment

Rules: a. A paragraph is a separate unit *only* in a one-paragraph composition. In a longer composition, each topic develops the theme in some way. If there is more than one theme (e.g., several chapters in a book), each theme develops the overall area of study in some way. Paragraphs must be read in relation to the total environment.

b. The idea expressed in a topic is also related to the total environment. It is not sufficient to look for *an idea* in the topic.

1. A paragraph must be read in context. That is, it must be recognized as part of a whole composition. A nonfiction book has three levels of context: paragraphs, chapters, and the whole book. In a paragraph, all the sentences are related to a *topic*. In a chapter, all the topics are related to a *theme*. In a book, all the themes are related to a particular *area of study*.

Example
1. Area of study (shown by book title)
   A Geography of the United States
   A. Theme (shown by chapter heading)
      The Middle West: Breadbasket of the Nation
      1. Topic (topic sentence of a paragraph)
         Kansas is known as a farming state.

2. The total environment includes all the levels of context. It gives additional clues for finding the topic sentence.

Example. In the last example, one of the paragraphs about Kansas is in a geography of the United States, as part of a chapter on the middle-western states as food producers. The first sentence of paragraph (a) fits the total environment.

Paragraph (b) about Kansas might occur in a book on business and economics, as part of a chapter on possible solutions to the fuel shortage. In this environment, farming cannot be the important point; so the first sentence does not fit as a topic sentence. The topic must relate to the fuel shortage in the economy.

3. Since ideas are expressed in topics, they must also be related to the total environment. The environment helps *interpret* the ideas.

Example. In the book about business and economics, the idea expressed in paragraph (b) could also be stated this way:

In the fuel shortage, Kansas may soon become better known for its fuel production than for its farm products.

Now suppose that the same paragraph appeared in a chapter on stereotypes in a book about ways that people's attitudes change. The idea expressed in the topic sentence might be put like this:

In the fuel shortage, the stereotype of a Kansas farmer may soon change to the stereotype of a fuel supplier.

But the area of study covers *ways that attitudes change,* and a stereotype is a kind of attitude. The Kansas situation is related to the total environment only as an example. On that basis, the author's idea could be interpreted this way:

> In a fuel shortage, a fuel supplier may acquire that stereotype in place of an established one.
>
> Or: Changing economic conditions may change a stereotype.

Continuity and the Topic Sentence

Rule: Continuity signals the relationship between a topic sentence and its supporting statements by showing a logical sequence from one sentence to another.

1. "Continuity" is another term for logical development. One sentence follows another in a sensible way.

Example.   Suppose someone is describing the things he does in the morning. He says:

> I eat breakfast.
> I go to class.
> I get dressed.
> I wake up.

His hearers will be a little surprised, because they expect him to list things in an orderly way. They would also expect him to use some connecting words to make the order clearer:

> I wake up at *7:00 o'clock.*
> *Then* I get dressed *and* eat breakfast.
> *After that* I go to class.

2. In written material, continuity is used the same way, to show how one sentence follows from another. This is helpful in finding the topic sentence.

Example.   Both the following paragraphs contain the same information.

a. The energy crisis has created many problems. There are certain points in its favor. We have to stay home on weekends. We wake in the dark. We dress in the cold. The energy situation is not completely bad. We drive to work crowded six in a car to save gasoline. We have to drive slowly. We get to know our families better. Our bills pile up. We can no longer afford frozen food. We have fewer accidents. Our purchases go down. We can go back to good home-cooked meals again.

b. It is true that the energy crisis has created many problems. We wake in the dark, dress in the cold, and drive to work crowded six in a car to save gasoline. Our bills pile up while our purchases go down. On the other hand, there are certain points in its favor. We have to stay home on weekends, so we get to know our families better. We have to drive slowly, so we have fewer accidents. And since we can no longer afford frozen food, we can go back to good home-cooked meals again. In short, the energy situation is not completely bad.

Paragraph (a) does not have continuity. It cannot be sorted out in a sensible way.

Paragraph (b) has continuity. It presents the information in logical order. The author has summarized two sets of facts, and has given examples of each. Then he has tied them all together in a general statement. The last sentence has to be the topic, because it is the only general statement that is related to all the other sentences. The idea it expresses might also be stated this way:

There are good things as well as bad things about the energy crisis.

Continuity and the Paragraph without a Topic Sentence

Rules:
a. If there is no topic sentence in a paragraph, continuity signals the relationship of all the sentences to each other. The way this relationship supports the theme and the area of study determines the topic.
b. Since the idea is not stated, interpretation depends on the whole environment, which includes *any other* environmental clues.

1. Occasionally a paragraph does not have a definite topic sentence. Then continuity helps in finding *a topic* by showing how all the sentences can be related to the total environment.

Example.   The following paragraph might be in a chapter on physical fitness in a book about health.

> Mr. Abercrombie is a farmer. At the age of 65, he works sixteen hours a day, but he does not mind hard work. He eats three good meals a day and he sleeps well. As a result, he is still strong and healthy.

Continuity puts the sentences together in a logical way. The whole paragraph could be expressed in one sentence:

> Mr. Abercrombie does not mind hard work, *even though* he is a 65-year-old farmer who works sixteen hours a day, *because* he is still strong and healthy *as a result* of eating three good meals a day and sleeping well.

But this is a summary, not a topic. The logical development must be related to the total environment. How does it support the theme? How does it support the area of study? What is the connection?

Theme: *Physical fitness*—Connection—Area of study: *Health*

| He eats right and sleeps well. | —as a result— | He is strong and healthy. |

Topic: Mr. Abercrombie is strong and healthy because he eats right and sleeps well.

2. If the topic is not stated in a sentence, then of course the idea is not stated, either. A paragraph without a topic sentence usually refers to an idea that is stated in another paragraph, as will be seen later. The idea is suggested in the topic, but interpretation depends on other clues.

Example.   The idea suggested in the above topic could be expressed in general terms, in relation to the theme and area of study:

> It is possible for an old, hard-working farmer to be strong and healthy, if he eats right and sleeps well.

But it cannot be assumed the author means that all old farmers will be strong and healthy under those conditions, unless there are other environmental clues to support that idea.

Important note. We have to be careful when we interpret ideas in general terms, especially when there is no topic sentence. We can only look for the author's conclusions. We cannot make them for him.

Summary

In order to find the author's idea, or conclusion, in any paragraph, we can:

a. Look for a topic sentence, following the rules of paragraph formation and using continuity clues.
b. Relate the topic sentence to the total environment.
c. If there is no sentence that fits the rules, use continuity clues to relate the sentences in a logical way. Then look for the way the paragraph supports the theme, the way it supports the area of study, and the relationship that continuity shows.

Clues for the Development of Ideas

Sequential Topic Sentences

Rules: a. If a topic sentence supports the idea expressed in a previous topic sentence, the new paragraph expands or repeats the same idea.

b. If a topic sentence does not support the idea expressed in a previous topic sentence, the new paragraph introduces a new idea.
(Exception: Contrasting points may be treated separately and then compared. Since continuity provides the clues, this is noted under "connectors.")

1. A supporting statement can repeat or expand an idea. An example was given earlier:

Statement of idea: Bright children need an extended curriculum for developing their abilities.
(Statement of facts)
Expansion of idea: Additional activities must be provided to remedy the situation.
This kind of expansion sometimes occurs within a paragraph, but it is more common in a series of paragraphs. Then all the topic sentences support the same idea.

Example.　　New York has two faces, one for the visitor and one for the native. The visitor comes to the city for a short time. He is happy to get away from his quiet neighborhood at home, and wants to see as much as he can. He envies the people who live in this entertainment center. He does not realize that the average New Yorker leads the same quiet, humdrum life as anyone in Oshkosh, Central City, or Main Street, U.S.A.

　　The visitor sees New York as a city of constant excitement. He usually stays in a hotel in the center of town, where he sees crowds of hurrying people and hears the steady noise of subway trains, buses, fire engines, and police cars. He goes to the theater district with its flashing signs. He sees plays, musicals, prize fights, and all the various kinds of entertainment that New York is famous for. He rushes from one big event to another. When he goes home, exhausted, he tells his friends about that exciting place, New York.

　　The native sees a very different New York. He does not live in a hotel, and may get to the theater district once or twice in the course of a year. He works at his job like anybody else and goes home to a quiet street or a large apartment building. This is his neighborhood, where he visits with friends, eats quietly with his family, reads his newspaper, and watches television. If he thinks about New York at all, he just thinks of it as home.

The topic sentences are:

a.　New York has two faces, one for the visitor and one for the native.
b.　The visitor sees New York as a city of constant excitement.
c.　The native sees a very different New York.
　　　(plus expansion in the last sentence)
　　. . . he just thinks of it as home.

There are three topic sentences, but only one idea: visitors and natives see New York differently. Topic sentences (b) and (c) support the idea stated in topic sentence (a). After finding that idea, it is not even necessary to look for ideas in topic sentences (b) and (c). One topic clearly refers to the visitor's view and the other to the native's.

　　2. The paragraphs still have to be related to the total environment. And that environment includes not only the theme and the area of study, but also *other previous topics within the theme*.

Example.　　Suppose the paragraphs about New York occur in a psychology book, in a chapter about different ways of seeing things. Then they might come after a paragraph like this:

Entire groups of people may see the same things quite differently. For instance, people who have lived in a big city for a long time do not even notice things that others come many miles to see.

Now the idea is stated in the first sentence of this paragraph. The whole section about New York just gives an example. The topics support the same idea; the "visitor" and the "native" belong to two different groups who see things differently.

This relationship will be true even if other paragraphs come in between, so long as their topics also support the same idea.

3. Sometimes the same idea will be continued in several paragraphs. But sooner or later a new idea will be introduced. Since it also relates to the theme, it will have some relationship to the previous idea. But the topic sentence will not *support* that idea.

Example.   Suppose the paragraphs about New York in the psychology book are followed by this one:

Of course, there are always individual differences. A person may visit a big city like New York to see how the people live. He is interested in the kinds of things city people do, or perhaps he is planning to move there and wants to know what it is really like. And another person may live there because he likes excitement; he spends as much time as possible doing all the things that most visitors do.

This paragraph is also about the visitor and the native. It is related to the earlier section about New York, as well as to the theme and the area of study. But the topic sentence does not support the same idea. The other topics supported the idea that *groups* see things differently. The topic sentence of this paragraph states that there are *individual* differences. It introduces a new idea.

Sequential Topics without Topic Sentences

Rules: a. If two or more paragraphs in series do not have topic sentences, they usually support the same idea. A general idea is suggested by the relationship of the topics to each other, but interpretation depends on a similar stated idea in the immediate environment.

b. If the topics appear to support the same general idea, and a similar idea is stated in a previous topic sentence, the paragraphs support the previous idea.

c. If the topics appear to support the same general idea, but not the idea in a previous topic sentence, the idea they support will be found in a subsequent topic sentence. (There may be rare exceptions to this rule. However, in expositional material authors are so anxious to make their points that it is very unlikely they will leave a conclusion unstated.)

1. Relationships between topic sentences show whether a paragraph continues the same idea or introduces a new one. The topic of a single paragraph without a topic sentence can be related to other paragraphs the same way. But when a series of two or more paragraphs do not have topic sentences, the relationship may be harder to find. It will depend on a general idea that all the topics *seem* to support.

Example.   The earlier paragraph about Mr. Abercrombie occurred in a chapter on physical fitness in a book about health:

Mr. Abercrombie is a farmer. At the age of 65, he works sixteen hours a day, but he does not mind hard work. He eats three good meals a day and he sleeps well. As a result, he is still strong and healthy.

The next paragraph might go like this:

Mr. Abercrombie's son Bill also works on the farm, but he likes to spend his evenings visiting with friends. He often has a sandwich for dinner and then hurries into town. He gets home so late that he has trouble getting up in the morning; he often does not have time to eat a good breakfast. Consequently, we are not surprised to learn that he tires easily and is often sick.

The topic for the paragraph about old Mr. Abercrombie has already been determined: he is strong and healthy because he eats right and sleeps well. The second paragraph has no topic sentence, either, but continuity shows that young Bill tires easily and is often sick because he does *not* eat right and sleep well.

If the two paragraphs are read as separate units, they look very different. But when the topics are related to each other, they seem to support the same general idea in different ways.

Theme		Area of Study
+ eating and sleeping	→	+ health
− eating and sleeping	→	− health

General idea: Eating and sleeping habits are directly related to health.

2. The series may support an idea that has already been stated. Then the general idea can be fitted into the stated idea, and the topics can be seen to support it.

Example.   The paragraphs about Mr. Abercrombie and his son might follow this one:

A balanced diet and plenty of rest are essential for good health at any age. Anyone can lead a happier, healthier life if he follows a sensible plan for diet and rest. An old person can keep his health because of it, and a young person cannot be healthy without it.

The general idea is not exactly the same as the idea stated in the topic sentence, but it is similar. It fits into the stated idea, and both topics support that idea. In this simplified example of a complex problem, the topics alone would suffice. The relationship is not likely to be so clear in a college text.

3. A topic sentence can come at the end of a series of paragraphs, just as it can come at the end of a single paragraph. The author gives several examples, and then states his conclusion. In this case, the general idea will have to fit into a later stated idea which will probably give a slightly different interpretation. It may even show that the first interpretation was wrong. Reading *toward* the author's conclusion requires an open mind.

Example.   Suppose the two paragraphs about Mr. Abercrombie and his son do not support a previous idea. They are followed by several other paragraphs which seem to support the same general idea, and then this paragraph:

It is clear that eating and sleeping habits have a definite effect on health. Although no one is free from the possibility of disease and crippling accidents, an old person who eats sensibly and sleeps well has a better chance than a young person who does neither. And a person of any age can lead a happier, healthier life if he follows the basic rules for diet and rest.

Now there is a topic sentence which states the idea. It shows that the earlier interpretation was not exact, but fits into the stated idea. This example illustrates why the general idea must be just that—very general. If the different ages of the men had been included, the general idea would have to be reinterpreted. Age is mentioned in supporting statements, but not in the statement of the idea.

Interparagraph Continuity: Connectors

Rule: If a sentence connector appears in the first sentence of a paragraph, it acts as a paragraph connector. It shows continuity from one paragraph to another, but the kind of continuity may depend on other clues.

1. An important part of continuity within a paragraph is the use of connecting words like "also," "however," "for example," and limiting expressions used as connectors like "consequently," "then," "in this case."

Paragraphs are connected to each other the same way. In fact, an author often has to choose between putting material into one long paragraph or separating it into several shorter ones. If the long paragraph compares two different things, the separate topics may seem to state different ideas. But since even a long paragraph contains only one idea, the shorter ones will, too. Connectors give clues to the development.

Example.   The paragraph about the energy crisis can be separated into three. Two sentences are added at the end, but they just summarize the information in the two sets of facts.

It is true that the energy crisis has created many problems. We wake in the dark, dress in the cold, and drive to work crowded six in a car to save gasoline. Our bills pile up while our purchases go down.

On the other hand, there are certain points in its favor. We have to stay home on weekends, so we get to know our families better. We have to drive slowly, so we have fewer accidents. And since we can no longer afford frozen food, we can go back to good home-cooked meals again.

In short, the energy situation is not completely bad. If we set the points in its favor beside those against it, we might come out about even. The advantages balance out the disadvantages.

The connector "on the other hand" shows that the same situation is presented in two different ways. The connector "in short" shows that the author is going to state his conclusion about the whole situation.

2. Paragraph connectors often signal continuation of an idea. But they may also introduce a change in ideas. This is a different kind of

continuity. Connectors like "on the other hand" and "nevertheless" can be used either way. Other clues are needed.

Example.   Suppose someone reads only the new version of the energy selection. The connector "on the other hand" shows him that the second paragraph presents the same *situation* in a different way. But does it express the same idea? He looks for clues in the third paragraph, and he finds the connector "in short." But suppose the third paragraph started this way:

> Let us take those weekends at home, for example . . .

The connector "for example" shows a continuation. But the example that is given refers only to the second paragraph. It shows that the author is not developing the idea that there are good and bad things about the energy crisis. He is developing the idea that *there are advantages*. In this case, "on the other hand" introduces a new idea.

Interparagraph Continuity: Transitional Sentences

Rules: a.   If the first sentence in a paragraph refers back to the previous paragraph, but does not expand the idea or state a new one, it is a transitional sentence.

       b1.   If the last sentence in a paragraph refers forward to a subsequent topic, it is a transitional sentence.

       b2.   If the last sentence in a paragraph does not support the topic, it is a transitional sentence that signals a change in ideas.

       c.   If both the transitional and topic sentences come at the beginning or end of a paragraph, the transitional sentence displaces the topic sentence from initial or final position.

Since the function of a transitional sentence is to be just that, the rules are concerned with the problem of distinguishing it from a topic sentence.

1. Connectors give helpful clues for the development of ideas, but they are not always dependable. A more reliable clue is a transitional sentence between two paragraphs. This is a special kind of connector that definitely states either a continuation of an idea or a change to a new idea. It always comes at the end of one paragraph or at the beginning of the next. It may include a connector: the sentence "Let us take those weekends at home, for example," was a transitional sentence with a paragraph connector. The connector gives an additional clue, but only as part of the transitional sentence.

Examples

a. Continuation of the same idea: When we think of communication, we think of language. But language is only part of it. We use our heads, our arms, and even our whole bodies. We show our attitudes by smiling, frowning, or biting our fingernails. We run to people we love and draw away from people we do not trust. In fact, our actions often tell more than our words.

The following incident will illustrate this point. In a recent program to help young drug users, one of the advisers came to the director for advice. He said that his group was hostile toward him, even though he was sincerely trying to help them. The director attended one of the adviser's sessions, and soon found the trouble. The adviser spoke in a friendly and encouraging way. But without realizing it, he would draw away if one of the boys approached him. He showed by his manner that he did not trust them near him. The boys were reacting to his actions rather than his words.

b. Change from one idea to another: The women's liberation movement has gained many things for American women. More women are employed in high-paying jobs. More women are active in politics, at both the local and national level. An increasing number of married women are showing their independence by going back to school, taking jobs and, in general, refusing to be "just housewives." *But, as we shall see, it is still a man's world.*

Men still hold the power and the purse strings. The President of the United States is a man, and few people take seriously the suggestion that a woman should hold that position. Men hold most of the seats in Congress. Almost all of the top executives in large corporations are men. And, although statistically women own more wealth than men, the greater part of it is managed, and controlled, by men—in banks, in law offices, and on the stock market.

2. A transitional sentence comes in normal topic sentence position, at the beginning or end of the paragraph. It may displace a topic sentence that would normally come in the same position. Their sequence can be recognized because they follow different rules.

Example. *But there is another way of identifying birds in flight. Every species of bird has a different way of using its wings.* The hummingbird beats its wings so fast that they are almost invisible, while the hawk rides gracefully on air currents, hardly moving its wings at all. The pelican flies straight ahead, raising and lowering its large wings slowly, as if it was almost too tired to fly. And the wren flutters about nervously as if not sure which way it should go.

Summary

When we read for ideas, we have to look for relationships. Ideas are expressed in topics, which are related to the theme and the area of study. Since the topics within a theme all support the theme, they are related to each other in a general way. Topics which support the same idea are related in special ways. In order to tell whether two paragraphs contain the same idea or different ideas, we can:

a. Look for the relationship between the topic sentences, or between a single unstated topic and a topic sentence.

b. If there are no topic sentences, use continuity clues to relate each paragraph to a topic and the topics to a general idea; look for a related topic sentence in an earlier or later paragraph.

c. Look for connectors and transitional sentences that relate the paragraphs to each other.

d. Always relate both paragraphs to the total environment.

Purposeful Reading: The Overall View

In following clues for identification, it is easy to lose track of the basic purpose in reading for ideas. Every author has a reason for writing a particular book. Exposition deals largely with facts, but the organization of the material depends on the author's point of view, which is shown in the overall progression of his ideas. In order to understand what the author is driving at, the reader must be able to follow that progression.

One helpful exercise is to give the Preface and Table of Contents as the first reading assignment in a new text. Class discussion will consider what they show about the author's plan for development. Then, with the aid of formal clues, the students can see how the plan progresses as they read. This is another aspect of reading in context, which is what the whole thing boils down to in the end.

Archibald A. Hill (1966) has pointed out that "the only way of arriving at a matching set of interpretations among a number of . . . readers is to take the maximum content from the context, and the minimum from the item examined." Hill was discussing imagery in poetry, which allows some leeway for interpretation. In dealing with nonfiction, the concept can be extended to include the author as well as the readers in the area of ideas. The only way the readers can arrive at the same interpretations as the author is to recognize *within the total context* how many ideas he is actually developing, what they are, and how they are interrelated. Formal clues alone cannot guarantee arrival, but they are signposts along the way.

CHAPTER 12

Analytic Syntax: A Technique for Advanced Level Reading

Ruth Berman
Linguistics Department,
Tel Aviv University

Background Comments

With the shift away from the strictly audio-lingual techniques in foreign language instruction over the past few years, attention has been refocused on the reading component—particularly at more advanced stages of the course of study. In this connection, see the very clear and thought-provoking chapter by Muriel Saville-Troike in this volume. Increased interest in the reading skill is manifested in the following articles—all of which appeared in recent issues of the *TESOL Quarterly*: Eskey (1970), Lackstrom et al. (1973), Norris (1970), Pierce (1973), Oller (1972), Wilson (1973). This chapter sets out to illustrate a technique whereby it should be possible to enhance the student's awareness of the grammatical and rhetorical structure of the target language—in this case English, to facilitate and hence deepen his understanding of the material he reads in English, and, it is hoped, to improve his proficiency in his own writing of English.

The technique in question may be termed "analytic syntax"—a notion which should become self-explanatory in the course of the exposition which follows. This technique is demonstrated by reference to the following 250-word excerpt from an article which seems fairly

First published in *TESOL Quarterly*, Vol. 9, No. 3, 1975. Copyright 1975 by Teachers of English to Speakers of Other Languages. Reprinted by permission of the publisher and Ruth Berman.

typical of the kind of prose college students are expected to read in the humanities and social sciences. Note that the excerpt itself was to a large extent picked at random; for I am claiming that any passage selected for intensive reading study can and should serve a similar purpose.

THE STATUS OF WOMEN IN THE MIDDLE AGES

After the decline of the Roman Empire, nearly all of the economic activities connected with the production of food, clothing, and shelter were carried on in villages and their outlying fields everywhere in Western Europe. Whether the village was a free community, or property
5   belonging to the lands of a great feudal lord or lady, it was mostly able to produce enough for itself. Its inhabitants supplied nearly everything they needed to maintain life. Furthermore, the industries of households and fields were not like the modern "heavy industries": women could handle nearly all of them alone, or with some aid from men.
10   Thus there was no sharp division of labor, as a rule. Men and women worked together for the most part. The responsibilities for spinning, weaving, and cooking were mainly women's tasks, and woodcutting and digging ditches were generally men's tasks. However, men and women commonly worked side by side in the fields in all the processes
15   of changing raw materials into goods ready for use. Whether the workers on the land were slaves or free, men and women worked under similar conditions and enjoyed similar rights. After the birth of children, both parents had their services to help them in their work. In the records of medieval rural life, we find that women, because they were
20   women, had no specially hard labor to do—nor did the men, because they were men, lay specially hard tasks upon the women. On the contrary, the records show a fairly equal sharing of the difficult tasks.

In the following analysis of the text, two major components of the reading skill are deliberately ignored: vocabulary and general content. With respect to vocabulary, it is assumed to be already familiar to the students—either through prior explanation and practice, or by some device such as dictionary exercises or appropriate glossing of the text. With respect to general content, comprehension at three different and interrelated levels should be required: first, an understanding of the factual information contained in the text, which could be achieved by short yes/no questions or true/false items the answers to which can be directly lifted from the text itself; second, an understanding of a more inferential kind—possibly through open-ended questions handled orally in class and then in writing at home, or by means of probing multiple-choice-type items; finally a stage of elaboration and evaluation in which class discussion could be conducted on topics arising out of the text, where students would contribute their own ideas on such matters as whether the status of medieval woman was really equal to that of men and how the rights and duties of medieval woman compare to those of her modern counterpart in both urban and rural areas.

As for presentation, I would recommend the following sequencing—though maximal flexibility is desirable in relation to the specific text selected, the nature of the overall course of study, and so forth. I would start out by making sure vocabulary is understood, then go on to the first type of comprehension question noted above (factual information); at this point students should be ready for the "analytic syntax" type of treatment proposed below. And this would then be followed by the two more sophisticated comprehension activities: inference and elaboration, respectively.

The crux of the technique proposed here is the use of *structural paraphrase,* where phrases and whole sentences are reworded and juggled about with a minimum of change in lexical content and hence in lexical load. This technique can and should be effected with virtually no reference to technical terminology; thus, whatever the teacher's own view of the usefulness of "labels" such as Subject and Predicate, NP and VP, or Preposition and Particle, the method itself needs no recourse to such terms. The subheadings listed below are more for the edification of the teacher—rather, the readers of this chapter—than for the student.

It should be noted that not all the activities outlined below are intended for use with one short text. A text such as the one analyzed here could be the basis for a treatment of at the most two to three of the nine points listed below.

Demonstration of Rationale and Technique

1. Title

Rationale: It is important for students to be clearly cognizant of the theme of what they are going to be reading about, something which is often explicitly formulated in the title. Moreover, the title often uses key words which recur in the text and hence are important to a general understanding. And a by-product of this dwelling on the title would be an awareness of the conventions of punctuation and capitalization specific to headings and titles.

Technique: Which of the following says the same thing as the title?

a. The Status of Middle-Aged Women
b. The Status of Medieval Woman
c. The Status of Medieval Women

Students should, of course, select both *b* and *c*. The meaning of *a* is easily explained along the following lines: a middle-aged person, someone who is middle-aged, is neither young nor old; in our society the term generally refers to people in their late forties and fifties or sixties. The term "the Middle Ages"—spelled always with capital M and A—refers to a period in history; and anything which is "medieval" belongs to or describes the period of the Middle Ages. Both the singular form "woman" and the plural "women" can be used in this general sense—not a specific woman, but "woman in general," not a certain group of women, but "women in general."

2. Nominalization

Rationale: Reference is to a device typical of more formal style, particularly in writing: the use of abstract nouns where a more conversational spoken style would use the corresponding verbs. An abundance of abstract nominals—very often of Romance origin and with some degree of morphological complexity—tends to impede understanding when compared with the more concrete, and syntactically as well as morphologically simpler, form of verbs.

Technique: Read both the nominal and its corresponding sentential form, possibly writing the latter up on the board. Thus, line 1: "after the decline of the Roman Empire"/"after the Roman Empire had declined"; line 2: "activities connected with the production of food, clothing, and shelter"/"activities connected with how food, clothing and shelter were produced"; line 10: "there was no sharp division of labor"/"labor was not divided up sharply"; lines 11 to 12: "the responsibilities for spinning, weaving, and cooking were mainly women's tasks"/"women were mainly responsible for the tasks of spinning, weaving, and cooking"/that is, "women spun, wove, and cooked" (an incidental review of past tense forms of these verbs); lines 12 to 13: "woodcutting and digging ditches were generally men's tasks"/"the men were the ones who generally cut wood and dug ditches"; lines 14 to 15: "the processes of changing raw materials into goods ready for use"/"the processes by which raw materials were changed into goods ready for use"; line 17: "after the birth of children"/"after children were born"; line 22: "a fairly equal sharing of the difficult tasks"/"the difficult tasks were shared in a fairly equal way."

Note: In more advanced classes, this could be the basis for a brief consideration of the distinction between gerundive-type nominals and the more noun-like abstract nominals in such pairs as: *producing/production, dividing/division* compared with those verbs (generally of native Anglo-Saxon origin) which have only a single nominal in *-ing*, such as: *spinning, weaving, cutting, sharing.* Similarly, work could be done on derivational morphology in treating abstract noun suffixes such as: *-ion*, *-ment*, *-al*, *-ness*.

3. Reduced Relative Clauses

Rationale: The tendency in English to delete WH + *be* combinations or—where the relative pronoun replaces an underlying object noun phrase—the relative pronoun alone is often a stumbling block for the nonnative reader of English. The reason is that the structural clues or "function words" signaling the relationships between parts of a sentence are not overtly expressed in such cases.

Technique: The teacher supplies—or has students supply—the missing elements: (a) WH + *be*—line 2: "the economic activities connected with the production of food, etc."/"the economic activities *which were* connected with . . ."; line 15: "changing raw materials into goods ready for use"/"changing raw materials into goods *which were, which would be* ready for use"; (b) VERB*ing* = WH + VERB in Simple Present or Past—line 5: "property belonging to the lands of . . ."; "property *which belonged* to the lands of. . ."; (c) Relative Pronoun deletion—line 6: "supplied nearly everything they needed"/"supplied nearly everything *that* they needed."

Note: This text is not particularly rich in such constructions, but it is not hard to find texts which manifest an abundance of one or more of the three types of relative clause reduction illustrated above. Possible exercises would include sentences where students are required to omit the relevant structural items, as well as sentences where they are required to supply items which have been omitted.

4. Pronominal Reference

Rationale: Another major obstacle to fluent and proficient reading is difficulty with relating pronouns to their relevant antecedents. This can lead to ambiguity of interpretation where none is intended, or to outright misinterpretation of parts of a text.

Technique: Have students state clearly what or whom each pronoun refers to and then replace the pronoun by its referent. Thus, line 3: "*their* outlying fields"/"the outlying fields *of the villages*"; lines 5 to 6: "*it* was mostly able to produce enough for *itself* "/"the *village* was mostly able to produce enough for *the village*"; line 6: "*its* inhabitants"/ "*the village's* inhabitants" = "*the inhabitants* of the village"; line 9: "nearly all of *them*"/"nearly all of *the industries of households and fields*"; line 18: "both parents had *their* services"/"both parents had *the children's* services."

Note: This technique should have the following by-products: (a) an intuitive understanding of the role of pronominalization—in English as in other languages—as a means of avoiding tautology and repetition of the same nominals; (b) a realization that pronouns do not replace nouns as such, but whole noun phrases and that they reflect the properties of their antecedent noun phrases with respect to such features as case, gender, and number; (c) an awareness of the nature of reflexivization—through the example from lines 5 to 6; (d) a reviewing of genitive constructions using "of" rather than the apostrophe—compare "of the villages" to "of the villages' (?)"; (e) a review of the following paradigm:

$$
\left.\begin{array}{l} \text{he} \\ \text{she} \\ \text{it} \end{array}\right\} \text{they} \qquad\qquad \left.\begin{array}{l} \text{his} \\ \text{her} \\ \text{its} \end{array}\right\} \text{their}
$$

with brief pointers to spelling: *its* compared with *it's*, *they* compared with *their* (unlike the homophonous *there* relating to *here* and *where*).

5. Sentence Connectors

Rationale: Here is another device which is typical of the more formal style of writing compared with colloquial speech. A full appreciation of the meaning as well as of the syntactic patterning and rhetorical function of such items is essential both for proficient reading and for the development of a mature style in writing.

Technique: (a) Consider the word "furthermore" in line 7: What does it tell us? That more information is going to be given, that something is going to be added. In this sense it is like the word "and." Do the same thing for "thus" in line 10 and "however" in line 13. (b) In each case, write up lists on the blackboard as follows:

AND	SO	BUT
furthermore	thus	however
moreover	therefore	nevertheless
besides	hence	notwithstanding
in addition	as a result	in spite of this

(c) Give students exercises where they have to replace *and, so,* and *but* by one of the above, and follow with further exercises where students have to choose a suitable expression in terms of the meaning of the context. (d) Point out that all these expressions—single words as well as phrases—can come at the beginning of a sentence (as they do in the text), at the end, or in the middle, in preverbal position. Note the punctuation conventions in terms of use of commas in each case. Then give exercises where students have to reword sentences by shifting the position of the sentence connectors.

Note: This area could then be expanded by going back to the text and noting other expressions which indicate logical and rhetorical linkings with what has preceded. Examples include: line 10—"as a rule"; line 11—"for the most part"; line 21—"on the contrary."

6. Whether X or Y

Rationale: The text contains two instances of this kind of construction—in lines 4 to 5 and lines 15 to 16; I have found that students rarely appreciate precisely what it means, let alone how it is used.

Technique: Here I would have students explain how they would render the same expression in their native tongue, first taking care to cut the sentence down to its basic constituents. Thus, lines 4 to 5: "Whether the village was a free community *or not* (i.e., it was property which belonged to a feudal lord or lady)"; lines 15 to 16: "Whether the workers on the land were slaves or not (i.e., they were free men)." This is an instance where, certainly in dealing with native speakers of Hebrew, I would give a number of simple statements in their own language and have them reword them in English, dividing the exercise up into two parts: first, *Whether X or not* types of elliptical expressions, and then *Whether X or Y* where Y is explicitly formulated.

7. Negation

Rationale: The special devices used for negation in English—such as the alternation between *no* and *not any* or forms such as *nor* and *neither*—are often an impediment to the quite advanced student, who may have achieved adequate command of normal sentence negation with *n't* in his own speech.

Technique: Rewording as follows: line 10—"there was *no* sharp division of labor"/"there was *not any* sharp division of labor"; line 20—"women had *no* specially hard labor to do"/"women *did not* have *any* specially hard labor to do." Then add other exercises of the same type, before going on to the next point: line 20—"*nor* did the men lay specially hard tasks upon the women"/"*and* the men *did not* lay specially hard tasks upon the women, *either.*"

8. Punctuation

Rationale: Punctuation provides clues to the underlying interpretation and constituent structure of written material in a way analogous—though not necessarily parallel—to the role of intonation in speech. The conventions of punctuation differ considerably from one language to the next, and lack of due attention to or appropriate interpretation of punctuation marks may impede understanding or even thwart it entirely. For example, in Hebrew a comma is very generally required *before* the markers /še-/ or /kiy/ which function much like the "that" complementizer in English noun clauses (e.g., some of them claimed *that* the idea was impossible; most of the students in the class informed him *that* they were not prepared to take the test). On the other hand, Hebrew does not mark the distinction between restrictive and nonrestrictive relative clauses by means of commas—as does English.

Technique: (a) Note the colon in line 8. What could it indicate? (That an example is to follow, that a contradiction is to follow, etc.) What does it indicate in fact? That the general statement which was just made is now going to be made more specific. (b) Why is the expression "heavy industries" in line 8 printed in quotes? (c) Notice the comma following the word "free" in line 16. How would the sentence beginning with the word "Whether" in line 15 be changed if we left out the comma after "free?" (d) Why is there a dash in the middle of line 20?

Note: Some reference was already made to punctuation conventions in discussing Sentence Connectors in item 5 above; see, too, the relevant comment in item 9 below.

9. Dialect

Rationale: Advanced level students should be aware of differences between British and General American usage in writing—irrespective of the particular dialect in which they are being taught—so as to feel equally at home with materials written by either British or American authors.

Technique: (a) Note the American spelling of the word *medieval* compared with British *mediaeval*, like *archeology/archaeology*, etc. (The origin of the digraph *œ* might be noted); compare *labor/labour*, like *honor, color, favor*, etc., using only words students already know. (b) Note the comma before "and" in the listing in line 2: "food, clothing, and shelter," and have students find another similar instance (lines 11 to 12). Then compare these with, say, "coffee, sugar and tea" in British style.

Summary

As noted earlier, I do not recommend that all the above be performed on one single short text such as the specimen chosen here. Such a procedure would mean that we "murder to dissect," and thereby depart all too far from the basic aim: to enhance the student's understanding and hence enjoyment of written English. Rather, I have tried to show that almost any text in some kind of standard English *can* and *should* be used to illustrate one or two selected aspects of grammatical structure and rhetorical usage. The text used here lends itself well to a treatment of such areas as pronominal reference and sentence connectors. Other texts might be preferable for handling topics such as nominalization, relative clause reduction, or negation. And in some instances teachers—or textbook writers—might wish to adapt or construct suitable texts to illustrate a given syntactic or rhetorical device. Thus, in the Advanced Level Language texts of the *English for Speakers of Hebrew* series of textbooks at present being constructed by a Tel Aviv University team, we have found it helpful to use both methods: in some cases we take advantage of available texts, which we may adapt slightly to include the particular structures we are interested in; in others, we have found it best to write our own original material.

Another point worth bearing in mind is the fact that any given text can do no more than illustrate a specific construction or constructions. It may then be necessary to add a few selected exercises to provide students with further opportunity for manipulation of the point being studied. Yet here, too, a word of caution is necessary: the essence of what is suggested here is an *analytic* approach to syntactic and other devices, and not a drilling of the ability to use these devices productively. That is, this set of techniques should not merely replicate the kind of carefully graded and organized teaching of grammatical structures appropriate for intermediate level studies. For, to recapitulate what I said at the outset, the aim here is first and foremost to promote proficient *reading*, in the belief that therein lies a key to improved ability in writing, too.

CHAPTER 13

Advanced Reading: Teaching Patterns of Writing in the Social Sciences

Salwa Ibrahim
University of Manchester,
United Kingdom

Reading may be defined as an act of information processing. This act of information processing may break down as a result of a galaxy of factors—an inadequate vocabulary, inability to handle grammatical structures, failure to recognize the logical connections between sentences, incorrect utilization of context, and/or complete novelty of the material. It follows that the positive counterparts of these factors are requisites for the successful achievement of this act of information processing. In other words, successful reading involves a large number of factors: lexical, grammatical, sentence connections, paragraph organization, and many others.

These factors are not mutually exclusive. Reading comprehension requires more than the understanding of the meanings of individual words. "You could go through a book backwards, from bottom to top and right to left, recognizing all the words there perfectly correctly, but we should hardly call this 'reading' and certainly not 'reading the book.' Nor would it be any adequate reply to the question 'Have you read so-and-so?' to say that you recognized every word in it." (Dearden 1967). Moreover, reading comprehension requires far more than the awareness of the surface and deep structure of individual sentences. Syntactic understanding of individual sentences is certainly a prerequisite to the achievement of total paragraph or passage comprehension. It is only a prerequisite in that just as students who read a sentence word for word usually fail to comprehend its total meaning, so students who read a paragraph or indeed a passage sentence by sentence usually fail to comprehend its total meaning. Reading comprehension, therefore, requires the skill to recognize the lexical and the structural relationships within individual sentences and to recognize the logical relationships between them.

In spite of recent developments in linguistics and the move beyond the sentence, most teachers and textbook writers have not moved beyond it in teaching reading comprehension. Those who find themselves possessed with a feeling of guilt for neglecting to teach logical relationships between sentences resort to giving a few exercises on the use of connectives, such as *therefore, nevertheless,* or *but,* hoping that by some mysterious process of fusing sentences together the students themselves will become able to comprehend paragraphs, passages, and longer selections. The failure of students to discover this mysterious process has led some of the more research-oriented teachers to consider the problems of teaching logical relationships more seriously.

Arapoff (1968) lists the kinds of logical relationships that various groups of sentence connectors are associated with and describes these relationships in terms of supposition rules. She stresses the importance of teaching sentence connectors on grounds that they serve a significant semantic function in written English. However, she does not suggest any teaching techniques. Although Arapoff meant her analysis to be of help to teachers of writing, it could be used for teaching teachers of reading.

Horn (1971) stresses the importance of teaching logical relationships in teaching advanced reading in English as a foreign language. She points out that the logical relationships between sentences could be contained in a fairly limited list: "It would presumably be reassuring to the student to know that the logical relationships he encounters in his reading recur constantly and are limited in number, and that consequently while he is reading expository, or 'study-type' material, he is dealing with a distinguishable 'set' and not just working out a puzzle with endless variations. In other words, if he learns to recognise a definite list of logical relationships, he is likely to cope with the relationships he will find in all his information reading." Horn suggests that students would first be presented with pairs of sentences illustrating each of the relationships she lists. When they have proved able to identify the relationships in that form, they would go on to identifying relationships as they occur in paragraphs with sentences presented in vertical order, then with sentences presented as they would be in conventional format.

I am inclined to accept Horn's analysis and her suggested teaching technique. However, I believe that besides the skill of recognizing the logical relationships between sentences and besides the other basic skills of recognizing lexical and structural relationships, the total comprehension of a reading passage involves:

1. The skill to glean the ideas that the author is discussing.
2. The skill to extract the organizational pattern the author has used to express his ideas.

Of these two skills the first cannot be successfully accomplished until the second has been achieved. It is this second skill that plays a vital role in reading comprehension, for it provides the content to be read with a frame of reference. Failure in depicting the logical framework or the organizational pattern of a paragraph or a passage entails by necessity failure in grasping its total meaning. The logical relationships between the sentences do not form the organizational pattern of a paragraph or a passage. It is the organizational pattern that the author of a paragraph or a passage has chosen for transmitting his message that determines the sentences he constructs and the kind of logical relationships between them. Therefore, in order that the reader may decode a specific message successfully, he has to subject his own logic or reasoning to that assumed by the encoder or author and to reconstruct the logical organization he had chosen as a frame for his message. Complete comprehension occurs when the recipient of a message becomes aware of the total content of that message. Total content in this sense means something like the exact message intended by the encoder.

Ausubel (1963) stresses the importance of conveying to the students the structure of the subject they are studying. This should provide them with the "optimal anchorage" that is necessary if they are to comprehend or learn a subject. The structure of the subject to be studied should be presented to the students before embarking on the subject itself so that it can act as an "advance organizer" and provide the needed "anchorage." He states: "One important variable affecting the incorporability of new meaningful material is the availability in cognitive organization of relevant subsuming concepts at an appropriate level of inclusiveness to provide optimal anchorage. . . . In meaningful learning situations, it is advisable to introduce suitable organizers whose relevance is made explicit rather than to rely on the spontaneous availability of subsumers."

If we apply these suggestions to the teaching of reading, we will have to find out the organizational pattern of a reading selection and familiarize the students with it before they read it in order to provide them with "optimal anchorage." To my mind, this is precisely what is needed in teaching advanced reading comprehension. When a native speaker of English reads a paragraph or a passage, he automatically falls back on his experience with patterns of written English. This experience will act as his "advance organizers" and will provide him with the "optimal anchorage" necessary for comprehension. His prior experience with patterns of written English has structured his thought processes, thus enabling him to anticipate the way the organizational pattern of the paragraph or the passage he is about to read will operate to convey ideas. This is what students of English as a foreign language lack, and this is what they need to acquire. They need to be taught the most common patterns of writing in English, how to read them, and how to develop ways of thinking about them. In other words, they need their teachers to help them acquire the experience the native speaker of English subconsciously uses when he reads. Teachers of advanced reading should consider this the main goal of their teaching. It is an immense one, and to achieve it they have to be specifically aware of two inextricable factors: who is to be taught and what is to be read.

I shall limit myself to discussing teaching Egyptian social science undergraduates to read social science texts written in English. Although English is not the medium of instruction in the departments of social science in Egyptian universities, students are required to read social science textbooks and articles written in English and to use them as references for any written assignments. In spite of having studied English for six years prior to university entry, most, if not all, have reading difficulties. The result of a diagnostic reading test administered to a sample of them revealed the following:

1. They are more capable of extracting information from tables than from passages. The obvious reason for this is that the former requires less linguistic skill.
2. They have more difficulty in answering questions related to information implied in a passage than in answering questions on details explicitly stated.
3. They have difficulty in locating and forming comparisons and contrasts.
4. They cannot depict cause-effect relationships.
5. They have problems in drawing conclusions from information given in a passage.

In constructing a teaching program to develop their reading skills, I considered it important for part of the program to include teaching them to recognize the most common writing patterns that social scientists use so as to provide them with "optimal anchorage." This entailed the necessity of finding out the various writing patterns used in social science texts before deciding which of them to include in the program. The following writing patterns were found to be the most commonly used:

1. Main Idea—Supporting Details and Illustrations: This is one of the basic patterns of writing. Examples, illustrations, and details are used to support a main idea. The main idea can come anywhere in a passage, depending on the writer's line of argument, but is often contained in the opening sentence or sentences.

2. Definitions: Most definitions in social science texts appear in the form of extended definitions. They can run to chapter length, but the most common ones are a paragraph or two in length. Often different authors may use the same term in a slightly different way; so each attempts to give a special definition of what he intends the term to mean in the context of what he is discussing.

3. Dichotomies or Comparisons and Contrasts: Dichotomies appear frequently in social science textbooks. They do not yield a single main idea, since the essential quality of a dichotomy is its twoness, not its wholeness. Their structure varies in degree of complexity in discussing similarities or differences or both.

4. Cause and Effect: This pattern of writing is the most prevalent in social science textbooks. Cause-and-effect passages are often quite complicated, involving long, complex sentences. They require the reader to follow each sentence closely and not to expect to pick out any single key sentence. The total significance of such passages lies in the relationships among the sentences. A writer might choose a whole paragraph for stating a cause for some phenomenon, then cover its effects in a following paragraph or paragraphs.

5. Complicated Arguments: In this writing pattern, just as in the previous two, it is not easy to extract a single central idea. Certain key words or logical connectors help the reader to think in the right way. These words indicate an addition to an idea, a contradiction, a change of ideas, an exception to the main point, or a summary. Passages of this sort usually end with a conclusion; however, it is the various points brought up in the course of the argument, rather than the conclusion itself, that form the core of a complicated argument.

6. Fact, Interpretation, and Opinion: Here the writer presents a fact or a series of facts, usually in the form of objective statements. His presentation could take a paragraph or more in length. This is followed

by discussion and interpretation, which essentially aim at increasing the reader's understanding of the fact or facts presented. Sometimes the writer follows this with a personal comment explicitly stated, but most often he suppresses an overt statement of his opinions. A skilled reader can sometimes find the writer's personal feelings of the facts implicitly given in the interpretation.

These six patterns of writing are potential organizational patterns of expression in the social sciences. They could occur in a great many combinations, some of them complex. In other words, a passage that is mainly concerned with the exposition of a dichotomy could also include a cause-effect relationship, and/or a definition. It is plausible to assume, however, that the ability to recognize, observe, and use each of these basic patterns is essential to the understanding of social science writing, and that without establishing this ability it would be impossible to expect the more complex patterns to be understood.

Let us consider the following passage as a sample of social science writing. The sentences are numbered for easy reference in following the discussion and the flow diagrams that follow.

1. Herbert Spencer believed that a society corresponds in many respects to an individual being. 2. He noted several similarities between the biological organism and the social organism. 3. Both grow in size. 4. A baby grows up to be a man; a small community becomes a state; a small state becomes an empire. 5. Both increase in complexity of structure as they grow in size. 6. Progressive differentiation of structure in both societies and organisms is accompanied by progressive differentiation of functions. 7. Evolution establishes for both society and organisms related differences in structure and function that make each other possible. 8. A living organism may be regarded as a ration of units that live individually; a ration of human beings may be regarded as an organism. 9. In both organisms and societies the life of the aggregate may be destroyed, but the units will continue to live on for a time.

10. On the other hand, he noted three important differences between society and the organism. 11. In the first place, whereas in the individual organism the component parts form a concrete whole and the living units are bound together in close contact, in the social organism the component parts form a discrete whole and the units are free and dispersed. 12. Again, and even more fundamental, whereas in the individual organism there is such a differentiation of functions that some parts become the seat of feeling and thought and others are practically insensitive, in the social organism no such differentiation exists; there is no social mind apart from the individuals that make up a society. 13. As

a result of this second difference, there is to be observed the third distinction, namely, that, while in the organism the units exist for the good of the whole, in society the whole exists for the good of the members.

The passage as a whole represents a typical social science writing pattern: comparisons and contrasts. The first sentence in the passage gives a general statement of comparison. The word "corresponds" signals this out. The second sentence supports the general statement. The key word that indicates this support is "similarities." The third sentence gives us the first of those similarities followed up in sentence 4 by an illustration. Sentence 6 gives another similarity, this time expressed in the form of a cause-effect relationship. Sentences 7 to 9 give us further similarities announced explicitly by the usage of "both . . . and" in sentences 6, 7, and 9, and implicitly by the usage of the semicolon in sentence 8. The usage of "on the other hand" in sentence 10 announces that a contradiction is about to be made. The rest of the sentence manifests this by announcing that what follows will be statements of differences expressed via dichotomies. Sentences 11 and 12 give us the first and second of these dichotomies, which are clearly signaled by the usage of "whereas." The noun group "as a result of this second difference" which introduces sentence 13 indicates immediately a cause-effect relationship between the difference stated in sentence 12 and the one to be stated in sentence 13. The rest of the sentence gives us the last of the dichotomies, this time signaled by the usage of "while."

This discussion gives us an extended description of the organizational pattern of the passage, which is what I ultimately hope Egyptian undergraduates would be able to observe. I am inclined to believe that following Horn's technique (1971) would not achieve this for me. The list of logical relationships she gives is quite comprehensive, but using it would not lead us to get an overall picture of the organizational pattern of the passage. It is adequate for showing the relationships between sentences, and the first step of her technique, which I accept fully, would be essential in teaching students to identify the various categories of logical relationships. However, to show the students the organizational pattern of the preceding passage by presenting them with an extended description of it would more often than not lead to utter confusion. The alternative, in my opinion, is to present them with a skeletal structure of the organizational pattern of the passage. This would act as "advance organizers" of their thought processes and would provide them with "optimal anchorage."

The following is the skeletal structure or the flow diagram of the preceding passage as I see it. The numerals given in the diagram represent the sentence numbers. The signs used in the diagram:

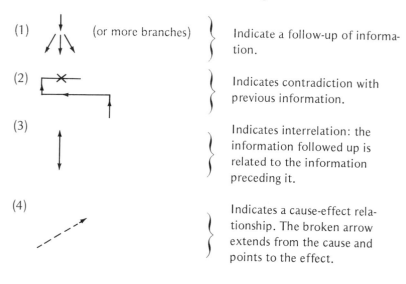

(1) (or more branches)   { Indicate a follow-up of informa-
                             tion.

(2)   { Indicates contradiction with
         previous information.

(3)   { Indicates interrelation: the
         information followed up is
         related to the information
         preceding it.

(4)   { Indicates a cause-effect rela-
         tionship. The broken arrow
         extends from the cause and
         points to the effect.

The outline on page 196 is the flow diagram of the logical relationships in the passage as well as of its overall organizational pattern. The outline on page 197 is a duplicate of the first, but it contains, instead of the logical categories identified in it, the actual sentences of the passage.

The following is a general plan for a directed reading activity revolving around the preceding passage:

A   Readiness

1. Vocabulary and Structure: The teacher decides which of the vocabulary items and grammatical structures used in the passage are likely to cause difficulty and accordingly impede comprehension. These stumbling blocks are paved before proceeding to the next step.

2. Logical Relationships: Here is where Horn's technique could be useful. The teacher finds out which logical relationships occur in the passage; e.g., comparison, similarities, contrast, differences, cause-effect, illustrations. Using uncomplicated controlled sentences as relevant as possible to the content of the passage, the teacher introduces these relationships to the students and gives them enough practice in identifying them.

B   Providing "Anchorage"

1. The First Flow Diagram: The teacher presents the students with the first outline—the flow diagram. This is read and discussed step by step. The concepts of comparison-contrast and cause-effect, and the linguistic structures that are used in forming dichotomies (similarities-differences) would have been covered by being taught in Step A: Readiness. The teacher makes sure that the organizational pattern is fully understood before proceeding further. This could be done by asking questions related to sequence, e.g.,

a.   Could the illustration given in 4 come before the first similarity given in 3?

b.   Could the third dichotomy given in 13 come before the second dichotomy given in 12?

These questions will ensure that the students understand that an illustration follows what it illustrates and that an effect follows a cause.

2. The Second Flow Diagram: The teacher presents the second flow diagram, which serves to complement the first. The two diagrams are used simultaneously at this stage. They are read step by step, sentence by sentence. The logical relationships within and between the sentences are noted closely.

C   Reading the Passage

1. Silent Reading: The students read the passage without reference to the diagrams. The first flow diagram will have already acted as "advanced organizers" of their thought processes and will have provided them with "optimal anchorage." They will be able to read the passage with a definite frame of reference in mind.

2. Discussion: The teacher discusses with the students the ideas in the passage, referring to the flow diagrams as much as necessary. The teacher gives the students the opportunity to ask questions on points or words they cannot understand. It is preferable that the teacher answer the questions rather than refer them to the class to avoid creating psychological problems which might lead to a setback.

3. Comprehension Exercises: The teacher prepares a number of exercises to ensure that the passage is fully comprehended. The students are required to do them in class. The exercises cover the following:

a. Contextual Reference (Multiple-Choice Format): This aims at drawing the attention of the students to the way pronouns, demonstratives, and other anaphoric devices are used to refer to something or someone already mentioned and so serve to relate one sentence to another. Apart from training the students in perceiving the cohesive ties

FLOW DIAGRAM I

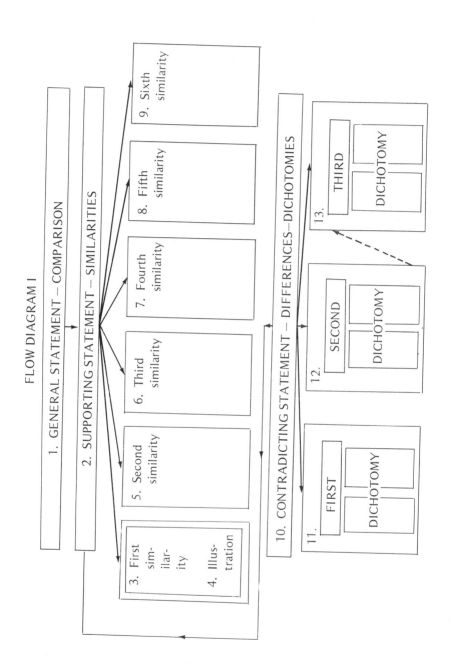

FLOW DIAGRAM II

1. Herbert Spencer believed that a society corresponds in many respects to an individual being.

2. He noted several similarities between the biological organism and the social organism.

3. and 4. Both grow in size. A baby grows up to be a man; a small community becomes a state; a small state becomes an empire.

5. Both increase in complexity of structure as they grow in size.

6. Progressive differentiation of structure in both societies and organisms is accompanied by progressive differentiation of functions.

7. Evolution establishes for both society and organisms related differences in structure and function that make each other possible.

8. A living organism may be regarded as a ration of units that live individually; a ration of human beings may be regarded as an organism.

9. In both organisms and societies the life of the aggregate may be destroyed, but the units will continue to live for a time.

10. On the other hand, he noted three important differences between society and the organism.

11. In the first place, whereas

in the individual organism the component parts form a concrete whole and the living units are bound together in close contact,

in the social organism the component parts form a discrete whole and the living units are free and dispersed.

12. Again, and even more fundamental, whereas

in the individual organism there is such a differentiation of functions that some parts become the seat of feeling and thought and others are practically insensitive,

in the social organism no such differentiation exists; there is no social mind apart from the individuals that make up a society.

13. As a result of this second difference, there is to be observed the third distinction namely, that,

while

in the organism the units exist for the good of the whole,

in society the whole exists for the good of the members.

binding the sentences in the passage together, it aims at referring them back to a close scrutiny of the passage.

b. Comprehension Check (True-False Format): The students are given a number of statements and are required to indicate whether each statement is true or false according to the passage. They are asked to correct the statements they think false to make them consonant with the information in the passage. This is meant to train them to be aware of what is involved in reading with understanding, which not only involves the understanding of individual words and sentences but often is a matter of recovering information from more than one sentence in the passage and drawing on implications.

c. Comprehension Check (Short Answer Format): The aim of this exercise is to train the students to use their understanding of the passage in writing answers to specific questions. It is meant to reinforce their comprehension of the passage and not to test their skill in writing. In answering the questions they could refer to the outlines or to the passage.

d. Comprehension Check (Blank Filling): The students are required to fill blanks in sentences by referring to the outlines and the passage. When they have successfully completed the sentences, they will have had a paraphrase of the main points in the passage. Besides aiming to check comprehension, the exercise aims at providing the students with practice in controlled writing as an intermediate step between writing lists of sentences and writing a free paraphrase.

The main objective of this chapter has been to point out the necessity of bringing across to students the organizational patterns of writing particularly characteristic of their field of specialization. Special reference has been given to Egyptian social science undergraduates learning advanced reading in English. A technique for presenting the organizational pattern of a social science passage and a plan for a directed reading activity revolving around it have been suggested. The points of view presented emanate from the research I am undertaking at the University of Manchester. The techniques are being tested at Ein Shams University in Cairo.

References

Aborn, M. 1959. Sources of contextual constraint upon words in sentences. *Journal of Experimental Psychology.* 57. 171-180.

Allen, J. P. B., and H. G. Widdowson. 1978. Teaching the Communicative Use of English, in R. Mackay and A. Mountford, "English for Specific Purposes," London: Longman.

Allen, Virginia French. 1973a. Trends in the teaching of reading. *English Teaching Forum.* 11, 3.

Allen, Virginia French. 1973b. Trends in the teaching of reading. *Culture and Language Learning Newsletter.* 2.7-11.

Altman, Howard B., and Robert L. Politzer (eds.). 1971. "Individualizing Foreign Language Instruction." Rowley, Mass.: Newbury House.

Anderson, Jonathan. 1971a. Selecting a suitable "reader": Procedures for teachers to assess language difficulty. *RELC Journal.* 2.35-42.

Anderson, Jonathan. 1971b. A technique for measuring reading comprehension and readability. *English Language Teaching.* 25.178-182.

Anderson, R. C. 1972. Comprehension. *Review of Educational Research.* 42, 2.

Anthony, Edward M. 1963. Approach, method, and technique. *English Language Teaching.* 17.63-67.

Arapoff, N. 1968. The semantic role of sentence connectors in extra-sentence logical relationships. *TESOL Quarterly.* 2, 4. 243-252.

Austin, J. L. 1962. "How to do Things with Words." London: Oxford University Press.

Ausubel, D. P. 1963. "The Psychology of Meaningful Verbal Learning." New York: Grune & Stratton.

Bander, Robert G. 1971. "American English Rhetoric." New York: Holt, Rinehart and Winston.

Barnard, Helen. 1971/72. "Advanced English Vocabulary." 2 vols. Rowley, Mass.: Newbury House.

Baudoin, E. M., E. S. Bober, M. A. Clarke, B. K. Dobson, and S. Silberstein. 1977. "Reader's Choice: A Reading Skills Textbook for Students of English as a Second Language." Ann Arbor: University of Michigan Press.

Baumwoll, D., and R. L. Saitz. 1965. "Advanced Reading and Writing." New York: Holt, Rinehart and Winston.

Bever, T. G., and T. G. Bower. 1970. How to Read Without Listening, in Mark Lester (ed.), "Readings in Applied Transformational Grammar," New York: Holt, Rinehart and Winston.

Binham, P. 1968. "How to Say It." London: Longman.

Bormuth, J. R., et al. 1970. Children's comprehension of between- and within-sentence syntactic structures. *Journal of Educational Psychology*. 61, 5.

Carr, Donna H. 1967. A second look at teaching reading and composition. *TESOL Quarterly*. 1.30-34.

Cazden, Courtney B. 1972. "Child Language and Education." New York: Holt, Rinehart and Winston.

Chomsky, Carol. 1970. Reading, writing and phonology. *Harvard Educational Review*. 40. 287-309.

Cohen, A. D., H. Glasman, P. R. Rosenbaum, J. Ferrara, and J. Fine. 1978. Reading English for Specialized Purposes: Discourse Analysis and the Use of Student Informants. Paper prepared for 12th Annual TESOL Convention, Mexico City, April 1978.

Coleman, E. B., and G. R. Miller. 1967. A measure of information gained during prose learning. *Reading Research Quarterly*. 3, 3. 369-386.

Collan, Y., S. P. Lock, D. A. Pyke, and W. F. Whimster. 1974. Medical English for Finnish doctors. *British Medical Journal*. 30. 627-629.

Corder, S. P. 1967. The significance of learners' errors. *IRAL*. 5, 4.

Croft, Kenneth. 1960. "Reading and Word Study." Englewood Cliffs, N.J.: Prentice-Hall.

Cziko, G. A. 1978. Differences in first and second language reading: The use of syntactic, semantic and discourse constraints. *The Canadian Modern Language Review*. 34, 3.

Davis, F. B. 1944. Fundamental factors of comprehension in reading. *Psychometrika*. 9. 185-197.

Davis, F. B. 1946. A brief comment on Thurstone's note on a re-analysis of Davis' reading tests. *Psychometrika*. 11. 249-255.

Dearden, R. F. 1967. Curricular Implications of Developments in the Teaching of Reading, in J. Downing and A. L. Brown (eds.), "The Second International Reading Symposium," London: Cassell.

Edinburgh Reading Tests. 1973. London: University of London Press.

Eskey, David. 1970. A new technique for the teaching of reading to advanced students. *TESOL Quarterly*. 4, 4. 315-322.

Eskey, David. 1971. Advanced reading: The structural problem. *English Teaching Forum*. 9, 5. 15-19.

Farr, R. 1969. "Reading: What Can Be Measured?" International Reading Association Research Fund Monograph for the ERIC/CRIER Reading Review Series.

Fawcett, R. 1977. The Use of Reading Laboratories and Other Procedures in Promoting Effective Reading among Pupils Aged 9-15. Ph.D. Thesis. Nottingham University.

Ferguson, Nicolas. 1973. Some aspects of the reading process. *English Language Teaching.* 18, 1.

Fry, Edward. 1963a. "Teaching Faster Reading." Cambridge: Cambridge University Press.

Fry, Edward. 1963b. "Reading Faster." Cambridge: Cambridge University Press.

Gates, A. I., and W. H. MacGinitie. 1965. "Gates–MacGinitie Reading Tests." New York: Teachers College Press, Columbia University.

Goodman, Kenneth S. 1967. Reading: A psycholinguistic guessing game. *Journal of the Reading Specialist.* 6. 126-135.

Goodman, Kenneth S. (ed.). 1968. "The Psycholinguistic Nature of the Reading Process." Detroit: Wayne State University Press.

Goodman, Kenneth S. 1969. Analysis of oral reading miscues: Applied psycholinguistics. *Reading Research Quarterly.* 5. 9-30.

Goodman, Kenneth S. 1970. Reading: A Psycholinguistic Guessing Game, in H. Singer and R. B. Ruddell (eds.), "Theoretical Models and Processes of Reading," Newark, Del.: International Reading Association.

Goodman, Kenneth S. 1971. Psycholinguistic Universals in the Reading Process, in Paul Pimsleur and T. Quinn (eds.), "The Psychology of Second Language Learning," Cambridge: Cambridge University Press.

Goodman, Kenneth S. 1972. Reading: A Psycholinguistic Guessing Game, in Larry A. Harris and Carl B. Smith (eds.), "Individualizing Reading Instruction: A Reader." New York: Holt, Rinehart and Winston.

Goodman, Kenneth S., and C. Burke. 1973. "Theoretically Based Studies of Patterns of Miscues in Oral Reading Performance." Washington, D.C.: U.S. Department of Health, Education and Welfare, Office of Education.

Goodman, Kenneth S., and James T. Fleming (eds.). 1969. "Psycholinguistics and the Teaching of Reading." Newark, Del.: International Reading Association.

Gough, Philip B. 1972. One Second of Reading, in J. F. Kavanagh and I. G. Mattingly (eds.), "Language by Ear and by Eye: The Relationships between Speech and Reading." Cambridge, Mass.: MIT Press.

Gougher, Ronald L. 1972. "Individualization of Instruction in Foreign Languages," Philadelphia: Center for Curriculum Development.

Greenbaum, S. 1969. "Studies in English Adverbial Usage." London: Longman.

Gunderson, Doris V. (ed.). 1970. "Language and Reading." Washington, D.C.: Center for Applied Linguistics.

Halle, M., and K. N. Stevens. 1964. Speech Recognition: A Model and a Program for Research, in J. A. Fodor and J. J. Katz (eds.), "The Structure of Language: Readings in the Philosophy of Language." Englewood Cliffs, N.J.: Prentice-Hall.

Halle, M., and K. N. Stevens. 1967. Remarks on Analysis by Synthesis and Distinctive Features, in W. Wathen-Dunn and L. E. Woods (eds.), "Models for the Perception of Speech and Visual Form: Proceedings of a Symposium." Cambridge, Mass.: MIT Press.

Halliday, M. A. K., and Ruqaiya Hasan. 1976. "Cohesion in English." London: Longman.

Harris, D. P. 1965. "Reading Improvement Exercises for Students of English as a Second Language." Englewood Cliffs, N.J.: Prentice-Hall.

Harris, D. P. 1969. "Testing English as a Second Language." New York: McGraw-Hill.

Harris, Larry A., and Carl B. Smith (eds.). 1972. "Individualizing Reading Instruction: A Reader." New York: Holt, Rinehart and Winston.

Hasan, R. 1968. "Grammatical Cohesion in Spoken and Written English," Part 1, Programme in Linguistics and English, Teaching Paper 7. London: Longman.

Hatch, Evelyn. 1974. Research on reading a second language. *Journal of Reading Behaviour.* 6, 1. 53-61.

Hays, William. 1963. "Statistics for Psychologists." New York: Holt, Rinehart and Winston.

Heaton, J. B. 1975. "Writing English Language Tests." London: Longman.

Herbert, A. J. 1965. "The Structure of Technical English." London: Longman.

H.M.S.O. 1975. "A Language for Life." London: H.M. Stationery Office.

Hill, A. A. 1965. " 'The Windhover' Revisited: Linguistic Analysis of Poetry Reassessed," *Texas Studies in Literature and Language.* 7. 349-359.

Horn, Vivian. 1969. Teaching logical relationships in written discourse. *TESOL Quarterly.* 3.291-296.

Horn, Vivian. 1971. "Advanced Reading: Teaching Logical Relationships." *English Teaching Forum.* 15. 20-22.

Hornby, A. S. 1954. "A Guide to Patterns and Usage in English." London: Oxford University Press.

Hosenfeld, C. 1976. A preliminary investigation of the reading strategies of successful and nonsuccessful second language learners. *System.* 5, 2.

Huey, Edmund B. 1968 (originally published in 1908). "The Psychology and Pedagogy of Reading." Cambridge, Mass.: MIT Press.

Johnson, Francis, C. 1973. "English as a Second Language: An Individualized Approach." Melbourne: Jacaranda Press.

Kaiser, H. F. 1970. A second generation little jiffy. *Psychometrika.* 35. 401-415.

Kaplan, Robert B. 1963. "Reading and Rhetoric." New York: Odyssey Press.

Kaplan, Robert B. 1966. Cultural thought patterns in intercultural education. *Language Learning.* 16.1-20.

Kaplan, Robert B. 1972. "The Anatomy of Rhetoric." Philadelphia: Center for Curriculum Development.

Kavanagh, James F. (ed.). 1968. "The Reading Process: Proceedings of the Conference on Communicating by Language." Washington, D.C.: HEW, National Institutes of Health.

Kolers, P. A. 1968. "Introduction," in Edmund B. Huey, "The Psychology and Pedagogy of Reading." Cambridge, Mass.: MIT Press.

Kolers, P. A. 1969. Reading Is Only Incidentally Visual, in K. S. Goodman and J. T. Fleming (eds.), "Psycholinguistics and the Teaching of Reading." Newark, Del.: International Reading Association.

Kolers, P. A. 1970. Three Stages of Reading, in H. Levin and J. P. Williams (eds.), "Basic Studies on Reading," New York: Basic Books.

Kolers, P. A. 1972. Experiments in reading. *Scientific American.* 227, 1. 84-91.

Lackstrom, John E., Larry Selinker, and Louis P. Trimble. 1970. Grammar and Technical English, in Lugton 1970. (A reprinting of this article includes a bibliography of related work by the authors and their associates. 1972. *English Teaching Forum.* 10.3-14.)

Lackstrom, John E., et al. 1973. Technical rhetorical principles and grammatical choice. *TESOL Quarterly.* 7, 2. 127-136.

Ladder Series. n.d. New York: R. R. Bowker Co. (for sale only outside the United States).

Lado, Robert. 1955. Patterns of difficulty in vocabulary. *Language Learning.* 6.23-41.

Lado, Robert. 1964. "Language Testing: The Construction and Use of Foreign Language Tests." New York: McGraw-Hill.

Lambert, W. E., and G. R. Tucker. 1972. "Bilingual Education of Children: The St. Lambert Experiment." Rowley, Mass.: Newbury House.

Lefevre, Carl A. 1964. "Linguistics and the Teaching of Reading." New York: McGraw-Hill.

Lennon, R. T. 1962. What can be measured? *The Reading Teacher.* 15. 326-337.

Levin, Harry, and Joann P. Williams (eds.). 1970. "Basic Studies on Reading." New York: Basic Books.

Longman Graded Supplementary Readers. n.d. London: Longman.

Louthan, V. 1965. Some systematic grammatical deletions and the effects on reading comprehension. *English Journal.* 54. 295-299.

Lugton, Robert C. (ed.). 1970. "English as a Second Language: Current Issues." Philadelphia: Center for Curriculum Development.

Lunzer, E. A., and K. Gardner (eds.). In prep. "The Effective Use of Reading." Report of a project carried out on behalf of the Schools Council. London.

Maberly, Norman C. 1974. "Mastering Speed Reading." London: Oxford University Press.

Mackay, R., and A. Mountford. 1978. "English for Specific Purposes: A Case Study Approach." London: Longman.

Mackay, R., M. Bosquet, A. Cyr, N. Spada, and E. Gatbonton. 1978. Theory and Practice in ESP: Case Studies. Paper presented at 5th AILA Congress, Montreal, August 1978.

Macmillan, M. 1965. Efficiency in Reading. A Survey with Reference to the Teaching of English. ETIC Occasional Paper No. 6. The British Council.

Macnamara, John. 1970. Comparative studies of reading and problem solving in two languages. *TESOL Quarterly.* 4, 2. 107-116.

Marder, D. 1960. "The Craft of Technical Writing." New York: Macmillan.

Markstein, L., and L. Hirasawa. 1974. "Developing Reading Skills: Advanced." Rowley, Mass.: Newbury House.

McArthur, T. 1973. "A Rapid Course in English for Students of Economics." London: Oxford University Press.

Menosky, D. M. 1971. A Psycholinguistic Description of Oral Reading Miscues Generated during the Reading of Varying Portions of Text by Selected Readers from Grades Two, Four, Six and Eight. Unpublished Ph.D. dissertation, Wayne State University.

Miller, G. A. 1967. The Magical Number Seven, Plus or Minus Two: Some Limits on Our Capacity for Processing Information, in G. A. Miller, "The Psychology of Communication." New York: Basic Books.

Moore, W. G. 1949. "A Dictionary of Geography." Penguin Reference Books.

Morris, Ronald. 1973. "Success and Failure in Learning to Read." Penguin Publications.

Morrison, J. W. 1974. "An Advanced Course in Listening Comprehension." The British Council and Newcastle upon Tyne University.

Mountford, A. 1971. "A Stylistic Analysis of Two Texts from the Scientific Register, from a Rhetorical Point of View," Assignment for the Diploma Course in Applied Linguistics. University of Edinburgh.

Mountford, A. 1974. "English in Agriculture." (English in Focus series) London: Oxford University Press.

Munby, J. L., O. G. Thomas, and M. D. Cooper. 1966. "Comprehension for School Certificate." London: Longman.

Nevo, Baruch E., and R. Ramraz Shor. 1975. ITANA III—A Fortran IV program for multiple-choice tests and item analysis. *Journal of Educational and Psychological Measurements.* 35. 683-684.

Newmark, Leonard, Jerome Mintz, and Jan Lawson Hinely. 1964. "Using American English." New York: Harper & Row.

New York City Board of Education. 1964. Reading in the subject areas, Grades 7-8-9. *Curriculum Bulletin.* 6.

Niles, O. S. 1970. School Programs: the Necessary Conditions, in K. S. Goodman and O. S. Niles (eds.), "Reading: Process and Program." Urbana, Ill.: National Council of Teachers of English.

Norris, W. 1970. Teaching second language reading at the advanced level. *TESOL Quarterly.* 4, 1. 17-35.

Ochse, J. J., M. T. Soule, M. J. Dijkman, and C. Wehlburgh. 1961. "Tropical and Sub-Tropical Agriculture." 2 vols. New York: Macmillan.

Oller, John W., Jr. 1972. Assessing competence in ESL: Reading. *TESOL Quarterly.* 6, 4. 313-323.

Oller, John W., Jr. 1979. "Language Tests at School: A Pragmatic Approach." London: Longman.

Oller, John W., Jr., Donald Bowen, Ton That Dien, and Victor W. Mason. 1972. Cloze tests in English, Thai, and Vietnamese: Native and nonnative performance. *Language Learning.* 22.1-15.

Oller, John W., Jr., and Nevin Inal. 1971. A cloze test of English prepositions. *TESOL Quarterly.* 5.315-325.

Oller, John W., Jr., and K. Perkins. 1978. "Language in Education: Testing the Tests." Rowley, Mass.: Newbury House.

Osgood, C. E. 1959. The Representational Model and Relevant Research Methods, in I. de S. Poole (ed.), "Trends in Content Analysis," Urbana, Ill.: University of Illinois.

Perren, G. E. 1963. Linguistic Problems of Overseas Students in British Universities. ETIC Occasional Paper No. 3. The British Council.

Perren, G. E. 1971. Specifying the objectives: Is a linguistic definition possible? *English Language Teaching.* 25. 120-131.

Pierce, M. E. 1973. Sentence-level expectancy as an aid in advanced reading. *TESOL Quarterly.* 7, 3. 269-278.

Pike, K. 1967. "Language in Relation to a Unified Theory of Human Behaviour." The Hague: Mouton.

Plaister, Ted. 1968. Reading instruction for college level foreign students. *TESOL Quarterly.* 2.164-168.

Praninskas, J. 1975. "Rapid Review of English Grammar." (2d ed.). Englewood Cliffs, N.J.: Prentice-Hall.

Quirk, R., and S. Greenbaum. 1973. "A Concise Grammar of Contemporary English." New York: Harcourt Brace Jovanovich, Inc.

Quirk, R., et al. 1972. "A Grammar of Contemporary English." London: Longman.

Richards, J. C. 1974. A Non-Contrastive Approach to Error Analysis, in Jack C. Richards (ed.), "Error Analysis: Perspectives on Second Language Acquisition." London: Longman.

Rivers, Wilga. 1964. "The Psychologist and the Foreign-Language Teacher." Chicago: University of Chicago Press. Chaps. 10, 12.

Rivers, Wilga. 1968. "Teaching Foreign-Language Skills." Chicago: University of Chicago Press. Chaps. 9, 11.

Rubin, Joan. 1975. What the "good language learner" can teach us. *TESOL Quarterly*. 9, 1. 41-51.

Rudd, J. C. 1969. A new approach to reading efficiency. *English Language Teaching*. 27, 1.

Rutherford, W. E. 1968. (Revised 1974.) "Modern English." New York: Harcourt Brace & World.

Saitz, R. L., and D. Carr. 1972. "Selected Readings in English." Cambridge, Mass.: Winthrop Publishers, Inc.

Saville-Troike, Muriel. 1973. Reading and the audio-lingual method. *TESOL Quarterly*. 7, 4. 395-405. (Reprinted in this volume.)

Scherer, George A. C. 1964. Programming Second Language Reading, in G. Mathieu (ed.), 1966, "Advances in the Teaching of Modern Languages 2," New York: Pergamon Press.

Science Research Associates. 1965. Rate and Power Builders. Chicago, Ill.

Searle, J. R. 1969. "Speech Acts." London: Oxford University Press.

Seliger, Herbert W. 1972. Improved reading speed in comprehension in English as a second language. *English Language Teaching*. 30, 1.

Selinker, L. 1972. Interlanguage. *IRAL*. 10, 3.

Selinker, L. 1979. On the use of informants in discourse analysis and language for specialized purposes. *IRAL*. 17.

Selinker, L., and L. Trimble. 1967. "Technical Communication for Foreign Engineering Students" (mimeo). Seattle, Wash.: University of Washington.

Shannon, C. E. 1951. Prediction and entropy of printed English. *Bell System Technical Journal*. 30. 50-64.

Shuy, Roger. 1975. Talk given at Ohio University on April 24.

Sim, D. D. 1973. Grammatical Cohesion in English and Advanced Reading Comprehension for Overseas Students. M.A. Thesis. University of Manchester.

Smith, Frank. 1971. "Understanding Reading: A Psycholinguistic Analysis of Reading and Learning to Read." New York: Holt, Rinehart and Winston.

Smith, Frank (ed.). 1973. "Psycholinguistics and Reading." New York: Holt, Rinehart and Winston.

Smith, Frank, and K. S. Goodman. 1973. On the Psycholinguistic Method of Teaching Reading, in F. Smith (ed.), "Psycholinguistics and Reading," New York: Holt, Rinehart and Winston.

SRA Reading Labs. n.d. Chicago: Scientific Research Associates.

Stauffer, R. G. 1960. "The Language Experience Approach to the Teaching of Reading." New York: Harper & Row.

Stevenson, Robert N. 1973. Using slides to improve reading comprehension. *English Teaching Forum*. 11, 2.

Stevick, E. W. 1973. Review of Curran, "Counseling-learning: A Whole Person Model for Education." *Language Learning*. 23. 259-271.

Stevick, E. W. 1974a. Language teaching must do an about face. *Modern Language Journal*. 58.379-383.

Stevick, E. W. 1974b. Review of Gattegno's Teaching Foreign Languages in the Schools: The silent way. *TESOL Quarterly*. 8.305-314.

Stevick, E. W. 1975. One simple visual aid: a psychodynamic view. *Language Learning.* 25.63-72.

Strevens, P. 1971. The medium of instruction (mother-tongue/second language) and the formation of scientific concepts. *IRAL.* 9, 3.

Taylor, W. L. 1953. Cloze procedure: a new tool for measuring readability. *Journalism Quarterly.* 30. 415-433.

Tempany, H., and D. H. Grist. 1958. "An Introduction to Tropical Agriculture." London: Longman, Green.

Thurstone, L. L. 1946. Note on a reanalysis of Davis' reading tests. *Psychometrika.* 11. 185-188.

Tuinman, J. J. 1973. Determining the passage difficulty of comprehension questions in 5 major tests. *Reading Research Quarterly.* 9. 206-223.

Tullius, J. 1971. Analysis of Reading Skills of Non-Native Speakers of English. Unpublished master's thesis. University of California, Los Angeles.

Twaddell, W. Freeman. 1973. Vocabulary expansion in the TESOL classroom. *TESOL Quarterly.* 7, 1. 61-68.

Valette, R. M. 1967. "Modern Language Testing: A Handbook." New York: Harcourt Brace and World Inc.

Walker, C. 1974. "Reading Development and Extension." London: Ward Lock.

Wardhaugh, Ronald. 1969. "Reading: A Linguistic Perspective." New York: Harcourt, Brace and World.

Widdowson, H. G. 1971. The teaching of rhetoric to students of science and technology in science and technology in a second language. *CILT Reports and Papers.* 7.

Widdowson, H. G. 1974. An approach to the teaching of scientific English discourse. *RELC Journal.* 5, 1.

Wijasuriya, B. S. 1971. The Occurrence of Discourse Markers and Inter-Sentence Connectives in University Lectures and Their Place in the Testing and Teaching of Listening Comprehension in English as a Foreign Language. M. Ed. Thesis, University of Manchester.

Wilson, L. I. 1973. Reading in the ESOL classroom: a technique for teaching syntactic meaning. *TESOL Quarterly.* 7, 3. 259-267.

Winter, E. O. 1971. Connection in science material in science and technology in a second language. *CILT Reports and Papers.* 7.

Wood, D. N. 1967. The foreign language problem facing scientists and technologists in the United Kingdom—report of a recent survey. *Journal of Documentation.* 23, 2. 117-130.

Yorio, Carlos A. 1971. Some sources of reading problems for foreign language learners. *Language Learning.* 21, 1. 107-115.

Yorkey, R. C. 1970. "Study Skills for Students of English as a Second Language." New York: McGraw-Hill.

Zinsser, Hans. 1960. "Rats, Lice and History." New York: Bantam Books.

Index

Newbury House invites you to consider the following books, aids to the teacher of English as a Second Language:

Effective Techniques for English Conversation Groups
Julia M. Dobson   0-88377-034-2
Tested methods of stimulating classroom conversation.

From Substitution to Substance
Christina B. Paulston and Mary N. Bruder   912066-82-2
A handbook for adapting structural pattern drills to your classroom.

The Gooficon
Marina K. Burt and Carol Kiparsky   912066-07-5
How to deal with the most common student errors.

English Style
Yoshimasa Ohashi   0-88377-103-9
While primarily intended for English as a Second Language courses, the book explores linguistic dimensions which will also fascinate researchers on a general level.

Memory, Meaning, and Method
Earl W. Stevick   0-88377-053-9
A remarkably lucid analysis of just what takes place within the psycho-dynamics of the language learning situation—how students learn and remember language components, how learning is affected by relationships to teachers and others, how recall and cognition work . . . and how the perceptive teacher can use this understanding of the language student's mind to increase the effectiveness of instruction and practice.

A Way and Ways
Earl W. Stevick
A penetrating deeply-felt exploration of the language learning process by the author of *Memory, Meaning, and Method.*

Teaching English as a Second or Foreign Language
Marianne Celce-Murcia and Lois McIntosh, Editors   0-88377-125-X
Maintaining a careful balance between theory and practice, this comprehensive introduction to the profession of teaching English as a Second or Foreign Language has sufficient depth to captivate the veteran teacher, but remains straightforward and fundamental.